THE WAY OUT
MUST LEAD IN

THE WAY OUT MUST LEAD IN

Life Histories in the Civil Rights Movement

William R. Beardslee, M.D.

Second Edition

Lawrence Hill & Company
Westport, Connecticut

THE WAY OUT MUST LEAD IN was originally published in 1977 in a limited edition under the imprint of the Center for Research in Social Change of Emory University. This second revised edition is published by Lawrence Hill & Co., Inc., 520 Riverside Avenue, Westport, Connecticut 06880.

Library of Congress Cataloging in Publication Data

Beardslee, William R.
The way out must lead in.

1. Civil rights workers—Southern States—Interviews.
2. Afro-Americans—Southern States—Interviews.
3. Afro-Americans—Civil rights—Southern States.
I. Title.
E185.98.A1B4   1982   323.4'092'2   82-12054
ISBN 0-88208-153-5
ISBN 0-88208-120-9 (pbk.)

Cover photographs courtesy of the Southern Regional Council

1 2 3 4 5 6 7 8 9

Printed in the United States of America

This book is respectfully dedicated to the men and women whose histories are herein described.

Table of Contents

Foreword to the Second Edition
by Vernon E. Jordan, Jr.

If ever a book needed to be done, *The Way Out Must Lead In* is it. The Movement was so important in the history of our people and our nation that every aspect of it needs to be recorded lest we or those who come after us forget the sacrifices and the courage that went into its making.

Black people are the barometer of America's social health. When Americans demonstrate a willingness to open their society to blacks, they demonstrate the health of that society. The 1960s were such a time; a period when the majority of Americans showed a generosity of spirit and a realistic understanding of what this country is all about. The American conscience was moved and it responded to black demands for equal rights.

But the pie was growing then, and people were willing to set place at the table. Today, the pie is shrinking, and we see an effort to push black people and poor people away from the table again.

The seventies were a time of national withdrawal from the drive toward equality. The deadly effect of white backlash and one recession after another has left black people sliding downhill. Just consider:

- Black unemployment is over double that for whites.
- One out of four blacks who want to work can't get a job.
- More black people are poor in 1980 than were poor ten years ago.
- Black income is down—for every dollar of income earned by white families, black families have 57 cents.
- The typical black family earns less than the government itself says it must have for absolute minimal living standards.

This national retrogression has bred a worsening climate of race relations and a national obsession with selfish interests to the exclusion of those interests that would unite us as a people.

It is hard for many to remember that there was a period when the civil rights movement harnessed the dreams and energies of the best among us, when it served as the catalyst for idealism and justice for many millions of white and black Americans.

Their efforts were successful. Because of their bravery and commitment laws were passed and old, time-hardened patterns of racist behavior were driven from the land. Today whenever a black person registers in a hotel, walks in a public park, attends a school, or votes, it should be remembered that these simple rights are in large part due to the people who sat-in, waded-in, marched-in, and laid their lives on the line in the 1960's.

By recording the experiences of a variety of people who were involved in the Movement, setting down their experiences, their thoughts and their emotions, William Beardslee has performed a most remarkable task for which we should all be grateful.

Their remembrances bring that brave era alive again and, perhaps more important, should spark a sense of rededication among those who either remember or participated in the events described here. For those too young to remember, this book is an important means of transmitting a legacy that must be kept alive in the minds and hearts of all white and black Americans who believe in the American ideal of justice and equality.

The Way Out Must Lead In is a readable and important book. It brings into focus a unique period in which great things were achieved through faith and determination. Dr. Beardslee has made a major contribution to the continuing struggle for freedom, and I congratulate him most sincerely.

Foreword to the First Edition

Looking back over the history of this nation it seems from the modern vantage point that slavery of Blacks could not have been practiced here. But it was. No nation, said a president, can exist half-slave and half-free and a terrible war was fought to end this terror. Now we know that slavery was only the worst of the visible forms of the problem—prejudice, discrimination, poverty, ignorance, plus the lack of freedom continued and still are present to some degree.

The 1960's will always be identified as the time of reckoning for our society. Although Black men had served in the armed forces of this nation in every war it has fought, equality still was denied by Federal and state laws, by custom, by prejudice and hate. The Allied victory ending World War II meant once again that freedom and democracy had been saved for the world, excluding Black Americans who found themselves still without either.

Slowly the Supreme Court began the process of destroying discriminatory laws, yet Black citizens in rural and urban America lived much as they had since the 1860's. The Civil Rights Movement proved to be the force that eventually chastened the courts and the Congress into removing all discriminatory laws; the final Federal law—legalizing segregated private housing—was not struck down until after the murder of the Reverend Doctor Martin Luther King, Jr., in 1968.

The change agent in the Movement was people, some white and the majority black. These were unusual human beings, courageous, dedicated, patient, ready to suffer all things and to sacrifice all things, who served as the precipitants emulating even unto prison and death the key proponents of non-violence in the world's history of social change. Eleven of these men and women are presented in this study by William Beardslee. These are real people who lived the experiences recorded here. What is this society's debt to these and all the others who set their feet and their voices and their hearts upon the troubled path to

freedom and equality within the American system? Their victory was America's victory. Until now, no one has asked them what their personal cost was in this struggle. It is time we all knew.

Fred Roberts Crawford

Author's Preface to the Second Edition

This book is a series of first person life histories of civil rights workers who stayed in the South and with the Civil Rights Movement for a long period of time, some now for more than twenty years. The current volume is a second edition of these histories, which were originally published in 1977 by Emory University's Center for Research in Social Change. That edition was based on in-depth interviews carried out in 1974. This second edition presents the original introduction, histories, and conclusion as they appeared. A new introduction by Vernon Jordan, this brief preface, and an entirely new chapter, "Continued Growth," which describes what has happened to these men and women since 1974, have been added.

It is remarkable that these men and women are all still active and involved in some phase of the Movement now, some twenty years after their original involvement. Ten of eleven were re-interviewed in 1980 for this second edition. As the workers, when they were re-interviewed, stood by their original statements about what kept them going, and as those statements are fully presented, only parts of the recent interviews, those which expand or add to what was said earlier, are described in the concluding chapter. In the First Edition, most of the historians did not want to be identified by their real names, and they were not, but for the Second Edition, several more did, and they are presented in the final chapter.

In reading over the Introduction, it is clear that some of the observations about the mood of the country and the political climate are dated. It was written just after Carter was elected, and he had been elected, in part, because of the strong support of Blacks like Andrew Young. There was a sense of expectancy in the air and the hope that the promise of the Movement would finally be fulfilled. That did not happen, and there was much frustration with the Carter administration for its lack of wholehearted support for socially oriented policies. If anything, the situation now is even grimmer, politically, for Blacks and poor people. The central piece of legislation of the entire Civil Rights

Movement, the Voting Rights Act, has not been fully supported by the Reagan Administration. Furthermore, massive cuts in educational and social programs have done huge damage to poor and black people. No one can tell what the future will bring to these committed civil rights workers and to those they represent, although further followup revealed that ten of the eleven remained in the South, doing what they had been doing, while one had continued similar work, but in a different area of the country. The long time interval of their continued work and their on going commitment remain remarkable, perhaps more so for being so clearly out of step with the current political climate.

My work on the follow-up of these men and women has been supported by the Harris Trust through Harvard University. Funds for the publication of this second edition have, in part, been provided by the Falk Foundation, and my thanks are due to them. As before, my deepest thanks are to the historians themselves. It has been a privilege to work with them, and they remain an inspiration to me.

William R. Beardslee
Boston, Massachusetts 1982

Acknowledgments

Many people have generously and graciously given of their time and energy to help me with this project. My work has benefited from fruitful discussions with colleagues, teachers, and friends. Pat Watters has been a source of advice and encouragement for this work from its inception. I met with him regularly while gathering the histories and have learned a great deal from his knowledge of writing and his deep sensitivity to people. I began this work while I was a resident in General Psychiatry at the Massachusetts General Hospital. Special thanks are due to Dr. Leon Eisenberg, who was then the Chairman of the Department of Psychiatry, for his support of the project, his reading of several chapters, and his encouragement to me to work on it while in residency training. I completed the manuscript during my residency and research fellowship in Child Psychiatry at the Children's Hospital Medical Center. Dr. Julius Richmond, Chairman of the Department of Psychiatry there, has given continued encouragement and invaluable support in many ways for the project. Dr. Peter Wolff read sections of the manuscript and his incisive comments helped me clarify my thinking. Dr. John Lemly, Dr. Howard Slyter, Dr. Gordon Harper, Ms. Evelyn Stone, Ms. Mary McHenry, Dr. Gregor Sebba, Dr. Chester Pierce and my father, Dr. William A. Beardslee, read parts of the manuscript, made useful suggestions, and offered encouragement at various stages of the work. Ms. Barbara Altman has edited the final draft of the manuscript and has made that process enjoyable and educational. Ms. Linda Haynes and Ms. Susan Finn have been responsible for the typing of the manuscript and in addition have assisted through their patience with my handwriting and with my various revisions of the text.

I wish to thank the Southern Regional Council, under whose auspices this work was originally undertaken, for its support and for a grant for some of the expenses of the project. I wish to thank Dr. Fred Crawford and the Center for Research in Social Change at Emory University for help with publication. I wish to thank Mr. Philip Hallen of the Maurice Falk Medical Fund for his encouragement and support. Publication has been made possible in part by a grant from the Maurice Falk Medical Fund.

My wife Barbara, through her companionship, encouragement, and humor, has been a constant source of support throughout my work on this project.

W. R. B.

Introduction
General Background

From the early 1960s until the present, a number of civil rights workers have continued to try to realize the goals of the Civil Rights Movement. They are unusual in having maintained their efforts for this long period of time, especially in light of the changes that have occurred in the Civil Rights Movement and in the country as a whole in this period. How these men and women have been able to maintain their commitments is the focus of this work. This is addressed by presenting a group of workers' own histories, their own descriptions of how they became committed and how they feel they have been able to remain so.

It is difficult, and certainly an oversimplification, to try to describe the Movement briefly because of its complexity and because of the variety within it. But it is necessary to review the history of the Movement to understand these histories because the workers' lives were inextricably bound up with the events of the Movement.

The Civil Rights Movement was clearly visible for much of the decade of the 1960s. It was a loose coalition of individuals and organizations, the National Association for Advancement of Colored People (NAACP), the Student Non-Violent Coordinating Committee (SNCC), the Congress of Racial Equality (CORE), and the Southern Christian Leadership Conference (SCLC) most prominent among them. At its high water mark, the coalition had the power to effect legislative change and was capable of mobilizing large numbers of people for demonstrations.

The most visible part of the Movement, especially through the news media, was the confrontation in demonstrations, enacted many times in places such as Charlotte, North Carolina; Nashville, Tennessee; Albany, Georgia; St. Augustine, Florida; and Selma, Alabama. In one group were demonstrators without weapons and uniforms; in the other, opposing group were armed men, uniformed, faceless, and powerful. The groups clashed, the uniformed beating the non-uniformed. There seemed to be bravery and simple courage on one side and armed, unreasonable force on the other.

What was visible in the demonstrations represented only a part of the attempts by the workers to break the pattern of segregation. They also registered voters, organized communities, brought

legal actions, and developed local and national organizations. Involvement often had a deep inner meaning for the workers. Especially within the South, the Movement drew in workers from all walks of life. "It kindled a fire in people" was the way one of the workers with whom I spoke described it. Becoming involved meant breaking with the past and starting a new way of living. Involvement gave the participants a sense of hope and a sense of their own ability to change the way in which they lived.

In terms of the chronology of the Movement, there had been many struggles for civil rights and social justice before the decade of the 1950s, and these laid the groundwork for the emergence to national prominence of the Movement. There were milestones in the 1950s. In 1954 the Brown vs. the Board of Education decision legally abolished the *separate but equal doctrine*. In 1955 the Montgomery Bus Boycott occurred, the first of the large scale nonviolent actions. In 1957 came the Little Rock school desegregation battle. In 1960 the first southern sit-ins occurred in Greensboro, North Carolina. In 1961 CORE sponsored the Freedom Ride. In 1963 there was the March on Washington, the first of many demonstrations aimed specifically at national legislation. In 1964 the Council of Federated Organizations ran the Summer Project in Mississippi, and there was a challenge to the National Democratic Convention by the Mississippi Delegation, as well as the Watts riot. In 1965 came the Selma March and the passage of the Voting Rights Act, and in 1966 the Meredith March, the emergence of the Black Power slogan, and the breakup of the large scale coalition of civil rights organizations. These events marked the waxing and waning of the Movement in a public sense.

The emergence of the Movement in the public consciousness coincided with a national sense of new possibilities. The Movement became visible at the time of the changeover in the presidency from Eisenhower, an aged war hero, to Kennedy, an energetic young man. Legislatively, the Movement was most successful during the early years of Johnson's presidency. Johnson, in spite of all his involvement in the war in Vietnam, did believe that a Great Society was possible, that America could confront and conquer poverty and inequality, and he did communicate this belief. The early years of the Movement coincided with economic prosperity for most Americans. It was a time without major war. There was a willingness to try to change and grow, both individually and nationally.

The mood of optimism contrasts with the mood of disillusionment that prevails now. There is a deep distrust of the visionary belief and commitment that those who joined the Movement demonstrated. Part of this feeling stems from the way the Movement seemed to fall apart. A great deal comes from what has happened to the country as a whole. Regarding the Movement, the simplicity of confrontation in demonstrations no longer exists. Dr. King has been killed, as have Robert Kennedy, Medgar Evers, and many others. SNCC no longer exists. The transition from then to now[1] has seen bitter public feuding between the various civil rights organizations. Some leaders have rejected two of the central principles of the Movement: (1) nonviolence and (2) integration. Instead, there has been the advocacy of armed resistance and separation. There have been many instances of pettiness and greed among those who came to power through the Movement. There have been many individual tragedies along the path from then to now.

Nationally, the effects of the war in Vietnam, the assassination of leaders, the large increase in crime, the Watergate scandal, and continued high unemployment have all contributed to the disillusionment. Moreover, there is an awareness of the limits on all resources, especially those related to energy. There is also an awareness of the complexity of problems that face the country. There has been a pulling back and retrenchment of the government in regard to many of the needs of the poor, minorities, children, and others. It remains to be seen what effect President Carter's administration will have on the disillusionment. It is noteworthy that his alliance with people who were part of the Civil Rights Movement, especially the Reverend Martin Luther King, Sr. and Ambassador Andrew Young, was an important part of his election victory. Both men represent in some ways the spirit of the Civil Rights Movement.

Although the people who have remained working for the goals of the Movement have been deeply affected by the changes within the Movement and the country as a whole, their commitments have not eroded. Seen against the backdrop of national disillusionment, their commitments are well worth trying to understand. In contrast to so many, they did not lose themselves or their will to work in the difficult, complex business of trying to bring about change.

---

1. For this phrase and for a moving history of the Civil Rights Movement, I am indebted to Pat Watters' *Down to Now*, Pantheon, New York, 1971.

A strong personal interest led me to this work and is part of the introduction to it. My family moved to just outside Atlanta when I was two years old and has lived there since. Neither of my parents is southern; both believe in integration, and have throughout the time I was growing up. I went to a segregated public school, and I lived in neighborhoods that were almost entirely white. In growing up, I gradually became aware of one thing that was very wrong with where I lived. It just didn't make any sense to say that black people were inferior: that they had to sit in the back of the bus, use separate restrooms, eat in different places, or sit in special sections in right field at the Atlanta Crackers' games in the ball park.

I went to Sunday school and church regularly, and I can never remember the minister saying that segregation was wrong or sinful, or that it was leading to the current and actual damnation and destruction of human life in the present, regardless of what happened in the afterlife. I tended to take church seriously, which made the lack of talking all the more puzzling. In studying Georgia history in school, much was made of the bravery of the men in Gray, but no one would admit that prejudice and racial fear were as much motives for the Civil War as were states' rights or economic factors. Much energy in the South was tied up in not hearing and not seeing, in denying the cost of segregation and in maintaining it at the price of considerable distortion. All this didn't mean that I knew what to do, or did anything, but I was aware of the situation.

There was a contrast between all that was good, the beauty of the people, the land, all the positive experiences I had in childhood, and the presence of segregation. It was like living with a lie and not talking about it. Because of what has happened since, I am all the more aware, but I was aware even then. Then came the clash about integration in Little Rock, then the sit-ins, and in 1961 the token integration of the schools in Atlanta, although not the school I attended. In high school I began to go to Quaker meetings and through that to get involved with people who were active in the Civil Rights Movement. It was a slow, gradual process for me. I began by doing volunteer work with the Quakers in Vine City, in a housing project. Curiously enough, in light of the fact that I am now a doctor working primarily with disturbed children, the first thing I was asked to do was to work with a black child who was deeply troubled. His father had been murdered,

and he had stood up in his church and said, "When I grow up, I'm going to blow this church up." I saw him many times, played with him, talked to him, got to know him and his mother, and through them many others in the housing project. It was like nothing I had done before and I was strongly drawn to it.

After that, I worked in the community in other ways. Then in the summers during college, I worked for the Southern Regional Council, first in their office and then in the field with the Voter Education Project. Several people there, including Dr. Leslie W. Dunbar, the Director of the Council, Vernon Jordan, the Director of the Voter Project, and Pat Watters, a writer who then was there, spent time with me, talked to me, and taught me. During this period I also met Robert Coles and read his work. I was impressed with both and have been deeply influenced by both over the years.

One of the people with whom I worked at the Council was a Morehouse student who was a member of Ebenezer Baptist Church. I visited his church with him, and I heard Martin Luther King, Jr. preach for the first time. From then on, I went to hear him whenever I could when he preached, on the first Sunday of every month. This also had a large influence on me.

In working for the Voter Education Project, I travelled all over the South, getting to know people, talking with them, doing whatever I could, and the Project could, to help with voter registration or whatever else was needed. I stayed in people's homes, went on marches, and came to believe strongly in the goals of the Movement. Being in the Movement gave me an opportunity to see what had been wrong with segregation and to try to right it. Above all, it gave me a chance to see how people very different from myself lived, to share with them, know them, respect them, learn from them, and in a small limited way to work with them.

Although I believed in what I did, and in the goals of the Movement, I emphasize that what I did was different from the people I am describing in this book. I did not quit school, or spend time in jail, or work full-time for several years in the Movement. In 1967 I decided to go to medical school. At the time I made this decision, many organizations, especially SNCC, were saying that whites no longer had a place in the Movement. It was also the time that the Vietnam War began to dominate the consciousness of the country. It was difficult for me to leave the Movement, in part because things seemed confused and unresolved, but I did.

Throughout my training, both in medicine and in psychiatry, I have had a strong interest in understanding healthy behavior,

in people's strengths as well as their difficulties and their ill-
nesses. A sense of the unusual strengths and commitment of the
civil rights workers I had known has remained with me from my
time in the Movement. Part of what led me to undertake this
project was a desire to know what had happened to the people
who had stayed in the Movement. I wondered how they had dealt
with the trials of the ensuing years. I wondered how they had been
affected by the profound disillusionment that gripped so many of
my generation. This, combined with my interest as a doctor in
how people cope in a healthy way with difficult situations, led me
to the project.

Method

I talked initially with a variety of people who had been involved
in the Movement, and with a number of physicians, teachers, and
colleagues who were interested in the project. I also reviewed
some of the literature on the Movement, although the large
amount of it precluded an exhaustive review.

There are analyses of the Movement from economic, political,
and social points of view, and many theories about why it suc-
ceeded at one point, did not seem to at another, and why it is no
longer prominent. Southern novelists and poets have contributed
a great deal to understanding the people of the South. There are
some specific examinations of civil rights workers by social scientists, including psychiatrists, but there is no in-depth, well-
worked-out set of psychological principles, or even framework of
understanding, that is easily applicable. Nor are standardized
psychological measures applicable to the question. Clearly, a
wide range of factors, economic, historical, political, interper-
sonal, and intra-psychic, have all played a role.

In reviewing the literature, I was most drawn to the first-hand
accounts of experiences in the Movement, either by the participants themselves, or conveyed through others, as in, not surpris-
ingly, Robert Coles' or Pat Watters' work.

In the selected readings which follow the last chapter, I have
included those works which have helped me in understanding the
South. Most deal directly with the South. Those that do not, for
example Erik Erikson's work, I have included because they provide a framework or perspective that is useful in understanding
what happened.

Given the range of possible answers, the lack of definitive stud-

ies, and the variety of factors that had an influence, I felt the starting place, the first approximation to understanding, had to be in the people's own understandings of what happened. I felt they could describe the pressures of the work and what helped them and hurt them. This would not provide a complete answer but would be an essential part of any answer to the question of how they were able to keep going over a long period of time.

As for objectivity, I undertook the work out of honest curiosity, and I tried to be as disciplined, careful, open, and rigorous as possible in doing it. I don't think that my personal interest in the work destroyed my objectivity or made the approach I used invalid, so long as the reader knows the position from which I undertook the work.

I chose to include in the project only people who had worked for at least ten years in the Movement and who maintained some significant involvement at the time of being interviewed. Involvement was defined as working at least part-time with a group of people on something related to the early goals of the Movement: voter registration and political power, economic development, and community organization. Involvement with these goals by necessity meant working at least part-time as an organizer.

All of the people were living in the South when I spoke with them. Most were living where they had done their work and are working now. I found them through my previous contacts with them in the Movement or through members of the Southern Regional Council. As the work progressed, I asked each person interviewed about others with whom it might be useful to talk, and thus found more people to include in the project. Most, but not all, of the people were black.

When I initially contacted them I explained the project and asked if I could come and talk with them. I told them about my background and that I was interested in learning about what gave them strength to keep going over time. All but one of the people I contacted consented to be interviewed. I told the people that in the reporting of the interviews they would not be identified by their own names. I did this because I felt that they would be freer with the details of their lives when not identified by name. Thus in editing, I have changed some of the people's names and the names of the places involved, and a few other details, in order to preserve the historians' anonymity insofar as possible. A few of the people decided after the interviews were completed to be identified by their real names, and in those few instances I have

done so. I have not included many of the specific names and places in their accounts, again, in order to protect them. These few are John Lewis, Thomas Gilmore, and Ken Dean.

In talking with the people, I asked about their early lives, about their initial involvement in the Movement and the reasons for it, and then the questions central to the inquiry: what kept them going over time; what did they see as their sources of strength; how did they deal with hard times in the Movement such as the deaths of close friends. I concentrated on their explanations and understandings of themselves. The role of an ideology, whether it was a religious faith, nonviolent philosophy, or political credo, the progression of each person's life, and what the person did after 1967, as it was a watershed point in the Movement, received special attention.

Essentially the same questions were asked of all of the people, although the order varied and the questions were general and open-ended. Each person developed the answers to the extent that he or she saw fit. Thus the histories differ somewhat from one another. Some workers emphasized experiences in their early lives as formative, while others pointed to the experiences early in the course of the Movement.

Many people described personal difficulties in their own lives or in the lives of their close friends, and these difficulties are a crucial part of the histories. They are by no means simply a series of healthy or successful reactions to the experience. I did not emphasize the public actions of the people involved, that is, leading demonstrations, testifying before Congressional committees, and so on, except where they are crucial in understanding the person's life history. Most of the interviews took place over several days. I spoke with almost all of the people after an interval of several months to review the previous conversations and to explore further areas that seemed to have been omitted.

I interviewed all the people in 1974. Although I have kept in touch with them, I have not tried to update their stories. One person has definitely left the South but still maintains his commitment to the goals of the Movement, while most remain doing essentially what they were at the time I spoke with them. Several have run for public office, and some have been elected.

Members of all the major civil rights organizations were included in the group interviewed. There are certainly more people who met the criteria than could possibly be interviewed. Moreover, I interviewed more people than I could include in this book.

In choosing which histories to include, I tried to choose representative ones, ones which reflect the range of ages, experiences, and
backgrounds of the people who have remained committed to the
goals of the Movement.

In editing I have not retold or rewritten the histories in my own
words, although the histories are not exact quotations in all
places. I have tried to be as true to the sense of the speaker's
words as possible. Notes from all sessions and tape recordings
from most sessions form the basis of the histories. I have reorgan-
ized the histories somewhat, and omitted the questions I asked
and the parts of the interviews that were repetitious or irrelevant.
In a few cases, I have included only the dominant themes of a
history or a person's perception, rather than the whole history.
Where it seemed relevant, I have included brief descriptions of
the people's current settings and how they looked and talked. My
own descriptions are set in boldface type to distinguish them from
the historians' stories.

The different historians faced some common problems in different places because their roles as organizers and leaders were
similar. Knowing these is helpful in reading the histories. One
problem was to learn to live with the constant threat of violence
to themselves and their friends. For some this also involved en-
during repeated beatings and jailings. Another was for them to
remain in touch with the people they were trying to change. Because they were leaders, they were constantly on the horns of a
dilemma between isolation from and attraction to the community. On the one hand, they were alienated from both their
communities and the larger society because they were attempting
to challenge and change both in major ways. On the other hand,
they had to be in close human touch with each other and with
their communities: to push too hard or to demand too much
change from a community meant to lose any relationship with it
and, therefore, any effectiveness. A final problem was to adjust
to the changes over time within the larger society and the Movement. As one example, tactics changed from getting people into
the streets for demonstrations to getting grants and to developing
firm economic bases and reliable, vote-producing organizations.
The skills required of the organizers were different in the two
situations. The people who stayed have had to change, develop,
and adjust their work accordingly. As another example, early in
the Movement, the workers believed totally in the vision of a
changed society. But to remain in the Movement meant to adjust

and adapt their vision to the realities of working and organizing, of politics and economics. This adjustment was all the harder because of the change in political climate.

What the historians themselves have said, their own individual conclusions about what kept them going, are the main conclusions of this work. The final chapter is not intended to supplant that, but rather is an attempt to pull together and indicate the common themes in the various histories, and to thus provide a way of looking at the common experience of all of the people.

In this work I have set as my tasks to gather the histories, present them, see what, if any, common themes emerge, and see what can be learned from them. Although I am a psychiatrist, I have not analyzed the histories in psychiatric terms, with the possible exception of a brief discussion of identity issues, nor have I tried to compare conclusions in detail from these histories with the work of other psychiatrists or other social scientists on the Movement.

I have not used these approaches, because to use them would have necessitated condensing and summarizing the histories, rather than reporting them fully. Clearly this work is only a part of a complete answer to the question of how the workers were able to keep working and this way of presenting the histories only one of a number of possible ways of examining the people's experiences.

Personal Reflections

Just as interviewing each person involved a physical journey for me, following each history was like following the historian's own journey, his or her choices at crucial junctions, like roads taken or not taken. Each had a kind of unfolding quality. In following these histories, I had to follow and know my own history. To re-examine what had happened in these other lives was to raise questions about my own life.

I had to resolve two questions for myself before I could get anywhere with the work. One was dealing with my own feelings about leaving the Movement in 1967, and the other was knowing what had happened to the intense vision of change, which had existed and which I had shared in the Movement. In going back I expected a lot of resentment, because I had left, because I am white, because I am now a doctor. I was acutely aware of the criticisms of social scientists who studied blacks, or the poor in

general, but never offered any real help for their problems. I was anxious not to over-judge, or over-analyze what I saw. I wondered if a white man like myself could do this kind of work.

What I found in talking with the people was very different from what I had expected. The people I spoke with were warm and open, and the anger and resentment I expected were not there. The people had many questions for me in the course of our talking, about what had happened to me and what it was like to be a doctor, about why I was doing the work, and about what others had said. I had many long conversations on either side of the more formal conversations about life history. The people were not interested in berating me for leaving the Movement, or in attacking me because I am white or a doctor. Instead, it turned out that the high point, the richest part of doing the work, was getting to know the people and their getting to know me. As I worked, I realized that it was impossible to work because of guilt, or to try to atone for leaving, or for being white or different, and that no one was trying to make me do that. The Movement people were not concerned with the past but with their needs in the present and future.

Concerning the second question, the vision of change, what comes to mind is my seeing the Mississippi River in flood for the first time. This happened on my first trip South to interview. In January, 1974, 500,000 acres of farmland were under water. The flooding was massive. In the Delta the water had enveloped the land like a huge brown blanket. Looking over the bluffs from Memphis, there was a vast, brown, opaque expanse, like a huge stage sliding laterally. Like a stage, except that all the play was underneath the surface, as the water ripped and tore the land apart, erased boundaries, killed animals, and carried things away. The power of the river fascinated me. I kept thinking that what was needed, hoped for, and even envisioned in the heat of the Movement was an event like the flooding—total, overwhelming, cataclysmic. The vision was to remake all the land and all the people, to erase boundaries and old structures.

I felt a strong wish to believe in the vision, to hope for cataclysmic change. I kept wanting to say that the rest of the country has deteriorated and has lost any vision or hope for the future, but the vision still exists here, in the first, and the most important, of all the struggles for freedom and self-worth in America of the last three decades. So as I started the work, I had to battle my own wish to believe in the vision of sudden cataclysmic change,

and to find that the Movement people had kept that dream alive.

I found I had to give up the wish for this kind of vision to be able to talk to the people. As I talked to them, I realized that having a vision, necessary as that was and is, was the easiest part of being committed and bringing about change. The people I talked with were truly remarkable, not in that they had a vision, for many people had that, but that they had worked for ten years in the cold, hard pragmatic business of organizing.

Beyond this, to return to the image of the flood, for me, watching the flood initially was awe-inspiring. It was almost poetic. As I was in Mississippi longer, I realized that the flood was a cataclysmic event, and that it did change people's lives immensely, but not in giving them new chances. The flood destroyed property. It prevented the planting of hundreds of thousands of acres. As in any natural disaster, those who were hurt most were those with the least resources: the man who had to clear a certain amount a year to keep his farm and could not plant that year, lost the farm. The gap between those who had wealth and those who did not was widened, and in Mississippi at least, this translates for the most part as the gap between whites and blacks.

For the organizers, what was important about the flood was not to be caught up in its image or with grandiose plans for change but to help people cope with the damage of the flood. For me, the issue was not getting back in touch with the feelings of believing in and being in the Movement, not in having a romantic vision, not in what had been in the past, but in trying to see, understand and respond to in an unencumbered way what was in the present.

THE WAY OUT
MUST LEAD IN

Chapter 1

John Lewis

John Lewis was Chairman of the Student Nonviolent Coordinating Committee from 1963 to 1966. When I spoke with him, he was the Director of the Voter Education Project, a group which works actively in the South in voter registration and citizenship education. The project carries forward one of the major, early thrusts of the Movement, that of political power for black people. Mr. Lewis's work with it involved much traveling and public speaking in the South, so he remained in close touch with many of the places and the people who were central to the Movement.

As with many people's history in the Movement, Mr. Lewis' history was bound up with one particular organization's work; his individual history is so completely intertwined with the organization's that for a period they are inseparable.

His history is characteristic in that it involves moving from a rural background to a position of great power and responsibility in a short period of time, and moving to the struggle on a national level for legislation, protection, and recognition by the government. Finally, his history is important because it encompasses most of the early political actions of the Movement: the use of nonviolent protests in the sit-ins, the Freedom Rides, and the large marches. For these reasons, I have included more detail than in some other histories.

We talked in Mr. Lewis' office. One thing more than any other set the tone for our talks. On the table in the office was one of the Voter Education Project publications, *Roster of Elected Black Officials in the South, 1974.* In 1965 there were less than 100 blacks holding elected offices. This publication lists 1,307 blacks holding elected office. There is a vast array of people in offices represented. The publication is a clear and simple statement that some real change has taken place.

He began by talking about his childhood.

I was born in Pike County, Alabama. It is primarily a rural county, located in southeast Alabama about 50 miles south of

1

Montgomery, only a few miles away from the area where Governor George Wallace grew up. I was the third child in a family of ten. My parents rented land from a wealthy white landowner, and each year they paid the rent in cash or in the form of a crop.

I grew up with a great interest in religion; I'm not so sure how I got involved in religion, but I recall when I was about four years old, I had such a strong interest that I even tried to baptize some small chicks. They became so wet I thought they were going to die, and I put them in the sun for them to dry. Later, between the ages four and seven, I continued to have a growing interest in the church, but at the same time I was also interested in raising chickens. Even though we had 50 or 60 of them, I could tell which one was which. I saw the chickens as innocent creatures. At night when it was time for the chickens to go to roost, I would go in and speak to the chickens, preach to them. My cousins, sisters, and brothers would come and play church. When a chicken was dead we had a funeral and we'd march down to the cemetery.

As a young child, I wanted to be . . . and I don't know why . . . I really wanted to be a minister in the Baptist Church. My mother and I always were very active in the church and all my sisters and brothers attended the church a great deal, and later my father started attending very regularly; but no one else in my family became a minister, although my grandfather is a deacon in the church and one of my uncles is a deacon in the church.

I never really got involved or excited about guns or pistols. I disliked those toys. My father kept a gun at the house; he would hunt with a shotgun, and he kept it over the door. I guess that had an impact on me, just seeing it there all the time.

I started protesting at an early age. I guess my first protests were over the whole question of killing the chickens. When my parents would kill a chicken, I wouldn't speak to them for days. I would refuse to go to the table to eat on that particular day. I wouldn't say anything to them about it, but not going was one way of saying, "You shouldn't have killed this chicken." I had gotten to know some of the chickens very well.

My next protest was about school. I had this deep desire to go to school. I wanted to go, and my parents wanted me to go, but at the same time they needed me to work in the fields. When I was four or five years old, I started going to the field to help pick cotton. I couldn't pick that much, but I did have to stay out to pick cotton or gather the peanuts, or pull corn, or chop cotton, or put out the fertilizer.

Some days when my parents wanted me to stay home and work in the field, rather than go to school, I would get up early and hide. We had a home raised on stilts, and I would hide under the house and wait until the bus came along. When the bus came, I would run out and get on and go to school. I did that many, many times.

Also protesting, I argued with my father that farming was just a weird gamble. My father would have to borrow money each year to get fertilizer and farming equipment, and then he had to buy seed. He would work and work and then come out in the hole year after year. He was not making anything. I used to argue that it was just a waste; we couldn't make anything with a small farm. Trying to raise peanuts and corn was just about impossible.

I started going to a one-room school in an old church. Sometimes we walked to school and sometimes we rode the bus. We had secondhand books that the white students had used and handed on down to us. The books were ragged, and we could see the names of the other students and the other schools.

In 1951 when I went from the sixth to the seventh grade, we started going by bus every day. We were transported by bus by the white school in order to keep the school system segregated. I'll never forget it. I think this was the first time that I really came to see the dual system of segregation and racial discrimination. We had to leave home some time early in the morning on our way to school, and we were supposed to be at the school by eight or eight-thirty. Sometimes we wouldn't make it until nine or nine-thirty because we had bus trouble. The area where I grew up was a prevalently black area. Although the white people owned most of the land, very few white people lived in this rural area. The roads were not even paved in some areas, particularly in the black section of the county. The bus always got stuck in the mud during the rainy season. Sometimes, it wouldn't go up hill, or it would run into a ditch. We had trouble getting to school or returning from school. So all of that had an effect.

In my junior high and high school days, the whole system of segregation became just as clear as anything. We couldn't go to the public library. It was a county library, and we were not allowed to even go in — white only. When we went to the movie theatre we had to go upstairs, and all the white people went downstairs. I came to resent that.

When I was about ten years old, I remember going into the drugstore and asking for . . . what we call today when we go to

the soda fountain and order a Coke, then we called it a combination. I remember when I wanted a combination, I had to, each time, come out on the street to drink it. I couldn't take a seat at the counter. I remember the water signs. I can see them now clearly, one saying "colored" and one saying "white" over the water fountains.

All in all, though, what had the greatest impact on me, what affected me more than anything during the early days of my life, I guess, was a religious upbringing code. We didn't have to go to Sunday School, but we wanted to go and we went. We went to church at least once a month, and it was a big occasion. I think it helped me.

In 1955 there was the Montgomery bus boycott. Montgomery was only fifty miles away. I was fifteen years old, in the tenth grade, at an all-black county high school. The black high schools were considered training schools, while the white high schools were considered high schools. Being in the training school, passing the white high school, and then seeing Martin Luther King Jr., and the black people of Montgomery organize themselves in such a way that fifty thousand people, for more than a year, walked rather than rode segregated buses had a tremendous impact on me. We didn't get a television until very late, but we followed the boycott on radio. We didn't have a subscription to the newspapers at home, but the high school did, so I would go to the library and read the Montgomery paper. I'd read all of the black papers, and I got very excited about what was going on. In a sense, I think that particular event probably changed the direction of my life more than anything else.

I had never met Martin Luther King, Jr., but I admired him greatly. I'd seen pictures of him, and I heard him on some Sunday mornings preaching on the radio. I'll never forget a sermon that he preached once, in Montgomery. It was something like Paul's letter to the American Christians. He took his sermon from Paul's letter to the church at Corinth. It was this whole thing about love. And it was really . . . very social . . . it had great emphasis on the aspect of this life and this world. He was saying to the black people in Montgomery, Alabama, and to his church in particular, that it was not enough for people to be concerned with streets that are paved with gold, and the gates to the Kingdom of God, but they had to be concerned with the streets of Montgomery, and the gates and doors of certain stores that discriminated against people, and places that refused to hire people in Montgomery.

In 1956 I told my minister that I had the call to preach, and I preached my trial sermon in February of that year. After that, I conducted the devotion, or the convocation at school on special occasions. I graduated from high school in 1957, and I wanted to come to Atlanta to college. My greatest desire was to come to Morehouse College, but it was impossible; I didn't have the resources. I just happened to be reading an old Southern Baptist newspaper, and it mentioned a seminary in Nashville, American Baptist Theological Seminary. Somehow it struck me because it said, in effect, that there was no tuition, and that a student could work and provide room and board. I applied there and was accepted.

I enrolled there in September of 1957. I was seventeen years old, and I had never really been away from home before for any period of time. An uncle, my mother's youngest brother, encouraged me to go to college. He bought me this huge trunk, an upright foot-locker. It was a great feeling to be packing things in the trunk to go to school. I left by Greyhound bus. It was early in September, the first week in September of '57, that I arrived in the city.

I had followed the Montgomery bus boycott and what Dr. King had done. On campus the first thing I tried to do was organize a local chapter of the NAACP. The college president objected to that because the school was jointly supported by both black and white church organizations.

At the seminary they paid me $42.50 for washing pots and pans three times a day and serving the food. Out of that I paid about $37 for room and board. I had a few dollars left. I had grown up on a farm, and I knew something about manual work and labor, but these pots and pans were some of the biggest and heaviest I'd ever seen. They were for cooking in the larger kitchens, and if they were full of water, they were almost impossible to lift. I did it for the first two years of school and I enjoyed it for I felt that it was necessary. It was a way of seeing myself through those few years of college.

The Nashville Christian Leadership Council started conducting a series of nonviolent workshops in the city during the school year '58-'59. I started attending some of these workshops, along with some of the other students from the schools in town. The workshops were primarily discussions about the philosophy and the discipline of nonviolence. Discussions were based on the New Testament, Gandhi, Israel, India, Africa, Thoreau, and the whole question of civil disobedience and passive resistance. We met

almost the entire school year.

The following year we started discussing nonviolence more or less as a social action, as a method of bringing about social change. In November, 1959, a group of students met with someone who was deeply involved in the whole Movement. He had been teaching and leading these workshops. We decided to test some of the large department stores downtown. We went in two different groups to restaurants and lunch counters. That was the first time that I could say that I was literally refused, that I had been denied, that someone told me, "No, you cannot be served." When I was growing up, people just knew better than to challenge. Your parents or somebody had said to you that you're black, you're supposed to go to that water fountain, you're not supposed to go to that lunch counter, you're not supposed to go downstairs to the theater. So you knew. You were conscious about it. You never really violated the customs or traditions. This was a deliberate attempt to violate it. It was the first time in my life that it was ever said to me, "No, you cannot eat here. We won't serve you." It was never said until 1959. In a sense, we expected it, but we wanted to establish the fact that the places of public accommodation did not serve mixed groups or did not serve blacks.

From that particular day in November when we had test sit-ins, we started regrouping, looking forward to more actions. We continued to meet in Nashville and continued to prepare for massive nonviolent sit-in efforts. In the meantime, on February 1, 1960, the students in Greensboro, North Carolina, had the first well-publicized sit-in. Then students throughout North Carolina started sitting in. We received a telephone call from one of the students saying, "What are the students in Nashville going to do?" Then, "What can you do to support the students in North Carolina?" We began sitting in downtown.

I'll never forget that series of days when we went down and sat there . . . I don't know . . . it was like a holy crusade, in a sense. Something told you just to stay there . . . the simplicity, the spirit, the sense of community that existed among the students. For the most part, during those early sit-in demonstrations in February, 1960, it was primarily black students, but there were some white students. We wanted to project the best image for the Movement. When some of the young whites would come up and put lighted cigarettes down our backs, or beat us, or spit on us, we never retaliated. We sat there. There was this great sense of

feeling on the part of all the participants that it was necessary to do. Even some of the people who felt that they couldn't be nonviolent, that they couldn't adhere to the philosophy and the discipline of nonviolence, would say, "Well, I will not come down and participate in the sit-in; but I will drive my car, or drive my father's car." They'd transport people.

That went on for several weeks until the last day in February. We all got arrested. A minister in the city, very active in civil rights efforts, had come to us early that morning and said that he understood from the merchants that we would be arrested. The minister said, "If you go down, you probably will be beaten. There are a lot of young hoodlums on the streets, and you will probably be arrested." That day a small group of us showed up. A few went in first and sat at the lunch counter. People came up and literally started beating the students or putting cigarettes out down their backs. They knocked people off the counter. The police came in and arrested all of the people sitting at the counter. They didn't arrest the people doing the beating, but they arrested all of the nonviolent students. Some of us that were at another variety store, only a door or so away, were asked to come down there and sit because the people had been arrested. We came, and we all were arrested. At the end of the day, 98 of us went to jail.

When the students on the campuses heard about it, about 500 of them came to continue the sit-in demonstration. More people got arrested. We went to jail. I didn't want to go to jail, but nonetheless it was a tremendous feeling to know that we had been able to dramatize the fact that segregation did exist and that there was something wrong about it. I guess many of us, most young black people, particularly in the South, grow up with a tremendous amount of fear of going to jail. Where I was brought up there was a street named Love Street. My mother used to warn us when we went to town, "Don't go down on Love Street." It was a bad place. Love Street is what Auburn Avenue is to Atlanta, or what Hunter Street is to Atlanta, what 125th Street is to Harlem. My mother would warn us that it we went to Love Street we would go to jail, the law would get us. We were told going to jail was the worst thing a person could do. It was a disgrace to go. First, it was bad for the person involved, then it was bad for the family, and it was bad for the family name.

I'll never forget the night in jail. It was just like a victory. For the most part, I don't think any of these people had been in jail before. In jail we became, in a sense, a bond, a circle of trust.

Even in Nashville there had been rivalry between the different colleges and universities, but going to jail and getting involved in the sit-in movement helped to cut across schisms. In my estimation, the people there literally grew up overnight in that sit-in. We organized ourselves. We elected a spokesman. We had an organization right there in the jail cell. During the period that we stayed in, we had committees for clean up, for exercise, and for people who needed to study or do their homework. It was a strong group of people.

My mother, after hearing that I had been arrested and jailed, said in effect, "You should get out of this Movement and get out of that mess." I remember writing my mother in jail and saying something about acting according to my Christian faith and my conviction, and that I must go through to do what I'm doing. From that time on, because of going to jail, I guess a schism did occur for a period of time between myself and my family. They really did not understand. I never tried to widen the breach. I kept trying to get them to understand. It was not until 1963 that my family began to understand me. The period 1960 to 1963 was difficult.

During that period the real family, in a sense, was not my family. The family was not my mother, my father, my sisters, my brothers, my first cousins, and my grandparents but the people in the Movement, a sort of inner circle. We were a circle of trust, a sort of band of brothers. Those people, the people that I struggled with, and went to jail with, and went to lunch counters and on the freedom rides with, these folks really became my family. I think Martin Luther King, Jr., himself, sort of being the symbolic leader, gave all of us . . . not just the participants in the Movement but to many more blacks and whites also, a sort of sense of somebodyness. Being involved tended to free you. You saw segregation, you saw discrimination, and you had to solve the problem, but you saw yourself also as the free man, as the free agent, able to act.

After what Martin Luther King, Jr., had to say, what he did, as an individual you couldn't feel alone again. You sort of destroyed a sense of being alone or a sense of alienation, the sense that you're just out there some place. I think the Movement itself, not just Dr. King, but this whole Movement, sort of integrated, brought different people together, and said, "You're not just so and so, here, or you're not just a student, but you're a part of something." It gave a sense of pride and it was a new sense of

identity, really. You felt that you had some sense of control over what was happening and was going to happen.

The community was tremendously important. There was a kind of togetherness which was one of the underlying, strong ingredients in nonviolence. If something happened to one person, it happened to all of us. If one person would go to jail, we all would go; and if one person would suffer, we all shared in that suffering.

We didn't concentrate on the violence that was done to us. We kept a telephone log. Someone might call in and say, "I saw so and so. He was beaten. The last time I saw him, he was bleeding, and such and such a thing happened, but he's all right." Even in meetings after something happened to someone, we didn't concentrate on the violence. People would just talk about what to do in violent situations, what to do with your hands, to take off your glasses and not to have any sharp objects on you if you thought there would be violence.

We used to say that our main goal was to bring about a desegregated community. In a sense we had to forget about ourselves. Somehow, we had to take our minds off particular incidents and concentrate on the goal. I think that was a sort of moving forth, knowing that we might have temporary suffering or physical pain or violence, but that we were there to bring about a desegregated and open community, to bear witness to a larger goal. We felt that the goal was an open community, a loving community in a redeemed society, and that the means must be in keeping with that. We felt that if the goal was integration, then we had to use an integrated means. We felt that if we were striving and struggling for the beloved community, then we could not use violent means to arrive at an nonviolent end.

Even before the sit-ins, I guess, I started giving serious consideration to becoming a conscientious objector. Later I got classified and had to say no to the draft. Nonviolence for many people was not just a method, not just a technique, but a way of life. It was so for me.

After the sit-ins I continued in school. In 1961 the Congress of Racial Equality initiated a program to test a Supreme Court ruling outlawing segregation in areas of interstate travel. They started recruiting people to go on the Freedom Ride in the spring of 1961, and I applied to go.

I was accepted, and all those who were going to start the Ride were supposed to be in Washington. We were supposed to get

there a few days early to go through a period of orientation. There were seven whites and six blacks going on the Ride. This was my first time in Washington, the week of May 4, 1961.

We went to a Chinese restaurant the night before the Ride. It was my first time having Chinese food. There were all these sort of weird things, for a country boy who had traveled little. It was just really strange. I was twenty-one years old in 1961. We went to dinner and it was like the Last Supper, all thirteen of us that went on the Ride. This was the night of May 3. It was really a very fascinating experience for me. We had Chinese food, all of the different pots and things, with people passing them, it was really good, different tastes and everything else. I enjoyed it. I didn't drink anything. That had something to do with my religious background. With the food, maybe I had tea or something.

We left the next day for Richmond, Virginia. We didn't have any problems in Virginia. Through North Carolina there were a very few minor problems. Two days later, we arrived in Rock Hill, South Carolina. We got off the bus, started walking toward the waiting room, opened the door, and three young white guys just came at us, really fist-fighting, and they literally knocked us down. That was the first violence on the Freedom Ride, and it was the first real violence for me. I had been arrested and hit here and there; but that was the first time I was really hurt, and it left a scar. We got up and stood there. In a matter of minutes the state police arrived and asked us if we wanted to press charges. We said no. I had to leave the Freedom Ride briefly, but I was supposed to rejoin on Monday in Montgomery. In the meantime, the bus continued through South Carolina, Georgia, and Alabama. At Anniston, Alabama, people burned one bus; on the other bus, people were beaten at the bus station in Birmingham. I was waiting in Nashville to rejoin the Ride. In Nashville we heard that CORE had cancelled the Ride. Some of us felt that the Ride should continue. A group of us—students in Nashville that were part of the student movement—started calling together different community people and ministers, saying that we must go. We had a meeting around nine or ten o'clock that night. We talked until six o'clock in the morning. We finally convinced the adult community to make the necessary money available for us to go on the Freedom Ride. We left that Wednesday morning, May 17, 1961. There were ten of us, two white students and eight black students. We started toward Birmingham. Right outside the city a policeman stopped the bus. He got on and said, "Where are the

Freedom Riders? I understand you have Freedom Riders on this bus." He arrested two of the people. When we got to Birmingham, other members of the police department got on the bus and said, "We're taking you in to the city jail, and we're placing you in protective custody of the Birmingham Police Department."

Early the next morning the sheriff came to the jail and said he was taking us back to Nashville. We said that we were on a trip, that we were on our way to Montgomery, and on to Mississippi and New Orleans. They put all of us and our baggage in two station wagons and a big limousine and took us to the Alabama/Tennessee state line. They left us there on the highway, saying that if a train or bus came by, maybe we could find our way back to Nashville.

We didn't know anybody. We walked across the railroad tracks and located a black family — they must have been in their seventies — and they were literally frightened to death. They didn't know what to do. They were staying on a white man's farm. They had heard about the Freedom Riders. They put us all in a back room in their house. When daylight came, the old lady sent her husband to two or three different grocery stores in the community to buy food for us. They didn't tell anyone we were there. We got on the telephone, called Nashville, and told them what had happened. We told them we wanted to continue, so they sent down a car. We rode by car to Birmingham. When we got to the bus station, we tried to get on, but we couldn't; they wouldn't let us board any of the buses.

There were delays; there was a mob threatening us at one time. I think Robert Kennedy was in touch with the Greyhound Company. We got a bus the next morning. We were given police protection from Birmingham to Montgomery. There was an arrangement that two officials of Greyhound would be on the bus, that a state patrol car would go with us, and that a small plane would fly above us. So we started out.

I was glad that the Ride was going to go on, but I just had an eerie feeling because I didn't know what to expect on the other end. It had been arranged that there would be transportation the moment we arrived in Montgomery to pick us up and take us to Reverend Abernathy's church. It was a strange feeling to travel down the highway on public transportation with that type of protection.

Before we got to the Montgomery city line, the state patrol car and plane disappeared. When we drove up to the bus station,

there was no sign of life. I had never seen it like that before, and I had gone to that station for four continuous years, going home for the Christmas holidays, Thanksgiving holidays, and returning sometimes in the summer. Nothing was around that station.

The moment the bus stopped, all the reporters and television people just sort of swarmed out there. Then out of the clear blue . . . I'm talking about just like a flash, and I don't know . . . to this day, I do not understand where the people came from, but there was a mob of about two thousand people that just came out there and literally just took the press people apart. They started beating one reporter and blood started gushing from his head. There was an NBC camera man who was working with Frank McGee at the time. They took his camera, one of these huge things, and just busted it across him. People were trying to get up trees or on top of the buildings to get away. We couldn't go anyplace.

When the mob had beaten the reporters down, they turned on us and they started beating us. I remember saying to the group, "Do not run. Let's stand here together." Our baggage was taken from us and burned right there on the street. I was hit and left unconscious there in the street for about forty-five minutes, according to the Montgomery paper. But I remember as I was lying there on the street and just bleeding, the Attorney General of Alabama came up and served an injunction on me for traveling through the State of Alabama as part of an interracial group. I thought that was the end. It was one of the most frightening experiences in my life. I was also quite concerned about some of the other people.

Before we were beaten we did make it a point to get the girls away. We got all the young ladies in a cab except two white students. This black cab driver refused to let the two white girls get in and said, "This is the law." One of the black girls challenged him and said she would drive the cab because they were trying to get away. The cab driver wouldn't let them. He just took the black girls. President Kennedy had sent down a newspaper editor as his personal representative. This man saw the mob trying to get to the young ladies. After the cab left with the black girls, and the mob started behind the two young white girls, he got between them and the two young girls ran toward a church. A church official let them in and that's the only thing that saved them. The editor was beaten in the street so badly that he had a concussion. A post office official hid some of the black students,

and some of the white fellows, in the basement of the post office. This was the white postmaster in Montgomery, in 1961, hiding people in the basement of the post office.

After the beating we all scattered all over the place; most of us had very few contacts and didn't know one another. I was taken to the hospital, treated, and dismissed.

What had I been feeling? Well, I guess it did come across to me . . . that this was possibly the final . . . but my greatest concern at that moment was that I was in charge of the people. I was sort of the spokesman for that group of people, and my greatest concern was what was happening to the group. I had the expense money, also. I think, and this was foolish, I had on me at that time, I think about $900, not travelers' checks. I probably didn't know anything about travelers checks then. I had never used them before. But I had $900 in cash for expenses. It was to take care of food and everything possible for the riders. I was concerned about that.

Nothing happened to the money; it was still in my pocket. My shirt and coat were covered with blood and I said, "God, is it possible for me to lose this much blood?" I started feeling the spot on my head—the cut. But I didn't think about it much after that. I didn't concentrate on it. I couldn't think about it because I felt it would be not only a waste of time, but it would be too much energy, going into what was happening to me personally, rather than forgetting about myself and becoming concerned about the main goal, the issue.

But although I didn't get overly concerned about it at the time, I do think about it now sometimes though. Sometimes, even to this day, I don't believe it happened. Sometimes I question myself, "How did it happen?" Some of these things come clearly to me. I guess they were dramatized to me again in '68 when I saw a particular picture—somebody put out a little booklet about Dr. King, and there was a picture in there of me. I was very small then, weighing only about 135 pounds. I've gained a lot of weight since then, but then I was small. I had on this sort of sport jacket, a pair of pants, and a tie, and the tie was thin, and . . . it was sort of frightening for me to see myself standing up there in this picture, with all this blood on me, and it sort of hit me, "How did that happen? Can you believe that it happened?" It brought it back.

That night I went to the meeting about continuing the Ride. I participated in the discussion like all the other people did. I went

back to the doctor just so he could look at the cut, but that's really all there was about it. That night we made plans for a mass meeting. In the meantime, Dr. King had been in contact with the Justice Department, and particularly with Attorney General Kennedy, and we made plans to have a big protest rally at the church. All of the Freedom Riders planned to arrive at the church at a certain time. We went to the meeting at the church; it was supposed to start around eight o'clock; by seven-thirty the church was full, and people were still coming. A mob came to the church. They threw stink bombs and overturned cars in the streets, right in front of the church.

It was at that meeting, that night at the church, that Martin Luther King, Jr. went down in the basement and made a call to Bobby Kennedy. He said that the lives of more than twelve hundred people were threatened and that Kennedy must do something. That very night, President Kennedy federalized the National Guard. General Graham of the National Guard in Montgomery came to the church that night. He ordered us all to stay in the church. We stayed there until six o'clock in the morning.

Two days later, Martin Luther King, James Farmer, Ralph Abernathy, and myself held a press conference and . . . I have a picture from that press conference today; I'll never forget it, I had a patch on my head in a shape like . . . it looked like a cross. We announced that the Freedom Ride would continue. We really wanted to complete the Ride and test the facilities. But we also wanted it to serve as an education for the community to get people involved in the Civil Rights Movement. So the goal was to complete the Ride.

We left Montgomery on that Wednesday. When we boarded the bus, we were escorted by the National Guard. In Montgomery we went into the so-called white waiting room, and the guards stayed with us. When we went into the restroom, they came in and guarded us. We went to the lunch counter. Dr. King and Dr. Abernathy sat with us at the lunch counter, although they didn't go on the Ride.

We rode to Mississippi with National Guard protection. When we got to Jackson we all got off and went to different areas of the waiting room. The police arrested us all and took us to the city jail. After the city jail got full, they transferred us to the Hinds County Jail. We went to trial and were sentenced to pay a $200 fine or spend 66 days in jail for refusing to move on. We refused

to pay a fine, so they sent us to the city prison farm outside Jackson. When we got there, one of the ministers was beaten by a guard, and that really created an incident. So they transferred us back to Hinds County Jail. The jail was crowded, and they segregated us. All the white guys were in one cell block and all blacks were in a different one. In the jail, in spite of the fact that we were crowded, we created a sense of structure. We organized ourselves. We also went on a hunger strike there.

They decided to transfer us to Parchman, the state penitentiary. They packed all of us into a big van truck. We had to sit on the floor, lined up the side of the wall, like horses or cows. By that time other people who had come in from all around the country had been arrested. They were all Freedom Riders, not from our particular bus, but different buses. We were singing all the way down the highway. When we got there, a white guard said, "Sing your freedom song inside. We have niggers here who are bad enough to eat you up. Sing your song inside."

It was really, really frightening. They lined us up on the wall and started walking us into the cells. They had us take off all of our clothes, every single person, each of us. Then we had to stand there for about two and a half hours in a long hallway, nude. You felt like you had been robbed of just all yourself. It was an attempt, I felt, to just dehumanize us. Then they started segregating people, all the blacks in twos and all of the whites in twos. A guard would come and get you in twos, take you to the jail cells, still with no clothes on. Then you would go and take a shower, and while you were showering, the guard would be there holding a gun. If you had a moustache or a beard or anything like that you had to cut it off. Many of the guys cut themselves trying to get their moustaches and their beards off because there were no mirrors. When you finished your shower, you were led back to your jail cell, and for about another hour and a half, left nude again. The jail cell was very, very small. Later we got Mississippi state penitentiary underwear, and that's what we wore.

We really couldn't communicate with one another. You couldn't get anything to read; you could only write two letters a week—a business letter and a family letter. All your mail was censored.

One day, on a Sunday afternoon, they brought the Governor of Mississippi, Ross Barnett, and a group of people down. It was like a tour for them, but for me, it was like being in a zoo.

I think the most difficult thing about it for me was being separated from the group. Sometimes you heard people's voices and you tried to talk to people but you really couldn't. It was very hard. All of us tried to get out within forty days so that we could appeal the case. So I got out in twenty-seven days. That finished the Ride experience for me.

What kept me going was the goal. I think a great many of us during that period were a little naive in thinking we could bring about greater change in a short period of time. Early in the game, I felt we had to pace ourselves. I didn't think it would be over quickly.

I went back to Nashville after the Freedom Ride. I took a train ride, and the rest of the summer I got involved in some efforts to desegregate the theaters and employment in some of the grocery chains. I became head of the local student movement. During the following year and the following summers, I continued to demonstrate nonviolently with a group of students, much as we had before, only there were fewer students. I worked as a field secretary for SNCC in the summers.

In 1963 we had a major effort in Nashville with many demonstrations, to make Nashville an open city. I was very active in that. Shortly after that, I was chosen as the chairman of SNCC. People didn't go around campaigning, saying "I want to be chairman. Elect me." It sort of emerged. I was elected by what was called the coordinating committee, made up of students' representatives from the different student protest movements throughout the South. After the second chairman resigned in June of '63, they invited me to the coordinating committee meeting. I never dreamed of it. I had no thoughts, ever, of being the chairman of SNCC, or any southwide or national organization, nothing like that. It was out of the blue, really, that they nominated me, and I was elected.

It was on that very day that Medgar Evers' body was in Atlanta. He had been shot a week before and his body had come from Mississippi to Atlanta, to the train station right out on Mitchell Street, where the train station used to be. We went by there and saw the casket, that afternoon, after the meeting. I moved to Atlanta the next week and got involved with SNCC full-time.

I gave up school. I really needed something. I became chairman in June of '63. School was out in May, and I didn't go back. It

was not until many years later, not until 1967, that I got my degree.

One of the first things I did after being elected was to get involved in the March on Washington. I spent a great deal of time working on plans for the March. I went to New York to discuss the March. At this meeting Whitney Young, James Farmer, Roy Wilkins, and others were there. There was a big controversy about who represented which organization, and what the March would be about. There was much arguing.

We continued to prepare for the March on Washington in 1963. I was asked to be one of the speakers. There was some controversy about the contents of my speech. I had prepared the speech, and our communication director, Julian Bond, had made advance copies available to a meeting. Apparently some of the people involved thought it was too radical. I thought the speech was very mild. I had suggested that the day might come when we might be forced to march through the South the way Sherman did, except nonviolently, splitting the South in a thousand pieces and putting them back together in the image of democracy. I said that we had to struggle for more than civil rights, to struggle to bring about a community of peace, love, justice, and brotherhood. I suggested that the day might come when there might be forces creating some national structure so that we would not have to wait for the Justice Department, or Congress, or the President, that we would take matters into our own hands. I had used the word "revolution," and some of the people said that using the word was extreme and inflammatory; I used the phrase "the masses," and some people said it was socialistic. I changed several parts of the speech, but even after the parts of the speech had been changed, some people still had some reservations. I really took it as an insult because I'd prepared the speech, and I was speaking out of the context of the Southern experience. I was speaking for the people that I was supposed to be representing, people that made up SNCC, and the people who were working in the South.

I recall in one part of the speech saying, "We cannot be patient, we cannot wait. 'Patient' is a dirty and nasty word to people who have been waiting so long." Someone objected saying, "John, the Catholics may be offended by that because they believe in patience." I'm not sure whether he was just saying this, but I took it quite seriously. I also said that we could not support the administration's Civil Rights Bill because it was too little and too late,

and because the bill would not protect the old women and young children involved in peaceful nonviolent demonstrations. It did not provide the right to register and vote for a person who lacked a sixth grade education. We in SNCC took the position, and I took the position in my speech, that the only qualifications for being able to register to vote in the United States should be those of age and residence. I said in my speech "One man, one vote."

During the March, when it came time to introduce me, I was tense because of all the pressure I had been under to change the speech. I gave the speech, and I felt good about it when it was over. In a sense, it changed my life. For the first time in my life, I saw that great pressures at the very highest levels could be used on you when you're saying something you're not supposed to say. Much later, I heard that some people within the Kennedy administration had put pressure on the Archbishop to say that he would refuse to give the invocation if I didn't change the speech. I had no way of knowing that. I was disturbed about what I saw, but under no circumstances did it make me bitter. I think I got a deeper understanding and maybe a better revelation of some of the things we were up against in bringing about change all over the country.

I still had a tremendous amount of respect and admiration for President Kennedy, in particular, and later for Robert Kennedy. But at the same time, I was not going to let that blind my criticism, because I thought that President Kennedy was being too cautious on the whole question of civil rights. Much later, after the March, Bobby Kennedy said to me, "John, the people, the young people of SNCC are educated, and I know and understand." I really believe that Bobby Kennedy, after the March and a series of events during the time that he was Attorney General, really did understand.

Less than a month later, the church in Birmingham was bombed and the four young girls were killed. It was September 15, 1963. What happened there was so devastating. I was in Troy, Alabama, visiting my parents when I heard about it. My parents had a great fear about what might happen to me. My uncle from Dalton wanted me to ride with him to Dalton and get on the bus there, so maybe no one there would recognize me as I came into Birmingham, and I did it; it satisfied his and my parents' concern.

There's not a set way or method, when someone dies or when there's a loss or when there's a death . . . each one is always

different . . . death itself is something that, in a sense, you never really get acquainted with, you never really understand. It's something I never understand, and never was able to understand, and never will understand. But I knew I wanted to do something. I wanted to express the sense of indignation, but I wanted to do it in some constructive way. We had a big debate in SNCC about marching on Montgomery and about a boycott of the State of Alabama. There was a search for some way to strike out in a nonviolent way to show our disapproval.

Martin Luther King, Jr., presided officially at the funeral of at least three of the girls that had been shot, and Martin had a beautiful way of comforting and providing a sense of release. Those young girls were four innocent human beings who became victims of the evil forces in the emerging society. I felt almost helpless that I could not do anything. I didn't know those young girls personally, but the killing still hurt me. We had the death of Medgar Evers, the four young girls in '63; in those early years there had been others. All of this continued to build up.

After the funeral of the young girls in Birmingham, I went to Atlanta. We started the big push in Selma—one man, one vote. On October 8, 1963, eight hundred people lined up at the Dallas County Courthouse all day long, trying to get in to attempt to register. That was the beginning there.

In November of '63, President Kennedy was assassinated. I was supposed to speak to a local union in Detroit on Friday night, November 22nd. When I heard that President Kennedy had died, I really felt bad, totally. This was the first time that something like this had happened to someone prominent, to somebody that I had met, admired, and respected. But it was more than that. The ideals of President Kennedy were a symbol. He had helped to create a climate that made it possible for some changes. In spite of his being so cautious, it appeared that the federal government emerged as a referee in the whole struggle of the Movement. His death had tremendous effect on me. I wanted to come home. In time of great crises, I really always wanted to go to a place that I knew best. I was thinking about getting back to Atlanta, but the meeting in Detroit was still on. So I went there, and I spoke, and we had a memorial service for President Kennedy. That was a Friday, and on that Saturday, I was supposed to go to . . . I guess it was Champaign, Illinois . . . the University, Urbana, some place, to speak to the student group. They still wanted me to come, so I spoke there, and I came back to Cincinnati from there

and spoke there. It seemed like I was never going to make it back to Atlanta. Finally, I got back to Atlanta late Sunday night and I was home. I watched the funeral and everything on television. I didn't go to the funeral. It affected me a great deal. When the Kennedy half dollars came out, I collected them — I still collect Kennedy half dollars — I have many, many of them and I probably should deposit them in a bank or draw interest, or something like that, but I collect them.

Near the end of '63, we were planning the big move on Mississippi, but even before then we had what we called a mock election in the State of Mississippi, what we called a Freedom Election, with people like Aaron Henry running. At that time there were only about twenty-four thousand black people registered in the State of Mississippi out of a black voting age population of about four hundred-fifty thousand. Almost two hundred thousand people turned out to participate in that mock election that we called, and that's where the whole Mississippi Freedom Movement got started. After the election we started recruiting students to come and be a part of the Mississippi Summer Project. In the early part of '64, I spent a great deal of time traveling to colleges all over this country. At the end of the recruitment period, we had at least a thousand people committed.

I had mixed emotions about the Mississippi Summer Project. We had been told that almost anything could happen there. There was a history of violence in the Delta, and we just didn't know what type of friction would develop between some of the black workers and the white workers. Another thing that disturbed me a great deal, as I went around the campuses recruiting students, was that in a sense I felt responsible for a lot of the people because I convinced them to come down.

We moved the SNCC office from Atlanta to Greenwood, Mississippi, and I spent most of the summer working out of Greenwood. After we got there, we had the disappearances and deaths of those three civil rights workers. I will never forget some of the problems and trauma that some of the SNCC people went through. I think we had all felt that the whites would do something and then this happened so early in the effort. It was unbelievable. It was really hurting.

Stokely Carmichael and I stayed in a house in Greenwood. People think there was a lot of bitterness between Stokely and myself, but it really was not the case. We stayed in the same house, and as a matter of fact, we shared a room with a black

family. Their son and daughter were very much involved in the local Movement there in Greenwood.

One of my great fears in Mississippi during that summer, and I think it's still a fear I have now to some degree, was the fear of being involved in an automobile accident. The people of SNCC drove like mad. All the guys had the fear that somebody was trailing them so they felt they had to keep the speed and that they couldn't let anyone be that close behind, and rightly so. But I was afraid of dying in an automobile, and I still am today. I'd rather travel by any other means of transportation. Later on, when I lived in New York, I always thought I would be hit by a car. It may sound silly, or psychological, or whatever, but I felt it would be very embarrassing to be hit by a car. I just felt that if I were hit by a car, people would just say, "Well, that fool got in front of a car. He should have stayed on the sidewalk." After all that traveling through the South and going to jail and being beaten, and all, then to get hit by a car would be awful.

Anyway, somehow we made it through the summer. I don't know, I really don't know how. But we made it. What happened that summer I think helped to change the direction of the Movement. It forced a great many people to rededicate themselves to the Movement. I often think of the mothers of those three guys that died helping us. They emerged as strong and brave. I still see them from time to time.

Particularly after the murders, we lived in Mississippi with the constant possibility that something could happen to any of us. During the summer many, many churches were bombed and burned, particularly black churches in small towns and rural communities that had been headquarters for Freedom Schools, for voter registration rallies, and workshops. There was shooting on homes, so we lived with constant fear. At the same time, we didn't become preoccupied with the fear. You got to feel part of a nonviolent army, and in the group you had a sense of solidarity and you knew you had to move on in spite of your fear. I think for many of us, that summer in Mississippi was like guerrilla warfare. You knew that you had to prepare yourself, condition yourself, if you were going to be there. You knew that you were going to stay for a period of time, and there were going to be disappointments and setbacks. What we tried to instill, particularly in the SNCC staff and also into the young people coming down, was that even as they came there, we weren't going to change Mississippi in one summer or one year, that it was a much

longer effort. In a sense we went down to help the people there, but no doubt they helped all of us a great deal; there's no question about that. Some of us, no doubt, literally grew up overnight because of being in positions of responsibility where we had to make decisions, we had to act. Our main purpose was trying to bring the local, indigenous black people of Mississippi to a particular level.

There was one thing about SNCC: there were all kinds of conflicts and debates about things, but in times of a real crisis people came together. I'm not talking about interim crises, like some organizational crisis, not that type. But if there was a crisis affecting a particular individual, or a particular city, or movement of people, then the SNCC people really felt together. Music and song really became a way of having people to sort of, I guess, escape immediate fears, the immediate dangers. I remember on many, many occasions where there was a threat of violence on the picket lines, when people were about to be arrested, and people knew they would be beaten, they were singing.

We sang songs like *"We Shall Overcome," "Freedom Is a Constant Struggle," "I Ain't Gonna Let Nobody Turn Me Around,"* and *"Before I Be a Slave I'll Be Buried in My Grave."* Sometimes when people were debating something, say whether we should go to Selma or not, there was a big, long discussion about whether we should go to Selma and march, then people would sing songs and they'd try to reach a consensus . . . would the circle be broken, people would ask. Songs tended to give people a sense of togetherness, a sense of unity and "sustaination." It also solved . . . music had a way of sort of quieting some of the feelings, disrobing people of some of their fears.

After the summer we sent a delegation to Atlantic City to challenge the seating of the regular Democrats of Mississippi at the National Democratic Convention. All across Mississippi there had been a real effort to organize a viable political structure under the banner of the Mississippi Freedom Democratic Party. A great many of us thought the delegation would be seated. Many other delegates from all across the country were sympathetic. Many people recognized that the regular delegation had been responsible, in so many ways, for keeping people from registering to vote.

We lost that round. The delegation was not seated. I think that was the beginning of a growing discontent and disillusionment within SNCC and on the part of a great many people, both black

and white, who had spent the summer of 1964 in Mississippi. People became very bitter and very hostile toward the government. I was very disappointed, but I felt we couldn't let it be our death blow.

Between the Democratic Convention of late '64 and the attempt in Selma, early in 1965, a group of 13 SNCC people who had been very active in the Mississippi effort, people like Fanny Lou Hamer, Julian Bond, and myself were invited to Africa. For most of us, it was our first time out of the country and our first time in Africa. I think the trip gave the group a new sense of determination. For the first time we saw black people controlling and running their own affairs. That gave us a greater sense of hope.

In late December of '64, SNCC held a series of meetings. SNCC had gone through a great many changes. A lot of people came out of that Mississippi summer very bitter, very hostile. Some people became very frustrated. It was not just clashes between blacks who made up the SNCC staff and some other people, like civil rights workers, volunteers who were not necessarily staff people, but those were part of it. One of the conflicts we had after the '64 effort particularly in Mississippi was, for example, like this. In some of the counties and some of the congressional districts where there had been a SNCC field secretary, black and a local Mississippian, who had been there as a secretary for weeks and months with very little attention from our side, someone perhaps able to type 20 words per minute. During the Summer Project, some white student had come down from the North who could type maybe 60 or 75 words per minute. When the work needed to be done fast, it would go to the white person and not the young black person who had been there all along. That dispirited the young black person.

As a result of the 1964 Mississippi summer, SNCC started turning inward as an organization. As long as there was a target, a Birmingham, a Nashville, a Selma, a Bull Conner, a Jim Clark, a nonviolent direct action, a viable movement, people could direct most of their energies and all of their attention toward it. When there was a low period without a target, sometimes frustration set in and people turned inward on themselves. During that time we had a SNCC staff meeting I will never forget. There was a great deal of debate about the future of SNCC and about what we should be doing. I think the frustration and the burden and weight of the Movement took its toll. It was so visible at this

particular meeting. After almost a whole night's meeting, some of the people suggested that we should give up structure, that we shouldn't have an organization, that we should have only a revolving committee. There shouldn't be a chairman, an executive secretary, or an executive committee, but only a revolving committee. During that time we had gone through the period that some people have referred to as the "Freedom High Period." After the summer of '64, everybody wanted to just do their own thing. We had a lot of discussion of women's rights. The whole question of decision-making became a problem, a factor within SNCC, and it had never happened before. Who decided who should go to South Georgia? Why did someone go to Mississippi rather than Alabama or to Atlanta? Who would make that decision? So the latter part of '64 and the first part of '65 were really considered the "Freedom High Period." It was a difficult period. It showed up particularly at the meeting, where people wanted to give up structure.

Then in the winter of 1965, we started getting more involved in Selma. That brought SNCC closer together. People started directing their concerns and energies toward the Selma Movement. The old SNCC people who had dropped out for a period came to Selma. This was the week of January 19. Then, in late February, we had a staff meeting. In a sense all hell broke loose at this meeting. There was a very strange scene that day.

One guy had remained in Mississippi and he'd become . . . not necessarily bitter . . . but very disappointed about what had happened in Atlantic City. He had worked in the field since 1961 and had put a lot of time and a lot of energy and spirit into there. He had sort of emerged in SNCC as a type of saint. People admired him and respected his qualities and feelings, and just his presence. The people who made up the staff were very, very close to him.

Some of these meetings that we had were like revivals, where people would sing and people would make speeches, some of them were fantastic sessions. This time this guy stood up and took a soft drink bottle with water — he said it was wine but it was not wine — and started singing and marching around the room with a lot of people. It was like being in a revival where the minsiter saves the souls of the sick.

He didn't want to emerge as the leader. But the local black people in the state where he had worked saw him, in a sense, as their leader. He didn't want to become a symbol. He didn't want

that responsibility and he felt that the only way to get away from that would be to leave. He said this. When he finished his statement, people continued to sing and other people stood and made statements and sang things like *"Will the Circle Be Unbroken?"* This guy went back to the field, but he didn't stay long; he just dropped out of sight. He eventually ended up in Africa.

We continued to have many demonstrations in Selma. Arrests occurred. All the SNCC people got back together on March 7. Some of the people at SNCC, particularly those who came from Mississippi, felt that we shouldn't march to Montgomery from Selma. SCLC said we should march. Jimmy Jackson, a black guy in Marion, Alabama, had been killed leading a registration march. People felt we should find some way to dramatize that killing and what was happening in Alabama. A march had been planned, so we had an emergency executive committee meeting. The executive committee took the position that we'd been leading people down the road, that they would get beaten and arrested. They said there had just been too much hurt and too much pain for people, and that we shouldn't do it. Others felt they had an obligation to be there with the people. The executive committee decided that those who wanted to march could march as individuals but not as representatives of SNCC. I decided to go.

About six hundred people from several counties in Alabama gathered the next morning at the church to participate in the March. I was asked to march with the group as an individual but not as chairman of SNCC. Six hundred of us lined up in teams, and the March started. Governor Wallace warned that the March would not be allowed. On that particular day I really don't think we planned to stay any place on the road at night, we were just going to march out of the city, come back overnight, and then continue the March the next day. We got across the Edward Pettus Bridge, and were met with a sea of state troopers. A major said, "This is unlawful, and you will not be allowed to continue. I give you three minutes to disperse." We stood there in a sort of prayerful manner. Not a single person in the line moved or said anything. In less than three minutes the major said, "Troopers, advance." They put on gas masks and started beating and pushing people. This time I felt it was really, really the end. It was hard to breathe because of the tear gas. It was choking me to death. I saw members of the sheriff's posse on horses with bull-whips beating people and just running over people. They left us lying all over the place. People were beaten all the way back down

to the downtown area. Many of us got back to the church and people came to pick us up. I made a little speech in the church. I made a statement to the effect that "the United States Government can send troops to Vietnam but cannot protect the poor people of Alabama." After that I was carried to a hospital where I stayed for three days. It was bloody, and a lot of people were hurt.

The next day hundreds of SNCC people from all across the South just emptied the state and came to Alabama. People who had disagreed with the March came to Selma to support it. I think that that was the turning point. What happened in Selma was the finest hour for the Civil Rights Movement.

In the hospital I remember thinking I was lucky to be alive. I really couldn't believe that it had happened. Some people would say that we were foolish, that we had too much faith, too much hope. I was just thankful to be alive. A few days later, Dr. King came to visit me, and that was a good feeling. There were cards and telegrams. One lady from Birmingham who died not too long ago and was living at that time in San Jose sent a beautiful thing of flowers with a little card that said, "A former Alabamian. We are with you." That was very touching, very moving.

It may sound strange, but I think someplace along the way I made up my mind that I would not become bitter or hostile. I think that's part of the whole philosophy of nonviolence. When you let the nonviolent discipline or philosophy become a way of life, it will control all aspects of your life. I recognized the fact that just by being in Selma and being in one particular march, that I was going to be there for a few days, a few weeks, a few months, and not eventually going to complete the chain; but that it was going to be a long struggle, that I had to prepare myself for a long and difficult struggle. You just couldn't afford to waste yourself. I disliked a great many of the things that occurred, particularly on March 7, 1965. I have never seen anything like that. Even today, when I watch the Martin Luther King film and see what happened there, it is hard for me to believe, but it is not something that I became bitter or hostile about.

I went back on the March. On the 9th, Dr. King attempted to lead a group of prominent ministers, priests, rabbis, and people from the academic community, across the bridge — more than a thousand people. He did get across the bridge, and there was a group of state troopers there. Apparently there was an arrangement with the Justice Department that this would only be a

symbolic action and that they would turn back. They did. In the meantime, we went into Federal Court, trying to gain the right to march. We sued the state of Alabama, and tried to get an injunction against the state of Alabama, Governor Wallace, Sheriff Clark, and the state troopers for interfering with a peaceful march. After I got out of the hospital, I spent most of my time testifying in Federal Court. In court they showed the film of what happened. Judge Johnson was so disturbed by what he saw that he called a recess. We asked for the right to march from Selma to Montgomery without interference from any county or the state. We presented a plan. For the most part, it was approved. In the meantime Reverend Reed had been killed in Selma. He had been beaten by a group of white men who saw him helping black people to gain the right to vote. That act and the other events created further indignation among many people throughout the country. During that time friends of SNCC in about 80 different communities and cities across the country engaged in protest demonstrations, reacting to what they saw in Selma.

President Johnson went on television March 15. He made a strong appeal to protect the right of black people in Selma to vote. He mentioned the fact that people had been beaten, and he mentioned that Reverend Reed had been killed attempting to support the voter rights effort. I remember listening to the speech with Dr. King. We had been invited to Washington by the White House to be in the halls of Congress when he spoke, but we decided we should remain in Selma. That night tears actually came to Dr. King's eyes when President Johnson said, "We shall overcome, we shall overcome." It was a great speech, probably one of the finest statements in support of voter rights for all people.

Later, when we got the order that a march would occur, President Johnson called Governor Wallace to Washington. He tried to get a statement from Governor Wallace saying that he would protect the marchers. Wallace said, in effect, that he couldn't guarantee it, so President Johnson federalized the National Guard. It was not until March 22, I believe, that we actually started to march from Selma to Montgomery. It took us about three or four days to reach Montgomery. The people that participated in the March — black, white, young, old, rich, poor, Protestant, Catholic, Jew — slept out in the fields, under those tents. About three hundred people walked the 50 miles. By the time we arrived in Montgomery, there were people from all across the country. I guess the total was about fifty thousand people. It was

a fantastic feeling when we got to Montgomery. It was a good feeling for all of us to make it there, stand in front of the Capitol, and demand the right of people to vote.

After that a great many SNCC people continued to work very hard in Alabama. They spent the summer of 1965 preparing for the election in 1966, and they used the symbol that the Black Panthers used later as a symbol. In a sense, that was where the Black Panther Party came from. The people in California picked up the symbol and gave the party a different kind of philosophy. Many people in SNCC at that time began to become very localized, to zero in on a particular community, mostly in Alabama.

This continued through 1965, and on August 6, 1965, President Johnson signed the Voting Rights Act. A group of us were invited to Washington to meet with President Johnson the night it was signed. We engaged in a long discussion with him. He was very happy about it, and so were we. We were invited to the White House for the signing of the Act, and that was a fantastic thing. We could see some of our dreams and hopes coming true. We felt the Act would make it possible for people all across the South to become registered during the latter part of the summer of 1965, and many more in 1966.

In the spring of 1966, SNCC went through some tremendous changes. In the February 1965 meeting, I had been re-elected to the chairmanship. After the summer of 1965, the U.S. Government was getting more and more involved in the Vietnam war, and more and more of the SNCC people were being drafted. A group of SNCC people put out a leaflet in Mississippi. They made a point about black people being drafted to fight for something they did not have yet at home. It started influencing people in SNCC, and the whole question of the war took on a different meaning. We spent a great deal of time in late November and December debating the question of Vietnam, and whether we should take a position on the war. Finally we had a staff meeting the last week of December and made a decision to take a position. Some of the people argued against taking a position. Some said that if we took this position it was going to hurt our fund-raising, and that it was just a bad position for us to condemn the United States Government for what went on in Vietnam. Some of us took the position, including myself, that if we were going to die, then let us die for something that is right. We shouldn't refuse to take a position because it might hurt the SNCC fund-raising efforts. The staff decided to make a statement.

On January 6, 1966, we prepared to issue the statement. It was a strong statement denouncing the war in Vietnam and denouncing the fact that many young black people, many civil rights workers, were being drafted. We called upon people to refuse the draft and do alternative service with civil rights groups and local poverty agencies in the southern parts of the United States. The press really played it up. Julian Bond was the communication director at the time. Julian was called about the statement, and he said he supported it.

After the statement I went out of town to speak in Virginia. When I got back, I saw a headline in the paper saying that there would be an attempt to keep Representative Bond from his seat for publishing that statement. I felt very bad about that. I felt that maybe because I issued the statement, I was responsible for the fact that Julian, after all this struggle, wouldn't be able to be seated in the Georgia House. Julian had been elected for the first time in the previous election.

The press tried to make it appear that we knew that the members of the Georgia House would react this way, that it was all part of a plot. We had no idea that issuing that statement would cause this great reaction. It just showed how naive we were. We stood behind the statement, and all of the people in SNCC supported it, including Julian; when it came time for him to take his seat in the Georgia House, he had to stand outside while the House debated it. When the vote came, he was denied his seat. The people in SNCC rallied to his support. Dr. King led a march to the state capitol. There was a special election and Julian was re-elected. He was still denied his seat. The case was finally taken to the Supreme Court, and his seating was ordered.

After the reaction to Vietnam had settled down, and we had been castigated by some of the older civil rights groups and certain members of the press, we were invited to speak at peace groups in the country. I also traveled a great deal. While I was away, there was a meeting of SNCC, in which the whole question of who made decisions came up. That was the first inkling that someone in SNCC would really get out and run for re-election. Never before in the history of SNCC had anyone campaigned for their position. I had been out of the country and came back when all of the preparations and plans had been made for the staff meeting. Stokely said he was going to be a candidate for the chairmanship of SNCC. I said, "Okay, that's good." Personally,

I had made up my mind on the trip that I wouldn't let myself be re-elected. I felt that it was time for someone else to become chairman of SNCC. I had been chairman for almost three years, and I also wanted to think about the possibility of returning to school in '66.

When I got back and started talking with people, the whole question of violence and nonviolence became an issue. I felt at that point that I had an obligation to stay there and try to keep that philosophy alive. My name was placed in nomination at the meeting along with several other names, and I won the election by a large vote. After the vote, two guys who were not even working on the staff at that time walked into the meeting. They said they wanted to challenge the election. That opened up a great deal of discussion on the whole question of violence and nonviolence, my relationship with Martin Luther King, the relationship with President Johnson, the fact that white people were taking over SNCC and it was time for blacks to work for black communities and whites to work with whites.

That meeting went on until four a.m. Saturday morning, and a re-election was held. I was nominated; Stokely was nominated, and he won the election on that vote, after a large number of people had left the meeting. It was a very bitter meeting. I didn't say very much during the meeting, and there were a lot of hard feelings, not necessarily between Stokely and myself. There were those who were very hostile to Dr. King and the whole nonviolent appeal. I think that weighed in the election. This happened on May 13, 1966. I resigned from SNCC on June 11, to become effective July 22, or something like that.

For six years, 1960 to 1966, SNCC and my commitment to and involvement in the Civil Rights Movement were my life. I wasn't married; I just didn't have any outside life. When I left, I had the idea that I would probably go back to school and maybe get a job on the side because I had very little money. After a while, after I resigned, I was offered a job with the Field Foundation. That was really the only offer that I received, and that's what saved me. I worked there for a year, and I enjoyed it. It was a fantastic opportunity to be there and work, but it was not really in the South, and I wanted to be in the South. I felt strange, cut off, separated.

After a time I came back to the South, to the Southern Regional Council. They called me and offered me a job as Director of Community Organization. I was working with Al Ulmer on the

cooperatives, the credit union, and community development. That was an opportunity, an opening, to get back in the South. New York was too big. To me, it was just hopeless, being in a place like New York; in the South there was a greater sense of hope. You could see people emerging. There was a sense on my part that I wanted to be a part of what was happening in the South, not just somebody on the sidelines watching, but one who would continue to participate in it. You know, I was born in the South, so I consider myself a southerner.

I did not want to run away from what I had been part of, simply because I had left SNCC. I felt that SNCC did a great deal for one particular period, but there were other agencies, other organizations, and other ways of going about changing the South. I wanted to see that change come about, and I wanted to be a part of it. I believed what I had been hearing some southerners say, that maybe the South could emerge as the model. Maybe it could work its way out of some of the most difficult racial problems and reach its potential. I accepted and believed that.

At that time Martin Luther King was still alive, based in Atlanta, and I was on the Board of SCLC. Bobby Kennedy was alive. I identified with what Dr. King did, so I came back and worked with the Southern Regional Council and the Federation of Southern Cooperatives. I traveled throughout the South.

In March, there were rumors that Bobby Kennedy was going to run for President. When I heard about Bobby Kennedy's announcement for the race, I sent him a telegram from my hotel, saying, "Senator Kennedy, if I can be of any help, let me know." I urged him to run. A few days later, I got a call from his office asking me to come to work in the campaign. I took a leave from SRC in March of '68. I only wanted him to pay my transportation and expenses because I really believed in his candidacy. I wanted to see him nominated and elected.

I went to Indianapolis to work with a black organization that conducted voter registration. People were very excited. I was in Indianapolis when Dr. King was assassinated. Bobby Kennedy was in Terre Haute on his way back to Indianpolis to speak at a rally. He had heard about the assassination, and there was a great debate as to whether he should come to speak. Most of the people at the rally didn't even know that Dr. King had been shot. Kennedy landed at the airport, and I talked to him on the telephone. I insisted that he come to this rally. It was in the heart of the

black community. People had showed up and it was a predominantly black audience.

He spoke, and it was a fantastic speech; he made an announcement that a good man, Dr. Martin Luther King, had been shot and killed. He went on to say that we didn't know who shot Dr. King but that apparently it was a white man. He asked the people not to hate, and not to fear, and to take a lesson from Dr. King. We went back to the hotel after the speech and had a talk; he broke down. We left that night, trying to get a plane to Atlanta.

I attended the funeral. After Dr. King's funeral, I remained in Atlanta for a few days. I felt that what happened was such a blow, such a tragedy. From the time I was fifteen to the time I was twenty-eight, the man had been a part of my life. He was a person that I trusted. He was my friend and hero, so it was a great loss. The grief was lessened to some extent by the fact that Bobby Kennedy was still alive, and I went all out campaigning for him.

After the Indiana primary, I went to Oregon and then to California. It was fantastic. He was defeated in Oregon, but the people in California just poured out for him. We knew, then, that he was just going to win. The night that he won the primary, I was in his room in the Ambassador Hotel. He suggested that I remain in the suite while he went down and gave his victory statement. I think Ted White of *The Making of a President* and several others were there in the room. We remained there and saw his speech on television. We were in the room when the shooting took place. It was really such a devastating thing. It felt so bad. The next morning, I checked out of the hotel. At that time Senator Kennedy was still alive, but there was almost no hope.

I started back, got to the airport, and got on a flight to Atlanta. It seemed to me it was the loneliest, just the longest flight of my life. This flight was really the . . . I had traveled a great deal all across this country from 1964 on. I traveled, speaking for SNCC, and I'd been on many, many planes, long trips, from California to Atlanta, from California to New York, but this flight was the longest . . . the most depressing and the saddest flight in my life. Coming back I didn't go to sleep, and I would look down, coming over the mountains. I could still see snow, and this was June. I would cry a little; I had to cry coming back on this flight. I felt all alone, just completely alone. I came back to Atlanta and then there was a service. Then I made plans to go to New York for the funeral at the church. I did go and attend the funeral and rode the funeral train from New York to Washington. All along the

way you saw children, young people, black, white, poor, rich, old, young, everybody. It was very sad, but at the same time I was very moved. I wanted the train ride to go on and on because it was the last hope, in a sense. It really took a great deal out of me, it really did.

After the funeral and the burial in Washington, I came back to Atlanta. For a few days I just didn't do anything. I came back to SRC and then went to Chicago to the convention. Kennedy was *the* candidate, and I couldn't really get excited about the others.

When the Republican Convention came around, I went to the hospital for a regular checkup, and I watched the Republican Convention for about three days in the Holy Family Hospital in Atlanta. In the meantime, New Year's Eve of 1967, I had met my wife-to-be. In October of '68 I became engaged and in December of '68 I got married. When I look back on it, if Dr. King had lived, if Bobby Kennedy had lived and had become President, I think my own life probably would have been different. I probably wouldn't have gone to the hospital in the summer of '68 for a checkup and probably wouldn't have had as much time. I probably would have been married, but I probably wouldn't have gotten married so soon.

I returned to work and was offered the directorship of the Voter Education Project. I've been working there since, and I enjoy it. I can see certain things that have happened since 1962. I can measure them; I can count them. I feel good about it. More and more people have been registered, and more and more people are getting interested in the political process. More and more people will eventually be elected. There's a change in the politics of the South. I'm encouraged about what is happening in the South.

I think my thoughts have changed from time to time. I have made certain adjustments along the way, but I don't think there have been any radical changes in the goal, or in the dream. Some of the things that we had to fight for in the early 1960s are realized now. Part of the effort now is to consolidate the gains that were made and build on them. Over the long haul, political involvement and economic development will continue to be the most important.

Those of us who were committed to the philosophy and to the discipline of nonviolence during the early 1960s are, for the most part, still committed. I think we went through certain periods of frustration and disillusionment, and some people became very

bitter. During the early '60s in the South, particularly on the part of the younger people, there was a great deal of interracial or biracial cooperation, working together. During that time, the only true integration that existed perhaps in the American society was that which existed within the Movement itself. Today, I think some people would like to think that because of what we went through during late '66 to about '68, when people felt that the black community wanted to go one way and the white community was forced to go another way, that there could no longer be any real and genuine black and white working together in cooperation. I think that period of the late 1960s was transitional. I think we're almost out of it. In the South today, the black people and white people are prepared and willing to work together. I see it in Atlanta, in the heart of Mississippi, and in some places in Alabama.

There was a schism, and a great deal of this came from black northerners who really didn't understand the psyche of the black southerners. They did not understand what made them tick. They participated in the Movement and they did a great deal to help, but they came with a lot of myths. Growing up in New York and Harlem is different from growing up in Atlanta, or in Alabama, or in the Mississippi Delta. It is just a different feeling. I don't think that those of us that grew up in the South had the same degree of bitterness, the same degree of frustration as the northerners. I don't think we could have developed a nonviolent Movement in the North.

The whole effort in the political development that is sweeping the South right now is helping to realize the dream. Just count the number of the elected black officials and the new breed of elected white officials. People are crossing the racial line to vote for the man and not for or against a person because of his race. That's a strong indication of what is happening in this part of the country.

I think for some of us the Movement itself became a family. In a sense it became more than a family because the people became one of you. That had really nothing to do with race, someone could be black or white, but every person, in a sense, became your brother or sister. I'll never forget some of those meetings, whether they were staff meetings, or parties, or singing, or playing volleyball, there was just the sense of kinship, a sense of fellowship. Even today, many of the people may not be involved in the same

organization or in the same structure, but there is that line of communication. People call, and talk, and write letters. They try to keep up with each other.

I don't spend much time looking back. Sometimes I engage in a period of contemplation or maybe meditation. Sometimes I go back and read a particular book, or a particular letter, or a speech that somebody made. I listen to a record every now and then and sing some of the freedom songs that came through the Movement. I play some of the speeches by Dr. King and John Kennedy from time to time.

I really feel that I have to continue to look ahead. It's difficult for me to really become depressed. During the Movement, at the height of the Movement, I sometimes got physically tired. I was walking around but sometimes I was literally asleep. But that was the pace that was going. It's sort of difficult to become depressed, because I feel I am in tune with something. I have an obligation to do something. I enjoy what I'm doing. It's necessary to do it.

It is a great source of inspiration to see the results of some of the work that has been done. When I go back to a community, the same people that I met in the early 1960s are still working and struggling. Things have changed a little for them, but not much; they still have the courage and the audacity to keep going. That is the greatest source of inspiration for me, and I think that, in a sense, keeps me going. We all build on the strength, the courage, and the fortitude of those around us. That's what I think the Movement is all about: you depend on your brother to help give you strength, and you help each other.

Chapter 2

Mrs. Anne Williams

Mrs. Anne Williams sat stiffly on the sofa in the office of the black lawyer for whom she worked. She spoke easily, without an accent. At the time I talked to her, she was 76 years old.

She was frail and her delicate bones were visible beneath the folds of skin. Though her manners were those of a fine, cultured southern lady, proud of her traditions and family, her perceptions and experiences were powerful, original, and by no means traditional.

She was born in 1897 in the county where we spoke. In 1914 she moved with her family to the Midwest, and then, in 1924, to one of the major cities in the North. She returned South intermittently in the 1930s and 1940s, and finally settled there permanently in 1952.

She spoke from an unusual perspective: she had personally witnessed and been involved with most of the major black political movements of this century. She had been active in the Civil Rights Movement. Several of the leaders of the Movement came to her for advice and counsel. She remembered people, names, dates, and titles of books exactly; I do not do full justice to that precision in this retelling.

We spoke first about her family.

My grandfather, my mother's father, was born in a rural county. He was a slave and still a very young man when slavery was over. He drove the coach for a white family. His young master taught him to read and write, and he taught him manners. Grandpa was always known for his courtly manners. In 1866, after Surrender, the black college where my father taught was founded. In 1867 my grandfather and some other ex-slaves walked from their homes to our town to enter the college. The people in the college were looking for leaders to train. Some couldn't quite make it, but Grandpa could, because, as I said, his young master had already taught him. So, he went to college in '67. He became a minister and then a politician. He preached until he retired at the age of eighty-three. In 1880 Grandpa went to the first general

conference of the Methodist Episcopal Church after the Civil War. He headed our state's delegation. He also went to the Republican National Conventions every quadrennium until 1928. He was a master politician.

What I remember most about him was the immense dignity he had. He was never caught off guard. He was a politician all the way, both through church politics and the Republican party. Next to his love for his wife and children, those were the two loves of his life—the Methodist Church and the Republican party.

He went to the Third Ecumenical Conference in London in 1901, and on one of the voyages, I don't know whether it was going over or coming back, there was a storm at sea. Everybody was afraid. When Grandpa asked the captain if he thought they could be saved, the captain took him to the hold, and he said, "Look down here. Do you see those men gambling?" Grandpa said, "Yes." He said, "Well, as long as those men are gambling, you are safe. When they quit gambling, you'll know the ship will be going down." My Grandpa had a slight speech impediment and when he looked down that hole he said, "Th-th-th-thank God they are g-g-g-gambling yet!" It was funny, the way the church fought gambling and all, and there he was, a Methodist preacher saying that.

As I grew up, politics was discussed all the time in our home. We kept up with things all over. My grandfather was a Taft Republican. At the convention in Chicago, Roosevelt attempted to split the Republican party. He did, to an extent, but he couldn't get the nomination without our state's vote. My grandfather was offered a bribe by a man from across the state. He came to my grandfather's hotel room and offered him a thousand dollar bill to switch his vote from Taft to Roosevelt. Grandpa wouldn't do it. He left the state with the delegation pledged to Taft, and he was determined to keep it that way. He did not change his vote or his endorsement, and a lot of people have said that that was really why the Bull Moose party was formed and why the Republican party split, because they could not get him to change his vote and take the delegation into Roosevelt's camp. It made a split in the party and naturally made a split among the leaders here in the state.

What I learned from him most was to be polite. He was a real snob. He didn't believe in being friendly except to certain people. He was that way until he died, and sometimes he and I wouldn't hit it off because he couldn't understand why I was so universally

friendly. I don't think he ever quite forgave me for it.

My mother's mother had been one of the house girls in slavery time, and she was quite a lady. Both of them were. They had come up, as they called them, "house people." They both had beautiful manners. All my grandmother cared about in life was her husband, her home, and her children. Those three were the center of her existence. I remember that she was very strict, as most people were in those days; but one time I asked her if I might go someplace and she said, "You don't have to ask me every time you want to go to some little girl's house or to play; you just come and say, 'Grandma, I am going to Bessie Tompkins' house, I'll be there such a length of time.'" Then she said, "If anybody tells me they saw you someplace else, I will know it isn't true because you have told me where you are going." She was very firm.

My father's parents were slaves, of course. They hadn't had any schooling whatsoever and never received any schooling. They married young, had five sons, and life was very, very hard. They lived on a farm in another part of the state. My father walked from that town to here at the beginning of the school year, and he walked back home afterwards. He wasn't able to take the train. His father was a good moral man, but he wasn't the aggressive type like my mother's father. They were farming people. My father's mother wanted all her sons to be professional men. She wanted one to be a doctor and one a lawyer and one a teacher. Several of them died of that awful malaria fever; two of them died the same summer, but papa survived.

Papa told us that mama could not read or write. But, when the children would sit around the fire at night after they'd come from this little old country school, they would be having fun and one might say, "Spell DOG," and the other one would say, "C A T." "Spell BIRD." "D O G." So finally, his mother got after them about misspelling words. So papa said, "Well, mama, how do you know we are misspelling words? You can't read or write." She said, "Now listen, son, when I was a young girl in slavery, nursing the white people's children, I listened to them when they would be spelling. I learned the Webster's blue-backed speller by heart from listening to the little white children because some day I hoped to be married and have children, and I wanted my children to know how to spell." Can you imagine—she learned the Webster's blue-backed speller by heart!

My father was a teacher at the college here; he taught ancient languages. Afterwards he went into the general work of the

church. We grew up privileged in the town because he was a professor. The church-related schools in those days had been founded for the purpose of training leaders. If any student showed any special talent, then a teacher would take the pupil under his wing. For example, there was a Dr. Black who got interested in my father, and he was a minister. He taught my father the full three years of theology. Just as he had received it, he gave it to my father.

My mother took this kindergarten course at the college. She took the stenography course that they had, and they used to stress elocution a great deal in those days. There was a teacher there who took a special interest in mama and worked with her on that; she played and sang, both very beautifully. She was quite an accomplished musician.

There was something about mama you find very, very seldom. She had a light touch. She could walk through dust and you couldn't see a fleck of dust on her. I couldn't walk on the sidewalk without looking like Weary Willie. She was naturally an extremely dainty person, what I call a very female woman, excessively feminine.

I grew up the oldest of four children. I began reading when I was three years old without anybody teaching me. I picked up one of the church papers one night and began reading, and my mother just fainted. I have been reading ever since. I guess the one love of my life has been reading. I read everything I could get my hands on. We had a reader called *Friends and Helpers* to teach us to be humane to animals and birds, and a little reader in third grade called, I think, *Fifty Famous Stories Retold,* which told about Bruce and Wallace in Scotland, King Alfred, and others. In other words, our teachers gave us what they had been taught. We got a real education. Papa had a wonderful library, too. We bought books when we didn't have enough for bread.

We grew up Republicans and Methodists, and I used to hear my grandfather tell how Frederick Douglass said that the Republican party was a ship, all else was the sea. At some meeting in Chicago, Frederick Douglass and Sojourner Truth were there, and at that time Mr. Douglass was very much discouraged. Sojourner Truth yelled out and asked him, "Fred, is God dead?" The answer was no. So it was the church and the Republican party that had a great influence on me.

When we moved to the town in the Midwest, the school out there was prejudiced, just like the one here. They wouldn't let me

take certain courses. I went to the principal and asked him about taking some education subjects because I wanted to teach. He said it wouldn't do any good because they weren't going to have any more colored teachers in the state. I think three colored girls had taught the year before. So every time there was something you really wanted to do, you'd find this roadblock up. Everywhere you would turn, it would be that same thing.

After I had taken a teacher's training course and taught some, I stopped. I loved teaching, but I didn't like the circumstances under which the average black woman at that time had to teach. I went back to my parents' house and just went to work—any kind of job I could get—because times were very hard then. For the most part, the average principal wanted to go with all his teachers. That was something I just wouldn't do.

I didn't take an active part in politics until after we were in the Midwest. People were working hard for women's suffrage, and I got in that fight. I got right out to it. When they passed the 19th Amendment, I was among the first who went down to vote. When I moved to the northern city, I took an even more active part, because I was grown then, married and all. I married when I was 27 years old.

I joined the NAACP first when we were in the Midwest. We had a mission church there; we had an immense building the white people had given us. We had no congregation, but we had the largest building. Father Jones, the Episcopal priest, got the NAACP off the ground there. For the first time I had the chance to attend their meetings. I had read their books and knew about it before, but I hadn't had the chance to take part. I remember having been told the NAACP grew out of the old Niagara Movement. DuBois and old man Trotter, J.M. Trotter, and a few others had organized the Niagara Movement and, of course, the NAACP came about after that awful riot in Springfield.

The NAACP were concerned. They went all out for what they believed, but in the true council they drew the color line. If they had any real dark people working there in the offices in New York, they were bookkeepers or somebody they kept out of sight. They had either real light colored people, or very light, olive-skinned people with good hair. The organization changed over time, because of pressure from the black newspapers, but it started out that way.

Until Mr. Garvey started his Movement, real dark colored people everywhere were just about looked down on. Unless some real

dark person by sheer force of intellect or personality was irrepressible, they were just kept out; that's all there is to it. My mother had a classmate, J. Smith, who was very, very black. They all went to Chicago one summer to work, just like young students do today. Chicago was an extremely color-struck town. Everybody got a job except Smith. It did something to him. To this day, he has never got over it. He's very shy and if you see him and try to talk to him, he'll speak maybe and then he goes right away. He stayed on in Chicago. He was ashamed to come back to school after that experience. Although he finally did get to work in the post office, he's still as shy as a wild deer because of that.

When Mr. Garvey came on the scene, he began drawing out these black people, these outcasts. He really made them feel that they were just as good as anybody. He was the first leader in this country who drew these black people into positions of leadership or even to take part in social life. I first got the book *The Mulatto in the United States* when I was in the Midwest. The author showed how the real leadership in this country was mulatto. That was why DuBois fought Mr. Garvey so, because Garvey set out to organize these black people and bring them up, and he said, "If Marcus Garvey had not drawn the color line on the black side, he and DuBois could have gotten along all right." I remember many battles.

Mr. Garvey's mistake was in organizing the Black Legion. The men were all sworn to protect their leader, and they would do it. He tried to have the Black Star Lines. There was nothing wrong with black people trying to have a line to bring imports and take exports, but they charged him $1,200 a day for dry-docking, or whatever you call it. Well, that was just impossible. Everything he tried was blocked. So finally, he hit upon this idea of the Black Legion. He had published a manual of arms, and he had not gotten permission from the authorities to do that, or to have that type of training, and so that was where they got him, for having this military organization. I met a cousin of his who told me that the President of the U.S. said to him, "We don't know whether he would be more dangerous if we let him stay here or if we deport him." His cousin said, "It did me good to see the President that worried about one black man." But he was finally deported. It was during the 1920s.

Mr. Garvey did have one further effect, though that was later. He wanted to come back to the country. A Republican president had sent him out, and they wouldn't let him back in. So he came

to Canada, and somehow got Al Smith's ear. He sent word for all the black people to vote for Al Smith. Now that was the beginning of the wholesale switch of Negroes from the Republican party to the Democratic party. Mr. Smith was going to try to see if he couldn't get Mr. Garvey back into the country.

While we were living out in the Midwest, I met my husband. A quartet was on tour. They had been out to California, I believe, for some sort of exposition. On their way back they were giving recitals, and they happened to give one where we lived. That's how and where I met him. He played the piano for them. He had that quiet dignity like my grandfather had, and he was an accomplished musician, even then. We worked and sacrificed a long time after we were married, before he was finally finished with his training. He became an organist as well as a pianist. We didn't have any children. None of my family have any children! I guess this is the last of the line.

As far as politics goes, my husband wasn't as aggressive as I, but he would go with me to some of the meetings. He never did hamper me.

When I moved to the northern city in 1924 with my husband, I liked it. For one thing, I was out of the parsonage, and that meant that I didn't have to be bossed by members of the congregation. I enjoyed it very much. Of course, it made a difference that for the first time in my life I was with working-class people, day in and day out. Politically, the first thing I did in the city was to register to vote. Then I followed the various organizations.

As far as work, well, in the city I mainly worked with the YWCA and the church organizations. But I still was interested in politics, and I worked with the NAACP there. I used to attend the UNIA (United Negro Improvement Association, Mr. Garvey's organization) meetings quite a bit because an old schoolmate of mine was in full charge of the organization. Mr. Garvey had taken him under his wing, and he was made acting president when Mr. Garvey went to prison.

In fact, I guess I was interested in anything political. I had gotten interested in the Communist movement before I left the Midwest. There was a little Jewish fellow who used to come by picking up laundry. He would talk about things that were happening in Russia. So I began going to the library to get books on Russia and Jewish history. When I went to the city, I would go to any kind of radical meeting. It didn't matter what it was. I learned quite a bit about Communism and the Communist party.

People would go over to Russia from the city, then they would come back and tell about it. I had quite a few colored friends who joined the Communist party and who went to Russia. One of them was West Indian. The Russians asked the Ford plant for an expert tool and diemaker. This fellow had just finished at the head of his class with an average of 98. Since they wanted the best, they sent him. When he got over there, some hillbillies from Tennessee refused to work with him. They sent the hillbillies home. He wrote and told me about it. In later years I read that he got a unanimous vote as chief deputy of that huge tractor plant at Stalingrad. The other year there was a long article in *Ebony* about him. He's the most influential black person in the USSR.

What the Communists were saying made more sense than what the other people were saying during the Depression. Hoover was saying that prosperity was right around the corner, and I saw those huge factories closing, plants being turned into lodges for homeless men. We had some friends who were masons. When the bottom dropped out, they lost everything because their money was tied up in other people's construction projects. Those friends of ours died in an insane asylum. They couldn't stand it. People lost homes. It was just pitiful. You might see a fellow you'd worked right along with, without a job suddenly, standing in a soup line.

I still read the *Daily Worker* when I get over to town and pick one up. I followed it very closely for a long time. I went to the meetings because they were open to the public. I went down when they would have the May Day demonstrations. I've seen mounted police run men down and split their heads. The Communists made a lot of sense. If it hadn't been for them, those boys at Scottsboro would all have been put to death in Alabama. It's just as simple as that.

The NAACP and the Marcus Garvey Movement had it very, very hard during the Depression because people didn't have the money. You know, they could only do so much. Eventually the government labeled Dr. DuBois a Communist. So he found out, as so many of my race found out, you never can be white. When he found out he really could not be white, it like to have killed him. Then he turned Communist. He left the country and went to Ghana with all his French and Dutch and Indian blood. He had to come home. He had to come home.

I learned in that period that lies were leading us down the road to war. We had no business in World War I and World War II.

We had become geared to a war economy. It took World War II to overcome the depression that followed World War I. If we're not fighting, we'll go in where somebody else is fighting.

I came down here to this county in '36. My grandfather retired from his ministry in another town and wanted to get settled back here. He wanted to come back home. I came and helped him do that. After that, I would come and go, because I was the only one who wasn't employed, and I always had the time. My husband indulged me. Well, in '36 when I came back with Grandpa, it was awful. I had never seen a place where people were so poor-spirited. I don't mean poor in spirit, but poor-spirited, and had such a deep-seated inferiority complex. It was pitiful. They even told me, "Don't dress up when you go downtown, because the white people won't like it." I said, "Well, they won't like it. I'm going to go downtown here just like I do in the city." When we were on the street, those white girls from the college would attempt to walk over us. On the streets, white people would force blacks off the sidewalk. So me, being a smart cookie, wasn't going to get off the sidewalk. If I was walking with any of the other girls, I would say to them, "Now, listen, we're going to walk single file. Do you understand? We're going to walk to the right. You get behind me, because I'm not getting off the sidewalk." I stayed on the sidewalk. One day I met three girls from the college, and they weren't going to force me off. I just dropped everything I had right on the sidewalk, and they had to get off while I picked it all up. I wasn't afraid of them. It would make me mad. I had an awful temper, and I wasn't going to be browbeaten. I never intend to be.

In the 1930s, there were a lot of lynchings and killings all over the state. Times were rough indeed. There were other things, too. One time the farmers were going to burn potatoes over there. Somebody got in touch with Washington, and they sent word to give those potatoes to the poor people. They were going to burn hills of potatoes! Another time, at the place over on the south side, they told poor people to come over because they were going to give them a whole lot of stuff at Thanksgiving. They gave those people two cans of beef!

During the war years, they had these curtains on the buses and trains to keep the blacks and the whites apart. I taught over at this little school. I think the first year I was there was the fall of '44. I happened to be down here with Grandpa, and they talked me into coming over there and helping. I had to take the bus. I

had to go all the way back and sit behind this curtain. I also had to stand there and wait until the white people got off. They even treated the black soldiers the same way. It still was pretty rough.

I was in and out through the years until 1952, when we settled here permanently. My husband had a stroke. There were some changes. The people seemed to have a little more feeling of really being human beings with a right to some things.

I worked very regularly with the NAACP when we came down here to stay. In 1954 when this edict was issued about the desegregation of the schools, well, then you could feel a stiffening of the attitude on the part of the white people. The superintendent of the Board of Education resigned here some years later when he saw they couldn't keep the colored children out any longer. He wouldn't preside over it, so he resigned. It made for an awful lot of feelings which still exist. I told some of the people that we hadn't seen any fight until they began putting colored children and white children in school together. I said that because I have lived in the North, East, West and South and I knew how white people felt about the schools. I went to a mixed school in that town out in the Midwest and I know how it is. I had suffered before.

I started with the kids from SNCC in 1960. Two boys came by my house one day. One of them was Stan, who had been so badly beaten down in the southern part of the state, and little Marvin Smith. I asked them in, and Marvin asked me if I didn't work with the NAACP. I said, "Yes, I do." He told me that they had been to the other people in the NAACP and had been turned down. They wanted to get some sort of organization started. So I started out from that, with them.

They didn't stay with me, but, you know, they would come by. I would go places with them, and counsel them. I just went all out with them and for them. The first Freedom House was right across the street from me. I was in and out of it all the time.

I could sympathize with them because, as I said, I knew the things that I had suffered. I didn't want them to lose their lives unnecessarily. I would tell them all the time, "No matter how crazy this other person acts, you be sure that what you're doing makes sense." The easiest thing in the world in this state was to get your hair parted, or get beaten to death, or thrown in jail for life, or killed. Since that is so easy, I prefer to do the hard thing, which is to stay alive and in one piece.

They would want to come downtown and demonstrate against Mr. Silverstein. I said, "Well, Mr. Silverstein was the only one here who did not have a 'colored' sign over the water and would let you sit anywhere and try on shoes." I said, "Now, you can't afford to demonstrate against him." They'd say, "We're going out and we're going to do it." I'd say, "Yes, but that is foolish. That doesn't make any sense."

Some of them came just like they'd go climb a mountain or anything else. I realized that in the next few months, or next year, they'd be just as totally dedicated to something else. But some of the workers, both black and white, were absolutely sincere and that attracted me.

I worked with voter registration. I'd go from door to door, into pool halls and barber shops to try to get people out to vote. When people have never done a thing, it's hard for you to make them realize how necessary it is. I have a little friend from Boston who had never registered to vote. So you can't be surprised if some field hand in this state isn't so wildly enthusiastic.

The Klansmen used to even come from other states and hang around that Freedom House. They tore down the tower for the two-way radio we had there, and they set the Freedom House afire. The police around here followed me from my house to the Freedom House, shining the light all through my house at night. They tapped my phone, so finally I just had an unlisted number. To this day, if anybody calls, I don't dare give my name because I'd have to get the number changed again.

The police would pick the workers up; they'd arrest them on all charges. We always had to get people out of jail right away. We didn't want them to stay in the county jail overnight. The city jail wasn't quite so bad, but if they went to the county jail, we knew what was going to happen to them there. So we would always get bond for them right away and get them out. They did get one of the boys and put him on the county farm. They beat that boy so. When he came out, he couldn't open his hands. They had to send him to the University Hospital for treatment before he could flex his hands.

I worked in different ways. I went on some of the large demonstrations. What they say happened at Selma, on the March, happened. It was an awful thing to me to see cutthroats, thugs, and that type of person on the March. They scraped the bottom of all those big eastern cities. Then I thought, "Well, I guess these are shock troops, because they don't care what happens." Everything

in the world was taking place.

It was hard there, too, because of the violence. That first night we were there, a young white boy from Wisconsin had his head split open. He was just trying to come into the compound, as I called it, where we were practically imprisoned. He had just come in, and they split his head. A young white minister died. A young black boy had gotten killed at Marion, Alabama, the first day they got there. Dr. King would go back from the March to the city everyday; they were supposed to have a trial but it never happened.

Through all this, I couldn't believe in nonviolence. I'm too violent a person. I didn't ever see any sense in nonviolence, even under Dr. King, because I knew that violence can only be conquered by another form of violence. It seemed as though my people had been so conditioned that they thought it was wrong to do anything to a white person. No matter what he does, we're supposed to overlook it. That really sets my back up. I believe in an eye for an eye and a tooth for a tooth. Oh, but I do! Nonviolence is definitely not the answer. In fact, sometimes it just doesn't seem that there is any answer. When you think how kings have been killed by their sons or daughters so they might ascend to power, or how kings have had their sons and daughters killed—what do you expect from just ordinary people? How in the world is nonviolence going to work for them?

All through the Movement, I was close to all those kids because I knew the need for what they were doing. I also knew how hopeless the struggle would be in some instances. But as Kelly Miller says, you can't afford to rob youth of hope. I fought and argued with them. I'm just an ornery cuss. I couldn't have stood it otherwise.

What I liked best about the workers was, first, their feeling like men and being aware of the things that kept them from exercising the rights of men. I thought about how much they stood to lose. Everytime they'd leave the Freedom House, no one knew whether they were going to come back in one piece or come back at all. They were young and away from home, and it took a lot for them to come out like they did.

I knew that things would never be altogether on the up and up, and I think that was really what disillusioned these kids. I knew that the kids in the Movement were going through the same things I had. These were things I wanted to shield them from, that I didn't want to tell them about. I noticed how the feeling

came about between the whites and the blacks. I saw the hatred growing, especially that time when Stokely Carmichael came out for Black Power. I read a very pathetic letter one of the Jewish boys had written him. . . "Man, what in the hell is the matter? What do you mean? To have this thing altogether separated?" Well, I've been through that, too, but I would die before I'd let them know it. You couldn't afford to.

In instances some whites in the Movement might say something, and I would take them right up on it. I would say, "We don't have time for you to get rid of prejudices. If you're prejudiced, then you have no business in the Movement." If some of the blacks would misuse some of the whites, I would say, "Now, because some white man did something to you years ago and you weren't man enough to knock his teeth down his throat, I'm not going to let you take it out on this little white boy from Wisconsin that you never saw before." I believe in being fair about the thing because I know that the black man was doing this because of what happened to him when he wasn't man enough to do anything about it. So don't take it out on the white boy now. I don't know how they stood me as well as they did, because we were constantly at loggerheads. There were things I just wouldn't stand for, and I spoke up for what I believed.

Even at that time of Black Power, as I said, I could understand how they felt. I used to feel it would be better if all of us could just be someplace by ourselves, or maybe, if people want to discriminate against us in stores, maybe it would be better if we could just have one black person do all the buying of the stuff we're going to need, rather than be humiliated. I felt the same as they have felt, but I couldn't afford to let them know it. I couldn't afford to encourage them because, after all, there is a difference in then and now, and I hate to see them destroy things. I knew that we couldn't get these things done ourselves. I was strictly against forcing all the white people out of the Movement. I still am because we don't have the resources that they have, and we cannot live without having access to those resources.

I don't like insincerity. Now, for instance, in the Movement here in town, the blacks wanted to drive all the whites out. They got up this manifesto and put every white person on their list. I'm bitterly opposed to any all black thing. I'm strictly for integration. They treated those white people shamefully until they got rid of just about every white person over there. Then these blacks came in. All they're doing is feathering their nests and filling their

pockets, walking over people with all this arrogance. That is hurt-
ful and harmful. I don't see how we can hope to have any real
culture or real education without integration. I don't want two
separate worlds, black and white.

**After our long discussion of the Movement and her actions
in it, we talked about her present situation, and then about
how she kept herself going through the hard times of the
Movement.**

I'm not active in any organization. The Voter's League is
strictly an Uncle Tom thing. They take people's money. The
preachers run it and they double-cross the people. I was at a
meeting where they had made their endorsement. After that
meeting, on the night before the election, they endorsed a completely different set of candidates. I can't fool with anybody like
that.

I am still reading. I've been reading *The Mission,* got interested
and excited over that Nazi business, and I went back and reread
The Deputy. It ties right in with what's happening now, you
know, Cardinal Mindzenty being betrayed by the Pope. I'm interested in that now, plus what's happening in Africa. It was ten
years before I could find a copy of Kenyatta's *Face at Mount
Kenya.* I finally ran across a copy of it. I just look into all the
political movements. I'll go anywhere they have a meeting. I even
went to a Klan meeting out here the other year. They said the
public was invited. Next time they put up a sign "white public
is invited." Sometimes I feel that there is nothing good on the face
of the earth. President Nixon was talking about establishing
peace in the Middle East. Well, he didn't establish any peace in
Vietnam. He didn't establish any peace here. How in the heck
was he going to come up like a genie out of a bottle and settle
everything in the Mideast? How could he?

Now, I went into the post office the other month to get a money
order, and this white lady jumps up in front of me, and I said,
"Now, wait a minute. I'll go to the ten cent store and buy a money
order, understand it? I'm not going to buy a money order after
that." I walked out of the post office and on to the dime store and
bought my money order. I said, "That stuff went out with the
Robert E. Lee." They never intend to give up, and I never intend
to bow my proud head. It's like the irresistible force and the
immovable object. I am not going to do it. That's all. All the
same, you've always got to be on the lookout.

Things are still rough here in the county. A year ago this past

October, there were three colored boys and three white girls together at a camp house. One of the boys didn't have anything to
do with one girl, but the other two did. They said that the girls
invited them into the place. It wound up with these boys being
charged with rape and bond set at $50,000. Those kids stayed in
that jail out at the county farm and were only allowed out two
hours on Sunday, visiting hours. Two of the boys received life
sentences. I have a feeling, from what I have seen in life, that they
will make a deal on the other boy. I don't know. The boys were
very young, and these girls were all grown, because eighteen is the
legal age now. The scuttlebutt was that that sort of thing had
been going on out there for a long time. Everyone knew it but they
were afraid to testify for the boys. The camp house belonged to a
very powerful man. When the lawyers asked to be allowed to take
pictures there, he told them, "Yes, take as many pictures as you
want." When they went out the next morning, the camp house
was burned flat to the ground. He was in and out of the courtroom
and in the witnesses' room during the trial, which you know is not
right.

People are still losing their homes and being threatened. In
other words, it's just the same, only different! In a way everything
is better just by being different. Now, for instance, if you go to
the courthouse and go to the ladies' room, you just go to the
ladies' room; you don't have to look for "colored" signs. There are
still places like truck stops where they'll refuse service to colored,
or they'll make them wish they hadn't gone in. But you can go
right downtown to the Holiday Inn and places like that. Human
beings being what they are, human nature being what it is, there
is still that residue, you know, at the bottom of things.

What keeps me going? I guess it is a feeling that there are just
certain basic human rights, and you're going to exercise them,
regardless. You hope that you can do something to cause somebody to see the error of his ways; and then maybe if he will do a
thing differently long enough, he may come to feel differently
about it. I still believe change is possible.

I was always a rebel in the family. The family believed in that
old strict way, and I was always the one to see everybody have
whatever they wanted. I don't get along with my family too well
yet on account of it; that's why I won't go live with any of them.
My sister and brother both want me to come live with them, but
I'm not about to. When I'm on the street here, I speak to everybody. Sometimes other folks don't, but here's the way I figure it:

that greeting I give a person, that smile, may be the only smile or greeting that poor devil gets the whole twenty-four hours. So I speak to everybody; it doesn't make any difference to me. But, you know, everybody's not like that. I figure that in the privacy of your own home, you can be as exclusive as you want, but the streets belong to everybody. All my life I've always felt that the bars ought to be let down a little bit and what you have you share with people.

In concluding, she spoke of a worker she had known who had been killed. He always felt very close to me, little Ralph did. We used to have some awful fights, but underneath everything I think he thought a lot of me. One day he said, "I've never wanted to be a nuisance to anybody. I felt that I was a nuisance at home, and I left home when I was ten years old. I took my belongings and went out into the street. There was an old lady who took me in, and I sold newspapers to support myself." He had really come all the way just on his own.

When our Freedom House was burned, he called a worker. He should have known his phone was tapped, but he called anyway. He said he was coming here and to tell me he was packing a box of books for me. I had lent him some books; he had been especially interested in reading the old books about the black Movement and he was returning them. He was blown up in a bombing on his way over here.

After I heard the news, I couldn't even relax. It seemed to me I could scarcely think. I was just one great sore inside. When you've known someone that well, and you've lived around them, and they've just poured out all of their life stories to you, and then something like that happens, sometimes you wonder if it's worth it. That life is gone and that person can't do anything anymore. Then you wonder if all he did really amounted to anything. You wonder if any of it is really worth it. It gives you just an all-gone feeling.

Those were hard times; I don't know what kept me going except that there is something in me. I don't know if it's because I'm just naturally born contrary and never say "die" or what it is. Sometimes I wonder myself why I would do such and so, or I wonder why I even stay down here in this state. I tell my friends that the first morning that I wake up happy, I'll know I'm a lost soul. Every morning I wake up miserable here, I feel there's some hope for me. It is miserable, but every now and again something will

happen. Somebody will say, "Mrs. Williams got me out of jail," or "Mrs. Williams got me off the county farm," and I'll say, "Well, maybe it's worth it."

Chapter 3

Reverend Caldwell

A problem in the Movement was that we had to act. We couldn't say, "Well, we're going to stop our actions on the grounds that we don't have enough information to come to a conclusion." That's what we accused others of doing. We couldn't do that. We did not have the choice not to act.

We wanted to destroy an evil society. The problem was, if we destroy, on what are we going to build? We have to think about this the whole time we are working, with every little problem that we solve. What are we doing when we help a union develop? Are we really helping the cause that we propose, or hurting it? If we get a union involved, we know that the national officers are fat, sometimes corrupt, and that they make deals with the corporations that we're fighting. We know all these things, and we have to wonder whether we're really helping our cause or hurting it. So, out of the old society we are taking some things to build the new. There's a problem if we do that, and we have to deal with that problem and come to a satisfactory or unsatisfactory solution and act.[1]

Reverend Caldwell is fairly tall and well-muscled, with a solid, bulging trunk and legs. When we met, he was dressed for work in a coverall and heavy boots. He spoke rapidly, his head bobbing up and down as he emphasized one point or illustrated another. He changed his mood and tone suddenly at times when speaking, either in unexpectedly looking at himself and laughing, or in directly driving home a point.

The Movement community in his area has been able to buy a large block of farmland. Acquiring the land is an attempt to realize the early Movement dream of communal sharing, in that Reverend Caldwell and the community hope those who live on it will farm it and share in the decisions about its use. Acquiring the land is also an attempt to secure a place that is safe from outside control, a base from which to work. As we talked, we drove along the boundaries of the land. The

dark soil was plowed in long, regular rows. Patches of red and white clay were occasionally broken by thickets of brush, groves of fruit trees, and ponds. Reverend Caldwell spoke with great pride of the land and the farm equipment. He knew every acre well.

He is the acknowledged leader of the Movement in the area. In the course of his 12 years of work there, he has organized the community in a variety of efforts, from challenging public accommodations, to voter registration, to school desegregation, and finally to acquiring the land.

He is unusual among Movement organizers in that he has remained in one place, working with one group. He thus has seen the various stages and changes in the Movement as a whole from the vantage point of their effects on his one area. In the troubled times of the late Sixties, he remained committed to the possibilities of blacks and whites working together, when so many turned away from those possibilities. The project which he leads now, as then, has both blacks and whites working on it.

Any decisions about the land are made by the Movement community as a group. In the early days of the Movement, the workers lived on a subsistence wage. They pooled their money to take care of the needs of the whole group. Reverend Caldwell, his family, and his coworkers still live this way. His wife is also a worker in the Movement. They have two young children.

He is caught up in the vision of what the farm could be and thinks entirely in terms of how to keep it going. As an example, when we talked of health care needs, he was interested in getting support for the larger farm project by using a clinic as an organizing tool.

As we talked, we visited the farm manager's office, where there is also a market and store. It was the middle of winter, and the Reverend and the manager talked at length about cash crops (truck-farming vegetables) to plant. They talked about marketing and plans to develop the store and market. The manager emphasized that the many people who work on the farm spend their earnings in the town instead of in the community. He wanted to change that.

What was striking throughout my visit was that the success of the whole undertaking was dependent on such things as the

shrewdness and the timing of the marketing, not just on the faith and efforts of the workers. Financial solvency was crucial in the first few years of the farm's operations.

Reverend Caldwell described the struggle to raise the money to buy the land. Some of the money came from private sources, some from foundations, and some from commercial loans. He spoke of the continued struggle to keep the farm going. He is embattled, accountable both to outside sources for funds and to the black community. There is pressure from both. By no means has the farm earned the money it is capable of earning. There are complaints of mismanagement in agricultural techniques. There is a lack of total support from the black community. There have been complaints about working conditions. To compound the problem, Reverend Caldwell led the Movement in the area for years before the land was acquired. He led the effort to acquire the land. Thus people have very high expectations of him, both in the community and in the outside organizations.

In talking of how he had come to the place he now holds, he talked first about his grandmother.

I've always said if the Lord called me, He called me through the mouth of my grandmother. I really believe that she had the greatest influence on my leaning toward the ministry, and I know that she influenced my going to church. I could talk all day about my grandmother. She was a human being. She had her faults, but she had an inside beauty. She was a mixture of Indian and white folk that brought out the American best. She was a beautiful woman, light-skinned with straight hair, and the rest of her characteristics were negroid. When she was seventy years old she could still jump in the air and kick her heels twice. She would get down on the floor and play with us. Grandma just had ways, I guess, that everybody wanted to mimic. It wasn't what she did so much outside. It was the inside that made you respond to her. We grew up poor, in a rough neighborhood, yet we weren't rough people. My grandmother wasn't rough, as such, but she wouldn't take no stuff from anybody.

I remember my mama, too. Since we were poor, we didn't have the things that we needed. I felt ashamed at school about my clothes, and the fact that I didn't have enough money to pay for lunch. But somehow my mama overlooked all of that and kept pushing me. She didn't try to get away from her responsibilities

as a mother as many young girls do these days, and I am grateful to her for that.

It took me a long time to understand the way my mother acted. That's something I have thought about for a long time and have finally worked out in my mind through introspection, rethinking, looking, searching, reading. My mother was quite young, and she and I grew up together.

I remember one time that my mother refused to eat when the rest of us were eating. I had a notion that she wasn't eating at all, so I made up my mind to watch her that whole night to see if she ate. She went to bed and didn't eat at all. The next day I demanded that she eat. I told her that I knew she hadn't eaten. So she did eat that time. That's the one thing I remember that really started me thinking about being responsible about things at home.

For some reason I was very visionary as a child. I guess I'd say that there were many times that I was just able to see further as a child than my parents and other adults around me. If there's anything that I believe would be a gift that's mine, it would be the gift of insight and sensitivity to people, a kind of ESP.

As a child, I used my imagination to ward off the bad spirits, or to bring the good spirits to my aid. I entertained myself. When I was scolded or made to stay inside, I would say I was going to be something. I was not going to be here. It was not going to be like this always.

I come from a basic Baptist background and a strict fundamentalist understanding of the Scriptures. I built a church at the age of about eight or nine with my group, but the whole thing was later converted to a tank.

He laughed and then continued.

There were a lot of other things we did as children. We made some inventions, whistles, for example. It was a group that went places together and stayed together. I remember that because it may have some connection with my feeling about how we operate on the farm now. That was a good experience, working with a small group, making decisions together. Not exactly as we do now, but there might be some connection.

I was superintendent of my Sunday school and taught the Bible there. I was convincing enough to adults to allow me to supervise them. I was exercising my mind in the Bible class very strongly. I was outspoken among adults, one or two of whom I really re-

spected for wisdom; not for their actions, but for their wisdom. **He laughed.**

I was a member of the Police Boys' Club. It kept me from being afraid of policemen. I learned boxing as a child, so I wasn't afraid to fight. I grew up in a neighborhood where I was beaten up a lot, but people knew that if they beat me they'd have to keep on beating me. I was small but they knew that if they ever beat me, they'd have me on their hands for a long time. I wouldn't give up. I'd keep fighting until I won.

I remember a teacher who said he was helping me. I was soft and tender-hearted. He saw weakness in that, so he really stomped me around. He hit me and cursed me every day. He'd throw something down on the floor and make me pick it up. He was a real Simon Legree, saying he was trying to help make me strong. That was strength, but I had already fashioned a kind of strength about myself. My strength was "stick-to-itness."

Before the Greensboro sit-ins, I got interested in sit-ins through a good friend of mine. For some reason he had the idea of going to churches to see if they really believed what they were talking about. This was 1954 or 1955. He wanted me to help him test the churches in the town where I grew up. We started going to various churches. On Sundays we were turned away from some of the white churches. One church let us in and sat us right in the front. I thought that they were trying to embarrass us. We got some threats, but we kept going. The point is that it was significant because it was before Greensboro. I did it and forgot it, no big thing. Nobody went to jail.

In my time I've had just about every job that a child could have and I've worked many, many jobs that any black man would have to work to exist. I've been everything—shoe shiner, waiter, dishwasher, bus boy, cafeteria worker—everything.

The greater part of my life was spent in school. I had a rough time in college. I had to work to earn money, almost full-time many times. In my last year of college I worked full-time at two jobs. One job was in the cafeteria, and I spent two hours every meal there—six hours a day. Then I worked at night in the college grill, the eleven to seven shift. I was making pretty good grades. too.

He narrated very simply the way he got involved in the Movement and did not elaborate on it.

While I was in college, a friend came to me and talked about the demonstrations. Then the SCLC made a call for kids who

were doing demonstrations to come to Greensboro, North Carolina. We had a meeting in Charlotte. That's where SNCC started. I thought it was a good idea to find out what other guys were thinking and doing because I thought we should get together on these things. Somebody else organized it, and I went and listened. I didn't have much to say, but I became a part of it. I went back to school but left to work with SNCC. I was sent to this area.

When we first came here, we decided to go to Rock Hill because some kids there were demonstrating and were doing what we had talked about doing—refusing bond. We thought we should go in there too and refuse bond. There were four of us. We went to participate with the 13 kids who were already in jail, and we went to jail in the same way. That was a big experience there. I learned a lot about nonviolent action.

He talked in detail about the transformation that took place in him because of that and other jailings.

By going to jail, I found out as much about the church as I did about myself. My understanding of the church started to change in jail. I was probably looking at things in a different way than most of the young guys there since I was fighting being a minister and at the same time knowing that I had to be a minister. I was looking for peace. The inward calling, at times, was greater than the call my grandma put on me because it had started internalizing itself and being more a part of me than my grandma. My grandma had died and I was still alive. Being in jail, the experience of Paul and Silas and others that I knew about became more real, and so Christianity became more real itself.

Actually loving your neighbor and doing to others became real to me only in the Movement. Before, it was just conceptual, and going to church on Sunday, and loving, you know, because it's wrong to hate, and feeling guilty if you hate because of the wrong. Whereas in the Movement, I moved from loving as a doctrine to loving as a discipline, to loving as a way of life, to now loving and hating as a healthy way of life.

We talked next about the general problems of being in the Movement for a long time.

It was difficult for us to reach the conscience of the nation. Dr. King did come, but when he left we were in the same situation. We never got the resources the other places got during and after the Movement. You don't see a lot of development down here, and that's the reason. We got everything inch by inch. It was hard in Mississippi, but then, after the explosions, after those three

guys died, things began to ease up and the people in Mississippi got more resources than we got here. People don't understand that. As a result, it has just taken us longer to develop what we had. We suffered for it, but I wouldn't say that I'd rather have it any other way.

Progress is misleading. It has been a stumbling block for us as organizers because the people became satisfied and weren't willing to take the steps that were needed. After all the fuss about public accommodations, it is discouraging to see that we're going to all those same places, spending all our money and coming out as poor or poorer for it.

All kinds of bad things happened in the Movement. On top of all the problems, there was the ordinary selfish greediness of individuals no matter who they were. If you couldn't comprehend all of it or enough to deal with it as it touched you, then you'd be overwhelmed by everything. You'd start over-reacting to things.

In many people's lives in the Movement, there came a time when support was needed, and in some cases there was no support. To be more specific, while a person was trying to understand himself, maybe he turned to his childhood for support, to make himself strong enough to deal with what was happening to him. Maybe he didn't find it there. He needed somebody to help him put it together, but there was no reinforcement from the predominant society or his family. A person in the Movement during those times was most likely just out of adolescence, suffering from the wounds that adolescence leaves. Maybe something in the Movement was not going fast enough for him or maybe his livelihood was threatened. He had a crisis because he didn't have the resources or the reassurance that he needed. If he was not able to deal with that particular crisis, it had a domino effect and shattered his image of himself. Many people left the Movement because of that.

A crisis also came in many young guys' lives in the Movement when they felt that all that they had done was in vain. They felt white folk were going to be in charge, and they saw what they had done going down the stream. My analysis of it is that they weren't able to regroup and devise new ways of living at that point. I advised people to find a way to take care of themselves while there was still a chance. That's what we're trying to do here.

I didn't lose hope, although it was and is a very troubled hope, and I kept a group. I think the group is the biggest thing we've got going for us, and I always told everybody else that. You can't

make it in this kind of thing by yourself. You have to have something to reassure you. Not only that, you have to have something to keep you straight so you don't give in to the rewards of this society. The group is working amid all the failures as the source of comfort and support for us. I am encouraged by the hope that someday we can join our piece of land with other pieces of land owned by other people. Then we will finally have the strength and togetherness that cannot be broken. I have not given up the idea of changing this damnable monster that we have.

The songs that we sang had more influence than anything else in enabling us to endure what the white people put on us. Without the songs we might have gone berserk. *Dark Song, Freedom, Oh Freedom,* and *Let us Break Bread Together,* were the songs we used to sing all the time before meetings. We would sing *We Shall Overcome* at the end of meetings. That was mostly sung in large groups when we wanted people to leave with the marching spirit and a sense of accomplishment. This song operated on me too.

Music is an opiate, a good opiate. Music does tend to bring the spirit together. Music kept the slaves together, enabling them to endure the lash. While I am sitting down here with you, our spirit is separate, you might say. When music moves, we move to the same spirit. So, in that sense, we feel that our spirit is moving together. We look at one another and communicate.

Music can tell what has gone on and what can go on. Music carries a depth charge with it. It can set off what we all know is there, the explosion that causes us to sing, "Goddamn it, I ain't going to do it no more." It's the rebel in us. It linked us with our past, it gave us a bridge from which to move during our present, and it hooked us onto the future. Through its creative aspect, it gave us a way to say where we were going. "I'm going to tear down your wall. I'm going to do this or I'm going to do the other." We all composed verses and songs. That music is something.

We concluded by talking about his own position, not about the Movement in general.

I don't think my vision has changed a lot over the course of time. I had been talking Black before Black Power. I had praised Garvey; at one point, I'd praised Malcolm X. I could see Malcolm coming into our camp, finally understanding that color is not the enemy; racism is. I think he saw that and he would have been a great resource for us. A racist is a racist. A racist can be any color,

that's what I'm saying. Anyone who uses race to a personal or group advantage is a racist.

As for hard times, I wouldn't want to describe the effects King's death, or Malcolm's, or other things had on me. My direction was clear; it wasn't changed. My vision was paradoxical. King's dream was part of my dream, but I also understood and had the nightmares that Malcolm had and the nightmares that Stokley Carmichael, Rap Brown, and others had. To keep healthy I have to be able to wake up out of my nightmare and have as much of the dream as I can and still be sensitive to reality.

I've always felt that I'm a potential fanatic. If I were to stop believing that we could change things and there will be a better day, for me it would be the same as dying, and I fear my dying would not be easy on white people. I mean what Rap Brown said about violence was nothing compared to what I would do. If he said to kill 10, I'd say 10,000. I'd say that, after all that's been done here. But for now I keep on believing.

He returned, finally, to a characteristic that he had used to describe himself earlier, one that sustains him now.

"Stick-to-itness" got me through the hard times in the Movement and gave me the hope that you can change things.

Chapter 4

George

George was born in a rural county in the South and grew up there. After a time in the North, he returned to the South to become a field organizer. He went to one area, worked for ten years, and saw major changes take place. At the end of that time, the pressures of the work overcame him and he left the area. When I spoke with him, it was shortly after he had left, and he was acutely aware of the pressures he had been under and of difficulties within his own life. Since our talks, he has resolved some of the difficulties and has worked for civil rights organizations again, although not in field organizing.

He is tall and lean, with a large head and large prominent eyes. He spoke very carefully. Talking about the Movement was hard, and we had to stop at times because the recollections were so painful.

I don't think there was any particular single event that led me to the Movement, although I must admit that I was deeply impressed by Dr. King and his Movement when it first began. There was a deep drive in me towards change, a basic concern ever since I was in elementary school. My initial awareness of the Movement came in the late 1950s when I was in high school. I remember that very little was said publicly about change in my neighborhood. Things were concealed. We did have one teacher who said that change was inevitable.

I remember asking my parents questions about why things were the way they were. Their answers would be cut short to let me know right away that asking was something that was dangerous, taboo. My father would say, "You just forget that; don't talk about that." I remember once as a child, I said, "One day I'm going to be President." He looked at me strange, like it was impossible.

One day something happened that dramatized the situation, that let me really know the difference between white and black.

I used to fight a lot, after school, in street fights. Once I had a fight with a white boy, and I mentioned it at home. My daddy whipped me and told me not to ever hit a white person. I was eleven. I can remember it very well. My father was the kind of person who thought we should fight, too. He'd say, "I'm going to hit you every day until you hit him. You stand up and fight." I learned then that there was a difference in fighting a black and fighting a white.

I think it goes even farther than that. When I was even younger, I used to stay with my grandfather and his two old-maid sisters. They were the only blacks in a rural county. He was surrounded by white farmers, not rich, just farmers. My grandfather had about 3,700 acres of land; he was among the biggest landholders in that section. I'd stay there in the summers and play with all the white neighbors. We spent the night in each other's houses, we ate together, and it was different than at home. I never heard the word "nigger" in that particular section; most of the whites were poorer than my grandfather. He wasn't rich but he owned the land, and the whites used to do sharecropping. I stayed with him sometimes during the school year because he'd get ill and need help. We would hire a ride into town every day to go to school and come back in the evening.

My grandfather used to sit and talk for hours. They called him "a lawyer." My grandfather acquired a lot of legal knowledge. He had volumes of law books. People from all over the area would come and ask him certain questions about law, and he could answer them. My great uncle, Cleo, was the first to own a general store in town, and he was killed by some whites. He was killed, and his store and property were just taken from him. I remember my grandfather being very bitter about that. My grandfather never worked for any white. My father has never worked on a public job, and my mother and my aunts have never been domestics.

We were a very poor family. My mother was always hostile toward whites. She still is now. She surprises me. She and my father own a restaurant and they will not serve whites. It is a nationalistic kind of thing built in us from my grandfather. All my grandfather's children, including my mother, finished high school. My uncle is seventy-eight years old and finished high school last year. My aunt was a teacher and one of the first to graduate from the college she attended. She built her own school.

My grandfather used to point out exactly what was wrong, and

I think he expressed some very intelligent views. I think that has had the greatest influence on me. He told me about Reconstruction and that there had been elected black officials. He told me about the Marcus Garvey Movement; he used to tell me about slavery. He always kept up with what was happening in Congress, and he used to explain how a bill was passed. He had a thorough knowledge of the whole process. He used to read the *Manchester Guardian* and other independent newspapers.

He never did say what was needed but he did predict what was going to happen. He's been very right. He had a lot of Indian blood and would talk about the Indians, about how they related directly to the land, how the white man was changing everything, and how it was going to lead to destruction. He was the first person to ever talk to me about life being a lonely existence. He said no people can be oppressed forever and that we were going to rise. He told me that I should always be proud if I was to survive. He talked about how he was promised 40 acres and a mule and it was never delivered. He was very proud of his 3,700 acres of land, and he used to talk about other blacks who were acquiring material goods. He was a materialistic person who felt that change would come through economics. He'd say black people would earn money and would become doctors and lawyers. He'd say blacks were going to be elected. He talked of what had been lost in Reconstruction. He used to talk about DuBois although he didn't agree with his philosophy. He believed strongly in Marcus Garvey's philosophy. He talked about the schools and said they would be integrated. He would talk openly about this with whites. There was no violence then, just talk. But my grandfather had a lot of old guns around, and he would shoot.

I remember that there was a prison near us. When the black prisoners escaped, my grandfather would feed them and give them money. He and my father got into a big argument about that. I think that most of my insight and motivation came from my grandfather on my mother's side.

Of his brothers and sisters, George said No, they were not involved in the Movement. I think it was, in part, because I was the youngest, and I see some of the things my grandfather said taking shape. Also, I wasn't married. My brothers and sisters were married and raising kids, and that is part of why they weren't involved.

In college in the South, I participated in demonstrations, and one in particular, a boycott, impressed me. After college I moved

to a big northern city, and I realized the problems were the same. The problem of employment for blacks was the same; there were subtleties, the excuses tended to be more logical, but the problems tended to be the same. In that city I became involved in a school boycott and a civil rights organization. I decided to return South and I did.

He felt an important factor in being involved was the kind of people in the Movement.

I was very impressed by the people, one man in particular. He was very sincere, quiet, and you could actually feel what he said. I never cared too much about the loud rhetorical speeches. I always related to the people, like Dr. King, and others.

He then described his early experiences organizing in the field

The first day I arrived in the county, there were four of us, and I was the only black. We stayed in the house of a widow, Dora Mae, who had a young boy, Joseph. About the fourth night, the house was fired on . . . a week later a cross was burned . . . there were a series of incidents. We had been having a series of mass meetings. I felt the more people we could bring to the meetings, the less harassment we would have. Sometimes we spent two or three weeks trying to get a meeting together.

The community was prepared for almost anything. There was a series of burnings, and some white businesses burned. Some black homes were burned, and everything was in chaos. Actually, there had been a small riot. Two of our people were killed that first year. The night they died, I saw them and I told them to be careful. They were going out into the rural, and I told them they shouldn't go. We lived in a big Freedom House, a place where there were about 12 workers. I used to go in at night and check everybody's room to see if everybody was in. Just by instinct, I used to get up at two or three o'clock and look. I noticed they weren't there that night. Then the sheriff came in with two wallets in his hand. He was dripping water and I just knew. I knew what had happened. They were just found drowned.

They never convicted anybody. They found a third pair of wet shoes but they never did anything. Then, you know, Jim's parents came in from out of state. His mother had just had an operation for cancer. The other guy was a local kid who just worked with us day by day; we considered him a staff member. You know, having to face the parents was very hard. . . . It seemed like

people already looked at me as though to say, "If you hadn't. . . ." It's a very, very strange . . . people almost never said it, although Jim's mother did . . . strange woman, she outright said it. That kind of takes you. Then you start wondering, you know, whether you want to be safe or . . . it was the turning point for a lot of people. Some people moved on, some stayed. I stayed.

I stayed and I worked. Over a ten -year period, I've seen a lot of changes. There was an emergence of new leadership in the whole community. The local people responded to issues. For example, once when there was a big trial the factories had to close because nobody went to work. It was estimated that four thousand people came to the trial. That's the kind of community it was. We had an information center, a legal assistance program, welfare rights organization, day care centers, a community cannery, a supermarket, credit union, neighborhood services, youth program. We didn't just have these on paper. They developed slowly over time. We built a swimming pool. Cooperatives were organized. We were the first or second county to have federal registrars. We had an effective organization, but it was a constant battle. Everything we've done has created a more organized community.

Over a long period I saw changes in both the white and black communities. The chief of police and I had confrontations, yet when I was in the hospital after an accident, he came to visit. The white minister from the white Baptist church sent flowers. I could feel the changes in attitude when I was standing on the street uptown; that's very important in a small town.

A wealthy influential white citizen joined us, becoming actively involved. He spoke out to the city fathers, telling them they had to start addressing themselves to the changes demanded by the Movement, that the town could no longer hope to deal passively with them. He participated. The Movement first attracted his daughter and then his wife. His daughter wanted to know what kind of society we were going to have. She raised the critical questions.

He was actually responsible for getting the funds for our day care center. He went to HEW. He carried the petition and had every white businessman sign it to send to the governor. His wife visited the governor. He served on our board of directors. He used his influence to get others who shared the same kinds of ideas and thoughts to run for public office. Over a two-year period he had

meetings with the liberal sector of the white community. The meetings got larger and larger. The more meetings we had, the more interested people became, and the more critical they were of the schools and other systems. This led to the election of an extremely liberal mayor. The campaign received much of its direction from me. I never did endorse the candidate. I told him, "You've got to work like I've worked." I told him he had to visit every stinking, dirty house in the black community. I said, "You have to go in those communities. You need to understand the problems. This will give you the opportunity." He actually put on his gym shoes and visited the pool halls and the homes in the black community. He would not have won if he had not had the support of the entire black community. So I have seen change.

For a black male in this society, who has had to endure the typical kinds of suffering that black males have had to suffer in terms of their own masculinity and the right to be a man, being in the Movement is a kind of a medicine. I don't know exactly how to describe it, but it's a great dose of medicine and it's very, very necessary to keep you healthy mentally. I think you'll find that that's why so many black people, even into old age, middle age, or young, are active now or have been active in the Movement. When the opportunity arose, they participated at some level. I've seen old women who threw down their sticks and canes and shouted to the songs of the Movement, that was the medicine. Seeing old people who were involved, that was the medicine. The people who were the drivers, more or less, of this caravan of people, got a huge dose of the medicine. It was a medicine of energy, it produced energy to see the responses in people . . . to look at the faces, to hear people talk, to hear them say that they knew this day would come, to hear people talk about the dark past, to say how an effort was successful, this was the medicine.

Now then it becomes a thing like other kinds of medicine, when do you know, or when do you determine that you have OD'd (overdosed). In an effort like this, dealing with, trying to change immediate realities as people were trying to do, perhaps people could have lasted longer. Certainly I wouldn't say that the Movement would have taken another direction, but people might have had a better change if there were some type of vehicle built into the overall Movement where people could have run away to catch up with themselves, mentally and physically, and evaluate and just brainstorm and try to clear up things and themselves.

I think the hardest, emotionally . . . . I used to fish a lot, anytime the thing would get . . . . A lot of people were very scholarly, and I'm not a very scholarly person. The Movement was surrounded with intellectuals who were busy continually searching for a long-range direction. I always looked at the things that we were immediately working towards. While many people used to look at the structure of things and say that, "You can't change it because of these things," my answer was always that, "I thought what we were doing was to try change immediate reality." I would say, "There is nothing that's absolute." That's about as far as I would tend to go. I was always interested in China and Africa and the Vietnam war was always a concern. But I limited myself with not trying to work in all of those areas. I'm basically geared toward the land.

There was much joy in participating with the people. If we built a building, I helped build it; if we dug ditches, I dug ditches. We set up the catfish farming cooperative, and I'd bulldoze. I participated and tried to become a total part of it. I think I became a part of the people. I never did try to assume leadership. I always saw myself as an organizer. Everything I've ever done in terms of a leadership capacity had to do with some other objective that included the entire community. The leadership was eventually assumed by the community. Most programs we established were spinoff programs; we did not try to control them. My time was spent in the field. I stayed in the rural areas.

The joy was talking with the old people. I always listened very, very closely to the old people. I'd fish with them at the same time we were still working on a problem. I've done a strange kind of organizing. I've picked cotton and talked with people. I've cut weeds and talked. I've fished. I've camped. I went to parties. I had dinner in their homes. . . . I found what made them endure, and I became a part of that. I never could relate to the church like they could, but I would always go the gospel singings. . . .

A number of incidents continued to pressure me in my work. I think I was arrested 36 times. Then I ran for public office, and one of the campaign workers was shot. He was the father of 11 children. I think that has been the most . . . it just about . . . it didn't get the best of me, but it started working on me, you know, seeing his kids and how things disintegrated. A white guy just walked up to him and shot him six times. He had the same name as me. He was dead on arrival at the hospital. I went to tell his wife about it. She just looked at me and started vomiting. She

did that four or five times, any time she'd see me. We got the
oldest son a hardship discharge from the Army, after he won the
Purple Heart in Vietnam, because of this. He's a total wreck now,
a junkie. He travels from St. Louis to Mississippi, just running.
He used to always come by the office or my house at one, two,
three or four o'clock in the morning to talk with me. He came just
to talk about, "Are we really doing the right thing?" What he had
learned in Vietnam was the only solution. He was arrested for
shooting a policeman in his car. He has been in and out of jail.
Some of the oldest girls moved away to northern cities. The
mother is real shaky. Her husband was well liked by everybody.
I think that that was the hardest thing for me.

It all started coming back on me one day. That was in '70. Later
I was in a car accident, and it seemed like from then on in my
health started going so I eventually had to leave.

Being out in the field, before I left, was not always easy. There
were days that I was so disturbed that I would . . . I used to go
stay inside for eight, nine days, just not come out. Why I don't
know, I just . . . sometimes it just got . . . I think that those were
the most terrifying moments. I got to where I was doing that more
and more often.

That's when I started having so many problems I just kind of
withdrew. That's basically . . . I imagine I lost a sense of direction. After you develop a community to a certain point then
there's a need for something greater, for a partner, you know, that
you can talk to. I was able to talk at a level that just didn't quite,
you know . . . there was no communication with the local people
about certain things. I would try but they couldn't see the relationship between national issues and our county. The war in Vietnam had no relevancy to them. I became very hostile about the
Christian concept of things. I would say, "That's a bunch of
bullshit." I think it sort of alienated people. They'd want to know,
"What's wrong with him?"

The community changed too. It took on a new sophistication.
After it became popular, the middle class started running for
offices. The people were not able to accept my theory of why they
should support someone. They would say, "This guy that used to
be the school principal locked us up, so why should we support
him now?" I tended to support the black candidate on the merits
of that alone. I would try to explain why and they would say,
"He's no different from a white man." Southern people, particu-

larly in the rural, have grudges that are deeply rooted, and they pass on from generation to generation. Children are taught to hate. Some people think that only applies to poor whites, but it's folk history within a community. Old grudges just never die. It's a great mental strain to try to deal with such complex problems. Then, there are many times that you need somebody to talk with, and after ten years, there are a lot of people that have moved on into other areas. If you call, they'll be brief, you know, "How're you doing?" There was a circle at first that added to the mental stability of a lot of people. You could drive maybe 50 miles away and just talk with someone. Most of the other workers have moved on now. But that's understandable. They don't want to identify with the Movement anymore. They don't want to become involved in it anymore because it's a frightening thing to them, too. I think it's frightening and tempting. It's tempting to become involved again.

It gets to the point where you can't have a personal life in a community. You become an emotional wreck. Sometimes I wouldn't sleep for three or four days. A lot of changes take place. You have to be able to relate to them in order to give some direction to your life. I think the mental problems were too much for some people to take. Some people didn't last two years.

I understand why some people from the Movement are in prison. . . . Some are involved in murders; some are involved in political sabotage such as bombings. Many times an ordinary citizen like the man on the street can't understand this. Even those people who have identified with the Movement can't understand what or why certain actions are taken. I'm saying that I can understand it. People have become drug addicts. I understand it because I know the pressures of awareness, of knowledge, of where things are. Knowledge can be destructive in this work. Knowing something specifically and not being able to change it or deal with it is destructive. Many people knew what was happening. People in the Movement knew of corruption in the FBI and the CIA—years ago. When I read it in the papers now, and see that people are shocked . . . it disturbs me a great deal to have known about it for a long time and to see that people are so slow to learn. I'm saying that knowing all this and not being able to change produces pressures.

At one time I felt that if true peace could be found in the grave, that it would be easy to take my life. It would be so simple.

He spoke softly and very slowly. And then looking at how cruel people are . . . it doesn't condition you to be more rigid or more like the people you have to deal with. It softens you after you have experienced the cruelty. It's impossible for you to do that same kind of thing to others. Yes, it does make you angry, hostile. It is hard to be gentle. But the true kind of hostility doesn't exist in you, because once you experience something that is so painful, there's no joy in doing it to another person.

All these things are intertwined in my mind. It may take years for me to figure out . . . I'm not where I'm supposed to be. . . . I have to get used to the world again. I have a family and I've got to give them some consideration. I've been married for years. My family has not been a part of my life. I'm about to drive my wife away. She's strong and attractive, but we didn't have a marriage. I was always gone, and when I wasn't out of town, I was at the office working. The house was like an office too. I'm saying that to do all these kinds of things, I had to have some kind of base to do it from.

I'd like to be back where I was, in the rural, but I can't. I recognize that, and I'm able to deal with that.

Where I work now, I'm not gifted. I don't understand the relevancy of meetings; I don't believe in conferences. So where do I go? I'm working on it. I've only been away two months. I'm working on it, day by day, and whatever happens, happens, and whatever falls in place, falls in place.

Chapter 5

Joe

Joe works on salary for a large human rights organization in a southern city. During the Movement he worked on a subsistence wage and lived in people's houses or Freedom Houses. We met and spoke in his office. He is slender and dressed casually. He is now in his late twenties. He was raised in a small city in the South. When he was in his mid-teens, he participated for the first time in civil rights demonstrations. This participation changed his life. He left school not long after that and worked for several years as an organizer. He literally grew up in the Movement, by his own report.

He stayed with the Movement through bitter times. He was especially close to Dr. King and was deeply shaken by his death, but managed after a period of time to continue working. In the course of his work, he met and married a woman who shared his commitment. He now has two children.

He began by talking about the experience of being a field organizer.

I'd get out early in the morning and walk through the little town, just visiting. Often the town would be so small that I could visit every home in the black community in half a day. I'd stop, sit on the porch and chat with people, or I'd meet them on the way to work and then again at lunchtime in the cafe. I'd make a circuit.

Ladies would be waving their husbands off to work. They would see me coming and call, "Hey, come here, where are you going? Don't you know you got no business out there in them streets by yourself. White folks would just love to catch you out there. You come in here." Then they'd ask me to stay and eat. Then they'd send me out the back way, warning me to be careful. I was out there by myself, and there was such caring. I just couldn't want for any richer experiences.

Literally, some of the greatest conflicts that I had to resolve in the black communities that I worked in was who was going to wash my clothes and where I was going to eat. I'd have to try to

walk a tightrope, making sure that I didn't spend too much time at any one family's home. If I needed a couple of bucks, or even a ride for a hundred miles or so, there would be people waiting in line. Their feelings would have been hurt if I didn't let them help me. When there's that kind of a push behind you, you can keep going.

I never went through the daily fear that a lot of people did, partly because I was young, and partly because I had good experiences with older people who were really concerned about me. Some of them had spent their lives in one place, perhaps never even going out of the county, but they were really concerned. I could feel their warmth and concern around me.

We could see change taking place daily, and we could see the community coming together. For example, after a demonstration, four or five hundred people might have been put in jail. I wouldn't know where to get the money to get these people out of jail—bail would be $100 minimum apiece and $1,000 apiece for the staff members. We'd try to scrape nickels and dimes together, and I would see poor people who had nothing pouring money out of socks to raise the money somehow. People would put up their churches, they'd put their homes up, they'd sign a bond with their life savings. They'd even put up their lives. They showed you their commitment—they couldn't verbalize it, but they acted it out all the time. People acted out love. Sometimes I would learn that someone from the white community had gotten word to someone that he wanted to give money as an anonymous donation, asking nothing in return. I wonder how I could take it, and how the people could stand it; then I remember these experiences, and I have some idea. The community would just open up, it would just embrace the Movement workers.

I like to describe myself as a full-time student. I pray that before my death, I may be able to say that I was a pretty good student, that's all. My life has been tremendously influenced by the Movement. I was thirteen or fourteen years old when I started in it, so I grew up being impressed. My mind was open; I hadn't had full schooling, so school hadn't dehumanized me so much that I couldn't learn.

I grew up in an extended family and a strong community. Our neighborhood was truly a neighborhood of one big family. The community as a whole looked after the children. I can remember that if I was away from home, and was in a fight or something with one of the other kids, and if an adult saw us, more than likely

both of us would get a tanning. The community looked after us.

An elderly lady who recently passed away at the age of eighty was my babysitter. She diapered all of us and babysat for all of us. There were times when she would have 14 or 15 kids that she was babysitting. She had raised four or five different sets of children in my neighborhood.

I was raised by people of that age. They had a tremendous influence on me. They gave me a very rich appreciation of life. If they're not the source, I don't know what a source would be in terms of my truly respecting and appreciating people. I often find as I look back on my own values that they were all handed down from older people. I can remember that I was carried to church by the ear; I was made to go. I can remember I would go in and sit through Sunday school, and as soon as the Sunday school was over, I would come up the stairs and straight out the back door. I would walk out of the church services. I can remember many lonely days sittting outside by the baptismal pool; I remember the emptiness out there. I was determined that I wasn't going to be forced to submit to the ritual; but simultaneously, I feel that I have learned to have a deep appreciation for Baptist Christianity. Sometimes I find that I'm unconsciously making biblical references. I gained this from these older people. I've never been able to really sit down on Sundays and read the Bible, but I know it fairly well. In my own life, my Movement experience has often been strengthened both in my own personal, internal struggles and in the larger struggle, because I have found I could look to the Bible for some example of where we were at that time. We talked about Daniel in the lion's den, and David facing Goliath. These passages from the Bible had immediate application to some of the struggles we were in, and I'd really grapple to see the similarity in the Bible.

I didn't know my grandfather because he died before I was born. My father and my mother were not married, so I grew up in a home where the women were the backbone of the family. I had a lot of uncles, but for one reason or another they decided against living in our area. Many of them volunteered for the Army or the Navy, and then they had spread out. I think I gained whatever would come from those experiences with men, from men of the neighborhood and the community.

In 1955 before he was a teenager, Joe visited family relations in Montgomery, Alabama. It was during the time of the bus boycott.

We were staying on a main street, and we saw Army jeeps with heavily armed soldiers coming down the street. Our neighbors were on the jeeps with them. It was a very shocking sight. Those people were being carried home by the Army because they had been to a mass meeting at Baxter Avenue Baptist Church, Dr. King's church, and the white goons had surrounded the church. Initially the goons had been across the street heckling, but for some reason they stormed the church. The National Guard had been called out, and I learned that in order for these people to get home, the National Guard had to load them on the jeeps and trucks and drive through the mobs. I'll never forget that sight. It made a real impression on me, and I think on other people my age who saw it.

The mental pictures of the bus boycott and all of the conversations about it prepared me, perhaps unconsciously, for my later involvement. A lot of times I personally find strength in falling back on those experiences of having been in the city where the Movement was rekindled. The people I saw on television in the demonstrations were not strangers—they were my neighbors and friends.

While Joe was in high school, he became involved in testing segregation in public accommodations. He also started to attend workshops on nonviolence.

I think I had my first eye-opening experience at that time. We had had workshops on the sit-ins, but I don't think any of that had really sunk in. I went on a citizenship education retreat, and on the retreat, a woman got up and talked about her town, Selma. She said that three or more black people could not be seen on the sidewalk without being in violation of an injunction against congregating. That was just the tip of the iceberg. She gave us some of the history of what people there had gone through trying to register to vote.

Later on, she presented a challenge to the meeting to come to her town and see what it was really like. We agreed to go. We didn't understand what we had been training for, and I don't think we even knew what an injunction was, but we went.

I'll never forget it. We rode on a bus to the town, a little old sleepy sort of town. We drove to the church. When we got there, the church was surrounded. Getting there was like driving through darkness and coming to a burst of light. It looked like half of the white men in the county were there on horseback. The

church was literally surrounded. I could see shotguns, too. That opened my eyes. Still, we didn't care. We got out, and we ran up and down the block. We knew that we were being totally defiant. I think we blew the sheriff's mind. First of all, he didn't know where we had come from. You could see the apprehension on his part. We lined up, marched into the church, and found seats. The people just clapped. All the people in the church welcomed us; they were glad to see us because they'd known what we had done. These people had gone a long way themselves in coming to the meeting, but they had all slipped in through the back door, or had come one at a time. They'd all meet at different homes and walk fifty yards behind each other for protection, so they could get to the meeting without getting arrested.

When we were all in the church, the sheriff marched up. I'll never forget his big burly self as he marched in the back door with three or four of his posse right behind him. He said, "Preacher man, I come to tell you all that the meeting's over, so break this up and go on home." Our leader told him, "Man, what are you talking about? You don't run this meeting. You better get on out of here, or take that hat off and put that gun down and take a seat." Then we all cheered. We got up and sang Freedom songs. You could just feel the spirit. We stayed and had the meeting. After the meeting, the tension did begin to creep in. Whites outside were taking the names of the people in the church, so if they worked for someone white they would be fired the next day. But the people's spirits were not dampened. It was the first time I ever believed nonviolence could work.

After that the more involved I became in the Movement, the more involved I wanted to be. As a result, I was active and always there when there was a meeting or a march or a sit-in. At the same time I was a high school student, so naturally that created a little conflict. I couldn't be at a mass meeting and in school at the same time. As a result of those conflicts, and getting arrested, I was repeatedly suspended from school. The Movement began to open my eyes to more worldly things and in much clearer detail than school had.

The Movement provided a very beautiful outlet for me in terms of my expressing myself and spending the energy that I had at that age. I really sort of fit, so getting involved came very naturally. I saw a place where I could feel that I belonged. Also I sought understanding. In school I constantly felt that people were trying to change me, and it was a breath of fresh air to meet

people who accepted me as I was. Dr. King stood out among those. It sealed a bond between the two of us and I often say, "To many people, Dr. King was their leader, but Dr. King never led me anywhere. He was my friend."

After Joe left school, he spent several years doing field organizing in several communities. In the course of his work, he participated in many of the large demonstrations of the Movement. He talked about the Meredith March in Mississippi in 1966. The March was really the last big civil rights march in which the several civil rights organizations tried to coordinate their activities. It was the march on which the slogan Black Power was first widely used.

Tragically, what was understood by others was not what was meant. I have to agree with what was meant. Stokely Carmichael stated that in order for black people in this country to be free, they must seize upon power and use that power. Unfortunately, Stokely was not given the opportunity to define power. I would say power means political participation in terms of registering, voting, and running for office, and the collective use of our dollars to develop business and industry. Stokely didn't get a chance to give any meaning to black power. He threw the words out, and before he could explain it, the press had taken it and used it as a bludgeon on our heads.

Through all his work, Joe developed and maintained a close relationship with Dr. King. He was well aware of the many problems of the Movement before Dr. King's death. Still, the death was a key turning point for him.

I guess Dr. King saw something in me that was worth paying attention to, and he attempted to cultivate it, to help develop, strengthen, and support it. I felt that he was genuinely with me and that he listened and paid attention to me. In a sense he was part of the male image in my life. It's possible that I may have even felt some fatherly interest in him. I've thought about that. The death of Dr. King really knocked the bottom out of me on a couple of scores. One is that I felt the loss of a friend very deeply. He was really down to earth, a beautiful person. He would listen to people, not only the verbiage of people but he listened to what they were communicating and expressing, and he responded to that. We were like a family, a group of us and him, and it wasn't like the loss of a leader, but it was the loss of a friend, a cohort, a counselor. He was a person who had his weak moments and his

strengths, all of that. I felt an immediate loss when my friend was gone.

I also felt a deep sense of bewilderment in that I couldn't understand how anybody could kill such a kind person. I do believe in nonviolence, but there are a lot of people I can think of who have probably earned a bullet for bad things. I couldn't understand why anybody would kill a person as kind and as good as he, with all the others around. Then, too, I went through a personal stage of anger and deep bitterness. I was extremely bitter and almost became very reckless because I just didn't care anymore for awhile. Things just didn't matter. I guess at my age and having had the kind of experiences I had, I was often brash and cynical. Dr. King had helped me to temper my brashness and had helped to root out some of my cynicism. I became awfully bittter to think about him having been killed by forces in this country that didn't even realize that what he stood for was their net gain in spite of them. I'm one who believes in and subscribes to a conspiracy theory. I really think there was a conspiracy to kill him.

I was still working when he died, and I kept working for a few months. I was almost working out a death wish. The work kept me so consumed, and I felt a deep responsibility to carry on the Poor People's Campaign because of the possibility that he was killed to stop that work. It seemed to continue would show that his death didn't stop the work. After the conclusion of a big effort and after the death, I spent a couple of years in limbo, going between deep bitterness and anger and not being very creative or productive. I wasn't going to do anything and didn't want anybody to bother me. I was going to sleep and be totally free from responsibilities.

I was sort of dying on the vine. I didn't do anything but float around the country involving myself in some hair-raising experiences. I lived in a commune for awhile. I hooked up with a group of people who talked about marching fifty thousand people to the United Nations and declaring that the country was committing genocide and that we were not going to be governed by powers in America. I worked a little with that group but at one point they were going to get up in the U.N., and everybody was going to pull off their clothes and get nude. So I decided they were not revolutionaries.

Finally I began to talk with myself. I remember that I had to ask myself, "Where are you coming from? If Martin Luther King were genuinely your friend or your brother, what would he have

you do? What are your responsibilities in that light?" That was probably the most difficult question I've ever had to deal with in my life, and it was really easily answered. I think that's where the difficulty came. It came to me that he would want me to continue; he would want me to build on the strengths that had worked, and to figure out why what hadn't worked, hadn't worked. In my own mind, my central answer was that he would have me to go on, and that's become my measuring stick. So I went back to work and kept working. When I get discouraged and I want to give up, I have to ask myself, as if I'm swapping places with Dr. King: "You and he were friends. Maybe if he were here now and you were genuinely friends, and your death was having this impact on him, what would you have him do?" Raising that question and answering it honestly for myself has been the greatest strength for me.

He summed up his experiences by first talking about the casualties of the Movement and then what he had learned.

In the final analysis, I think America will probably be the greatest Movement casualty. But there are a lot of individual casualities, too. A lot of people have literally burned themselves out. I see people now who are in their late twenties or early thirties who have literally lived all of their lives already. I can see ninety years of living in their spirit. We started out in the Movement with youth and zeal and the expectation that we could change the society, in essence, overnight. That did not happen, nor did years and years of challenging meet the early expectations. Some have become embittered and angry and cannot relate at all anymore.

For others there is no place to go. The society has become a closed society for them. The days of the big marches are gone. There's no place in the country where many of the Movement people can work with the same drive, the same motivation that they had in the Movement. There's no real place in the federal or local government. There's no place in industry. There's no place in the black business world, or the black church, or other institutions because these people will threaten the institutions if the institutions are not right. They are boat-rockers. Even if the institution is somewhat right, they will push to make it more right. Because there is no place, the people become bitter. They become bitter too because they worked hard to open doors for others, and now those others pass them by.

There is a double price. Not only is society closed for them, but
the organizations from which they came, to which they belonged,
no longer exist. Many people made the Movement strong through
creating an organization, a SNCC, a CORE, a SCLC; the organization was a child of theirs. The organization was like a family.
So when the organization was lost, the family for many of these
people was too. This hurt. All together, it caused the Movement
casualties.

Quite a number of homes have been broken because of a commitment to the Movement. When I decided to marry, I sought out
a special kind of person, a person who felt the same things and
was willing to make the same commitment that I was. That way,
there wouldn't be any possibility of having a conflict between the
two loves. I've learned that lesson from other people in the Movement. A lot of people in the Movement became quite embittered
because the deeper we dug in trying to root out evil in the society,
the more it seemed like the depth of the roots were endless.

I've structured my own life in such a way that I've learned, not
necessarily from the mistakes of others, but from the strengths
and weaknesses of others. I think the greatest teachers have been
the people I worked with. I think probably the most significant
thing I have learned in the Movement is just to be natural, to do
what comes naturally. I remember many times being in a position
of great responsibility and wondering what to do. I would be faced
with a decision that might affect four or five hundred people's
lives directly, and there were no books to turn to. The road hadn't
really been travelled before. So, looking at the road and trying to
decide whether to embark or not to embark—if to embark, why,
and to what extent—those kind of experiences toughened me up
to just do what comes naturally. In every instance when I was
faced with those kinds of decisions, I would take it to the people.
When we got a church full of people, I would just decide that it
was not my right to make the decisions for these people. This was
a question of their feeling, and they had the ability and the right
to make this decision. They would decide. I always felt a lot
better, because if these people made their own decisions about
what they wanted to do, then my conscience was clear. I've always tried to resist making my personal feelings the will of the
people, and almost every time it's been that we ended up being
on the same side.

I can decide now exactly who I'm going to work with and what
I'm going to work on. Young Americans are truly very beautiful

people. I find the same fulfillment working with high school students that I found working with older people in the Movement. It seems to me that many adults wheel and deal from the philosophy that the ends justify the means. They will use any means they choose. This is a situation that I did not find with young people. It seems to creep in, increasingly, in the college community, wheeling and dealing, but that's not true with the younger people. The Movement always had certain basic principles. Regardless of how great the price or how high the ante, there were just some things that the people in the Movement would not do. The young people have more morality, a very elementary kind of basic morals. Young people hold these in high esteem, and these are things that come naturally. So I chose to work with them.

I guess I had an awakening set of experiences in the Movement, earlier, as I described. The Movement, in my mind, is a natural occurrence and had to occur, and the people who were acting in the Movement did what was natural. To me it was natural to march from Selma to Montgomery, or to march from Selma to Galilee to China, to be free. That's a basic instinct of animals. Animals do not like being caged or to be cooped up. The essence of segregation was a cage for black people, and also a cage for white people. Living in a segregated society is just inconsistent with nature.

Looking back, I see Dr. King as the greatest articulator of the essence of the Movement. He talked about very basic but real things. He talked about love and even said, "Love your enemy." Dr. King talked about nonviolence. He said, "We want a society at peace and a society of humanity, and we want equality." If you stop and look at the simple prayers of the Movement, the Movement has never asked for any special provisions. We've asked for equal access and an equal chance.

It has a profound impact on me to visit a town where great struggles took place; towns where all the blacks once walked with a hump in their backs and had a little shuffle, when the theme of the day was blacks grinning when there wasn't anything funny. I go back and see they aren't grinning any more. I see their backs are straightened. They are cognizant of it, and they have recorded it. They know what a transition they've gone through, and they're proud of it. They sit and tell you how the Movement gave them a platform to stand on, gave them an opportunity to be an adult,

or to show that they were human. These people welcome you back. They've always got an extra plate, or they can always roust up a comfortable bed for you. It's good to stay in touch with them.

Chapter 6

Jim

Not all the organizers articulated a religious or political ideology as a basis for their continued commitment. Nor were all hopeful. Jim was fiercely anti-ideological and pessimistic. There was deep irony in my encounter with him; despite his feelings of disillusionment, he continues to do very important work.

He spoke and moved with intensity, as if there were a coiled spring behind each word or movement. He spoke clearly, without hesitation, each word almost bitten off. His organizing was concrete and pragmatic. Repeatedly, he had found out what a community needed at a particular time and had worked to realize that need.

He did not grow up in the South. He first became interested in the Movement through experiences in college. In the course of the Movement, he has married and has had children, has run for office, and has edited a journal. He has had to endure the stresses of the Movement and a near fatal illness in his wife. He constantly played down his own achievements, especially in his description of how he got involved in the Movement.

My initial activity started when I was a sophomore in college, the same time that the sit-ins started in the South. A group of us thought that we should lend some support to what was happening there, so we started picketing Woolworth's stores. From that effort we organized ourselves into ad hoc committees and just kept active for the next couple of years.

During the time I was going through school, I worked for a horse player. He had about 10 or 12 people, his assistants, out around the country who made bets for him. I was one of those. When I finished school, he didn't have anybody in the southern states. Since I wanted to go South, I asked him if I could be his man covering the southern tracks in Florida and New Orleans. He said yes.

In the last year of school, we had conducted a couple of polling drives for people in Hayward County, Tennessee and a county in South Carolina, Clarendon County. We were talking with other people who were also doing these drives, people in Chicago, and a group in Washington, D.C. We thought that the drives were successful.

Before I had started to work at the tracks, after college, I had time on my hands. Actually, one track didn't open until November, so I just thought I'd go in and talk to these people that I'd written to but never met. I met them, and they seemed like good people.

Not long after I went to work playing the horses, my boss died. I tried for maybe six months to just look at all the horses he had given me to play to see if I could figure out his system. I couldn't. This was the end of 1962. I was broke. By this time SNCC had been formed, so I came up to Atlanta to talk to one of the SNCC people. I told him that I was trying to get back home, that I needed some money for bus fare, and that I could either do some work for him to earn it or would send it to him when I got back home. He said that he would give me bus fare. He said I could fly, but I said, "No, I'd rather bus." So he said, "I'll give you bus fare home if you'll stop on the way. There's a guy who's running for office on your way, and he needs some help." SNCC was working for the guy. So I did stop. I just liked the folks here and I've never left. I've been home once since then.

When I first came to town, I started writing speeches for this guy who was running for office. Most of the people who were here and who were involved in the organizations at that time just seemed like a good group of people as far as I was concerned, the type of people that I wanted to be around. My interest wasn't political. I didn't think, at that time, that it was possible to bring about any meaningful changes operating with the system. I was not interested in voter registration, largely because of the way that the voter registration drive had started. It had come out during the Kennedy administration. I thought it was money that was handed out to get people off the streets, off the buses, out of the dime stores, or wherever they were. I thought that in other places, where people had the right to vote, the vote hadn't made any difference.

I was aware of the fact that there were a lot of people who were in need in the state. I was interested in seeing if I could do some-

thing for those folks. So, for awhile, all I did was distribute the clothing and the food that was raised outside the state. There were drug companies at that time sending vitamin pills down for some reason or other. I didn't know it at that time, but the vitamin pills were no good. Vitamins are dated. They are only good for about four or five months from the time they are put up for sale. After that they are no good, and the ones we got were probably no good. I really thought that they were good, though. I would take them around, and I always got a kick out of telling people that, "You might not be eating as much as you can, but if you take a vitamin pill a day, at least you'll get the proper nutrition." I did that for awhile. I couldn't tell anybody to register to vote, and I just didn't do it.

It was just the people that I liked. It was their sense of selflessness, their dedication, their trying to help folks, and their desire for no compensation for what they were doing. The people kept me here. Most of us were working for about ten bucks a week, and most of the people who came as volunteers were getting nothing during that period. The lack of emphasis on material things was important. Many of us living in Freedom Houses slept three to a room. We shared things.

In 1964, at times, there were just too many people for the kind of project we had. People didn't like waking up and not finding a T-shirt if they didn't know who had it on. It was all right if somebody took your T-shirt and you knew it was Joe, but then there were four or five other guys who could have taken it. The dishes in the sink started bothering people. The whole thing just seemed to deteriorate, and there was a lot of bickering.

After 1964 there was a lot of fighting among people from different organizations. It really had more to do with lifestyles, what they were seeking but not saying, or how they felt about the people they were working with, as opposed to what organization they were with. The fighting went along organizational lines. At that time I was undecided about what I was going to do, so I decided I would go home for Christmas.

About three weeks before I went home, a couple of people asked me if I could help them market products. A group of women had gone on strike from where they had worked and had started making shirts at home. They wanted to know if I could sell them. Another group wanted to start making quilts and wanted to know if I knew anybody who would buy them. There was a guy who had been supporting the Movement raising chickens. He couldn't get

a market for them and wanted to see if I could talk to some black grocery store owners to see if they would buy what he was producing. I went up and talked with him, and I got interested in raising poultry.

I went home, and on the bus all I could think about was raising chickens. It just seemed like a good thing. That's when I decided to come back. I must have decided before that because I left some things here. I came back and founded a marketing cooperative. I worked with that for five or six years. It was during this time that my wife was ill.

We always had a policy in the cooperative that we'd never accept government funds. After awhile bad things started happening. We were paying the people their salaries, but the salaries just kept escalating. In order to get good people, you had to pay for them. The problem was that they didn't have any sense of commitment. Their commitment was to a nine to five job. We just couldn't find the people to stay with the work. They didn't seem to even have, I don't want to say the morality, but the consciousness to stay on if they were given a better offer. If somebody came along and said, "We'll give you $2,000 more a year," they would just leave. The thing that was so bothersome was that the other offers and the salary increases came from people who were funded by government agencies. It got to the point where we thought it was a conspiracy on the part of the government to destroy the program. It wasn't, but that's the way it seemed.

So, a number of things made me decide that I had to get out. That's when I took a job editing a magazine about black economics. That was the first time I worked on salary. After a time there I quit and came to work where I am now.

Some of the high times in the Movement were being in mass meetings or rallies. We were trying to make them into political institutions, but they were also a form of entertainment for the people who had organized them and recruited the people. It was a time when some work was accomplished, but it was also a festive occasion for the organizers. It was the one time you got together with people, certainly after the thing, to talk about the meeting and if we weren't successful, what was going on. Most of the meetings were successful. There was always something accomplished in the initial days. There wasn't any bickering; we talked about what we thought had to be done, reported about how many people had tried to register last week, what happened over

in that community, what can happen in this community. You had
the feeling that you were really accomplishing something.

Other high times were just in the activities that I got into.
Being able to get people who'd picked cotton all their lives, whose
hands were swollen out of shape, to the point where they could
handle a needle, a very delicate operation, and make a leather
bag that sold out of some of the best stores on Fifth Avenue for
$30 and $35 was very satisfying.

The most depressing thing was to eventually find out that people who seemed to be committed to something at one time, or
were idealists who said that they were motivated a certain way,
turned out to be quite different. Some of the people were gobbled
up in government jobs, government-funded programs, or foundations. The behavior they manifested once they were in these positions could not be compared to what they said they were about
three or four years before. They just became agents of the system.
That's been the most depressing. There are people I don't talk to
now because of that. I guess a lot of the people who worked on
the voter registration drives did not have the same commitment.
Maybe some of them were just doing it for a job.

The fact that people left and went into other jobs didn't hurt;
it was the fact that they didn't stay motivated. They were here
to organize the people into groups so that the people could do
something for themselves eventually. Once these groups were
formed, they still needed some outside support in terms of resources, not just money, but human resources too. Many times
the only contact the people in these groups had with the outside
world were with the ones who left to work for the outside organizations. My feeling is that the people who left for those jobs could
have changed the guidelines within the organizations that they
were working in, so that the regular process of applying for aid
and that kind of thing could have been changed so that the groups
could have gotten aid. But that effort was never undertaken.

In other words, when they left, as far as they were concerned,
the Movement was over. They might write a check and give it to
some organization, and that would be their commitment for the
year. That was the extent of their commitment. They had gotten
the jobs they wanted, and if you asked them, "Well, what did you
do for the Movement?" "Well, I sent SNCC a $500 check." Noth-
ing was done in terms of ongoing activities, even within their jobs.
They were asking people to do things when they were here, like
saying, "Defy your boss man, go down and register to vote. Even

if you get fired, it's worth it. Do it." Yet they did not do those things themselves when they went to a job. They were just simply asking others to do something that eventually they were not willing to do themselves. With these people in this area, it was a question of survival; with the ones who left, it was just a question of changing their lifestyles.

I stayed with the Movement basically because I just like what I'm doing. That's all I can say. Whether I'm helping people or not, I like to think I am. As long as I think that I'm in a role that's doing something to help somebody, whether it is or not, I'm quite happy. I can't put it any more simply than that, and it's not really any more complicated.

I was never concerned about violence or nonviolence. I didn't take a position on it. I thought passive resistance was foolish, and I told people this, but I never actively advocated violence. I've never even said anything about being nonviolent. It was just something I never discussed. It was a discussion I wasn't interested in.

My personal utopia is nothing complicated: it's just to see a lack of deprivation; if not an equality of income, then certainly a more equitable distribution of income than exists now.

There are things that I take now that I wouldn't have taken ten years ago. There are some things that I do now that really make me ashamed of myself. I wouldn't even have thought of doing them before. I do them now because I'm trying to do something else. Just last week I went into a courthouse to look at some records. A clerk must have called me "boy" about ten times, but I never said anything. I just can't imagine myself doing that in the past. That might have happened whether I was here or not; I just might have mellowed. That's the only significant change that I see. I'm less than enthused about seeing any meaningful change being brought about, certainly not by me, nor my generation. I don't know what's going to happen with the younger people coming along. I think it's going to have to come from them anyway. Certainly the decisive action that needs to be taken is going to have to come from a younger group of people. In terms of the Movement, I feel that I have already made my contribution, and that the most I'd be able to do anymore is lend my support or give advice.

I stay because I can't go to Los Angeles or New York and really help people. The kind of help they need you really can't give. Here, if there's a guy trying to steal another guy's land, we can

help. We had a case recently in which a black guy owned 30 acres
of land worth $1,000 an acre. He couldn't read, and he could just
barely write his name. The black guy had done some work on a
white guy's tractor. The white guy said he was going to pay him
and wanted a receipt for the money. So the white guy asked the
black guy to sign the paper, the receipt, and he gave him $20 for
the tractor payment. Well, it turned out what he signed was a
deed for his property. A couple of weeks later, the sheriff came
by and said, "He wants you off his property." When the black guy
said that it was his property, the sheriff told him that the deed
was recorded in the courthouse. I think we can do something
about cases like that. But it's not changing anything—it's just
keeping one guy from stealing from another. It's the kind of thing
we will be able to do forever here, because it's just the way the
society is set up here. So I stay.

Chapter 7

Mrs. Johnson

Mrs. Johnson's county is rural and poor. Blacks there are in the minority. In spite of all the struggles of the Movement, there are no black elected officials in significant offices. Mrs. Johnson has been caught up in the Movement for the last 18 years and has gone through the changes in it as the county has. She began in the Movement by writing to the Federal Housing Administration challenging the prejudice in the giving of loans to farmers. She did this on her own but soon linked up with others to help set up a local branch of one of the major civil rights organizations. From that she began to challenge public accommodations, to establish a Headstart Center, to confront legislators, and to get county roads paved.

She is now in her late fifties. She lives in the county where she was born and has lived most of her life. She lives on land that her father left to her. She married when she was young, and she and her husband farmed for a living. She has no children of her own but did adopt and raise a child. Her husband died two years ago. She has relatives and friends in the county, and she spoke repeatedly about how the community had pulled together under pressure.

She works for the Headstart Program, and I spoke with her in the Headstart center. She is a stout, active woman, with a warm smile and sharp eyes. She spoke with pride of the children in the center, remarking that they were curious and unafraid of strangers. She spoke with warmth about the confrontations she had had, and won, with the local whites.

When I asked her what had kept her going, she answered by emphasizing experiences she had had in her childhood.

My grandmother was a slave. After she was freed, she was brought here with nothing. A drove of them were brought here. She had to hire out to a white man as a housecleaner. She stayed around and waited on the children. She was so good around the house that when his daughter married, he gave my grandma to

his daughter for a gift. My grandma was named Anne. They named me after her. He told his daughter not to whip her and not to let her husband whip her, but if she got disobedient to let him know and he'd whip her. When she'd do something, he would whip her. He used her, and she gave birth to my father.

My grandmother sat on our porch everyday, facing North, and told us stories about slavery time and "the old master" and "the old miss," and how they would get the whippings, and how they would have to work, and the hardships they had. This really made me angry with white people. I just couldn't stand white people.

As I was growing up, another thing made my angry. I remember my mother in labor from childbirth, and how the doctor just talked to her so brutal and treated her so mean. This doctor also owned a lot of land and had a big mansion near here. When she died, my father couldn't pay the doctor's bill for her care. He harassed my father, and that just stayed in me. He would come around our house to see how my father was doing and if he was making enough to pay him. We were working like the devil to pay him. Finally we couldn't, and we lost most of our land to him.

Where I live now, I have to sit and look across at that land my father owned and had to give up. I have stayed so angry about the land because my father had worked most of his life for it. We had all worked, and then this doctor came and took it. It made me angry.

When I was thirteen years old, I remember the doctor throwed a quarter down and winked his eye. He said, "There's a quarter," and I said, "Thank you," and he said, "Don't tell your father." My father protected me from the doctor. He was . . . kind of mean . . . I don't know why he didn't get killed.

Other whites would harass young girls. Like on wash day, these white boys would cut you off from the crowd in the woods and do all sorts of things. That never happened to us. My father would say to them, "Don't come around my girls when I'm not here. When you want to see them, I'm here." Several times he ran people off with his gun.

When I was growing up, I felt that if I could make it to him, I was secure. . . . I felt that nobody was going to bother me, because my daddy said they wouldn't. I think that . . . that's what made me not afraid, because he wasn't afraid.

He was a pastor as well as a farmer. He would ride all over on his horse, James. He pastored at one church for maybe 32 years,

but he didn't do it for the money. Whatever the church raised, they would give him. Sometimes during the Depression he would come back with just 40 cents. He just had a lot of guts. He didn't fight; he didn't even raise his voice. He whipped me only once in his life he didn't hit his children.

The Ku Klux Klan would ride through at night. This was when I was a very small kid. They'd have some kind of special noise they'd make, a noise like WOOP! WOOP! WOOP! WOOP! You could hear it miles away. Everybody else would run to our house, and when they did, my father would say, "Oh, it ain't nothing." The only time he would stop my grandmother was when she started telling hairy tales about how they killed a black man, how they hung him up, and they beat him to death, but his spirit came back. My father would say, "No, no, no, the spirit can't come back."

All of this stayed in me, and even before the Movement, I was outspoken. I was just never afraid. I'd go anywhere I wanted to go and say anything I wanted to say.

My husband and I had a hard time making it. We struggled, and we were very poor. We worked so hard. My husband and I worked together pretty close. We both had to be pretty strong. He was very mean. He didn't let anyone do anything to him. He would fight back, but I never did. I just didn't believe in getting out and fighting. When we'd go testing public accommodations and they'd start coming in with clubs, I'd just sit there. Many times we would go in through a group of Klansmen. My husband couldn't go because if they hit him, he'd hit back.

I don't know if the relationship between blacks and whites is every going to work out. It's going to have to come in another generation, a young generation. If the schools continue to work with integration, maybe in the next 8 or 10 or 12 or 15 years it will work out. It's not to come about soon. I don't know about small places like this, but I believe there will still be more violence. There have nearly been riots here several times. I'm really nonviolent, but I will defend myself, and I do take care of my home. If anyone comes down there, I will even shoot to defend myself. I wouldn't say violence hasn't helped change. I know one thing though. It looks like every time there is a riot, you see blacks suffering the most.

In order to keep on, it just takes a kind of courage. You've got to have something in you that makes you want to do something

for yourself and for your fellow man. Every now and then you find somebody that wants to do that. My motto is, "I pass through this life just once and any good that I can do anybody, let me not defer, for I shall not pass this way again." I had this in my husband's obituary. When you just think about it, you've got to do something while you're passing through. Get an education, get out and grasp for a job, work, get a car, ride around, die, and you've done nothing. I've lived a good life. It's hard, but I like the life I've lived. I know how it is to be left out, and I know how it is to be depressed. I know how it is to live under a threat all your life, to be afraid of dying, to be poor. I know how it is to be treated by people that have a few dollars more. I just know a whole lot about that. I'm proud about that. I'm glad about it. I don't have an education, but I'm able to master educators. Once in the late part of the 60's, I filed a complaint against the superintendent of education. I had written to Washington and Atlanta about free lunches and managed to get a few free lunches through a good friend. He was telling people, "Somebody wrote a letter to somebody in Washington," and I said, "It was me." "Somebody's holding up this money that we're already getting to feed these poor people!" "It was me." "It was you?" And he said, "The trouble is, there's too many folks that don't even know how to run their own homes, and they're trying to tell me how to run the schools!" And I said, "I know you're talking about me. Yes, I can run a home, and I can run a school. I've never seen the inside of it but I know you're making a hell of a mess!" We got to be pretty good friends after all that.

The farm relaxes me. In weather like this I have to go home, get in my old boots, get my dog, and go around the fences. It worries me, but when I come home, it relaxes me to see old cattle laying around, and to see my dog get after the cow. I have to holler at my dog, and it rests me. I fish every now and then, I just raise cattle on the farm. I was into the milk business, but they took our milk, so I turned them into beef cattle some time ago.

After I lost my husband, I was so torn up that I started to leave everything. After I settled down, I decided to keep this farm. I don't have a whole lot of money, but I can live on what I can pick up until I get old enough to retire. That's about five years.

I wouldn't live anywhere else but in this community because I've suffered too long and too hard to run away from what I've done. The only thing is that I've got a whole lot to do. I've got to

deal with lawyers, and then when they leave, it'll be somebody else. It's an everyday thing, but I kind of like it. My husband said I was crazy, and a lot of my other relatives say it's crazy to be bothered with other people and to be cursed out for it at times, but I kind of like it. I like the way we challenge the white power structure. I went uptown yesterday. I went in one store, and I saw a black girl working there. I went in another store, and I saw two black girls. They said they'd never hire blacks, but they did. We have a black policeman. That's not enough, but that's better than nothing. It's not near enough, but it's a start.

Chapter 8

Reverend Ken Dean

Reverend Ken Dean is a tall white man. He has worked extensively in the white, as well as the black, community over the years. We spoke in the city in which he had worked and lived for a number of years. Although he sees himself as a minister, his work has carried him far from the traditional minister's role—into politics and even into business. He spoke slowly, weighing his words carefully. We concentrated on why he got involved and what had sustained him over time.

My initial activity was not much different from anyone else's in the Movement, but I have found myself subconsciously asking why I got involved. One night in 1967, in March, something out of the past hit me as to why I was doing what I was doing.

I'd started school when I was five years old, a year early. At that time in public school we had what was called Blue Ribbon Day, which came on the first of May. When you started school in September, the school had a chart that listed all the health examinations and shots you had. It even listed periodic health reviews such as fingernails and hygiene. If you had all those things accomplished, you got a blue ribbon at a big ceremony on Mayday. There were seven children in my family, and I was next to the youngest. My father could never afford to have seven kids get all the exams, so none of us ever scored high enough to get a blue ribbon. I didn't know what it meant not to get a ribbon. This was my first experience at such things.

Mayday came, and they lined up all the kids that had blue ribbons. I was the only one that didn't have one, but it really didn't bother me. They marched down to the town square. I recall running on the sidewalk while they marched through the streets, hollering at my friends who hollered back. That was fine, but then they assembled in the square. I was standing off to the side. When they got through some speeches, they rang a bell. All the kids with blue ribbons could run into the drugstores and get free ice cream. I was calling back and forth to my friends, but when

95

they rang the bell, everybody ran. I got my three buddies, and we ran into a store. They got ice cream, but I didn't. I didn't know why. It hit me that night in March that this experience in my background probably had been more determinative than many others. To my knowledge, I had never ever recalled that incident from the time I was five years old until 1967. The realization was that if that kind of thing happened to me, a white kid, you can imagine what happens to black children every day. I realized the injustices of a society and a system in which people are discriminated against. I've understood my involvement in light of that experience.

Another important thing happened to me when I was six years old. I lived in a village of 250 houses, built for people who worked at a defense plant during World War II. It was what we would now call a federal housing project. In 1942 there was a polio epidemic, and some of my playmates got polio. One of them died and one was crippled. At the age of six years, I had to face the idea of life and death, a confrontation which normally comes to people at sixteen, seventeen, and eighteen years of age. After I went through that experience at such an early age, I made certain commitments concerning my life and vowed that it would not be wasted. That experience always stands in the background, even today, in terms of an appreciation for life and an awareness of death.

Another thing happened that had something to do with it. When I was in graduate school, *Life* listed 28 characteristics of poverty. I had never thought of myself as poor, but I checked off the points which applied to me and 26 of the 28 applied.

Then, too, as I was growing up, my parents always taught me to appreciate work. They also let life's mysteries be mysteries, and that created a kind of optimism for me. So, I believe that with hard work and optimism one can really go far.

In talking of his work over the years, he said, I consider my work to be a ministry. I really had no interest in going into the ministry as I saw it. I felt that there were fundamental claims that were made by the ministers of the church that were legitimate, but I also felt that people, as I knew them in terms of the ministry, were not living out those claims. I had an agreement with myself that I would follow out that claim as I understood it for me.

One of the things that I learned from my theological education was to be able to measure my own needs in terms of the com-

munity, and also to know something about my own boundaries. I keep a pretty close personal check on that because I see people who are destroyed in this kind of work. In many ways, I probably have the most lonely existence of anybody here. My initial identification was with integration, but I also thought that it was my responsibility to deal with the white community because it was the oppressor. I tried to be a broker in developing programs for blacks through the federal government, lawyer groups, legal suits, and foundations; at the same time, I have always had my living quarters and my primary institutional identification in the white community. It's the white institutions I'm trying to change, not the black. This is another thing that says something about what makes me move: I've always felt that, for me, the fundamental religious conviction, the essentials of faith, boil down to loving one's enemy. When you look realistically at the situation, the blacks weren't and aren't my enemy. The whites often were and are my enemy. So the question is, "How has it been for me to live in a community of enemies?" For me it has been just like it would be for anybody else—hellish.

My wife and I were kidding about it the other day. I was going to one town on Sunday, and she was going to another, so we would both miss church. My wife said to me, "What are they going to do at church?" I said, "What do you mean?" She said, "Neither one of us is going to be there. Who's going to scare the people today?" That's kind of the way it is, because if church is the place where you discuss the primary questions, which is the way I consider it, that means you confront the issues every time you go. I usually try to precipitate that discussion if nobody else does, but it's hell because I get very little support. When you come into a community and you become identified with a stance of protest, the question is, how long and loud can you protest and still come back to embrace that community? In a way I have always embraced it; but the protest has always been very real, and I find it a problem for me.

I have a scattered community. I think one's existence in a community allows one to survive, to find support. My family means a great deal to me. My wife is basically a person who shies away from controversy, and I'm a person who functions best in the midst of it. So our sharing and contact doesn't really gain a great deal of strength from the kind of work that I do. Insofar as I can, there are a lot of things that I try not to bring home with me. I have to be careful about that, because if I leave everything

at work, I lose communication altogether. That's a constant struggle. My wife has worked with me and has enjoyed it, but she gets very angry when people attack me. I don't get angry; I usually have what I call the moment which has the most potential in it for learning and for teaching. So we're different.

What sustains me? My life in the church is still very important to me. Even though the experience at the church is, by and large, a struggle and oftentimes a strain, there is still a kind of community support that comes from it. Some people from my community may say, "Dean may be a crazy nigger-loving son-of-a-bitch, but he's mine and I'm his, and we belong to each other." I'll give you an example of that kind of thing. When I lived on State Street a few years ago, there was a man living next door to me. This was when Martin Luther King, Jr. was shot. My wife and I went to Atlanta, and we marched. Afterwards, a guy was talking to me about "those damn niggers over there marching all over town." He was talking about us. We lived next door to him, we marched, and he didn't know it. So I had this long discussion with him. I was working for Robert Kennedy at the time.

A few days after that, I was interviewed on TV. The guy that was interviewing me asked me how much money I got paid for my work in civil rights. It was an attack on me, but I answered him. My neighbor saw me on TV. The next day he came over and said, "You know that son-of-a-bitch yesterday asking you how much money you made? That's none of his business, how much money you made." Later I heard this neighbor telling another guy that I was a civil rights worker who did everything he didn't like; but I was his neighbor, and it was all right for him to talk to me about it, but he didn't want somebody who wasn't our neighbor grinding me up about it. By God, I was his neighbor! I belonged to him, and he belonged to me! There were enough of those experiences, and they helped me.

I don't believe it's possible to arrive at an integrated society without dealing with the violent people on the right. It's absolutely stupid to take any other position. This really comes back to my basic understanding about man. I think within all of us there lies the potential for human development, and that man who is hooked off on the black side is no more fully human than is the one on the other side. As far as I am concerned, they stand equal distance, from a different perspective, from being human. That's where I've been and I'm still there, and my experience for the last fifteen years indicates that. I said publicly today, "A lot

of people would have me hate, but I'm not going to hate." Because you can't get there that way.

I have had some rough moments. A black man who was a friend of mine was killed. Before he was killed, he had told me that some people tried to kill him, but he couldn't tell me who they were. He was killed right after that. Now, I find that I have had a counseling relationship with one of the men convicted of killing him, who's in the penitentiary. It's very difficult for me when I am with such people who are in prison, and they talk about people who have bombed and blown up churches. It's difficult for them too, because they don't really glory in that.

The most difficult thing I've had to deal with here, though, is getting accused and attacked by parts of the white community because of my relationship with the violent people on the right. The one thing that people don't understand is that they think that if you relate to somebody that you're pro their political position. I don't support a violent position because I tried to reach these people. For about three months last fall, some white people tried to put out a contract on me, to have me killed, because of my attempts to reach out to the violent white men. That was the most shocking thing that's happened to me. It was an experience that I've never gone through before. In fact, it made me break out in bumps, because that was the only time that I was ever profoundly angry. I didn't get emotional; in fact, I was very calm. It calmed me for a period of three weeks, and I think it was because I was absolutely, totally angry. I didn't act out. I didn't talk with anybody about it, and I was consumed with anger. I had a sense of this being a country in which life could be worked out and lived on an orderly basis. Yet, when I moved in on the heart of this problem, half of the support community fell off. Then, when the other half tried to put out a contract on me, I felt pretty damn shaken.

People sustain me. My closest friend is involved in work similar to mine. He's a very intense, very critical guy who has opinions and who moves. He doesn't get invited out for a lot of light social life and neither do we. My wife and I have only been invited out three times in two and one-half years. I do talk with him frequently. There are other friends here, journalists mostly, and I have real anchoring lines of support outside the South that are very important to me.

My relationships with the people on the right are sustaining,

too. They mean a great deal to me. Conversations with them are gratifying. There hasn't been an attempted bombing or act of violence here since I started dealing with them in 1968, except those instigated by an FBI plant. You know, a double agent. I think that means something. I understand it, and it is how I understand myself and how I understand that, that becomes meaningful to me. I don't have to have people line up and thank me for that, because I know what the hell it means.

In summing up he said, In the same sense that our life is sustained through interlocking systems of blood vessels, as the blood would not be worth anything if it didn't have structures through which to flow, so I feel the same way about life. Structure seems to be necessary for life. I think that a central quality for life is structure, and I think an essential quality for meaning is order. What I'm saying is that folks who are involved in protest must also maintain some involvement in structure. I've always been aware that social change is never an end in itself. Some sort of order has got to be recreated out of the change. I think that awareness has probably meant a great deal to me, because I never was protesting as an end in and of itself. I think that it was very easy for people to be caught up and to make two mistakes. One is to think that protest should be based on hate. It should be based on love. I've always understood protest in that nature as a positive thing. The second mistake is that some people come to see it as an end itself and in a negative fashion. I think those two things are always destructive for everyone. I have a great deal of sympathy for the Weathermen because, while I might disagree with some of the tactics that they use, I think that they still have possibility for life and creativity. They haven't fallen apart. It's the same thing with the Symbionese Liberation Movement. I think it's damn tragic that that has to be an alternative, but nobody has really contested the claims of those kids in terms of the issue of food. In all the different work I've done, business, the church, or politics, I consider myself a minister who is working in structures. In every instance, the only thing that I do in my ministry is try to get people to realize their own potential. I can't do it for them. I try to get them to communicate so they can realize their potential for themselves.

Chapter 9

Reverend Rockwell

Some of the members of my church aren't for freedom. I don't mind telling them about freedom, though, because I feel like I'm working for the Lord. The Lord told me to preach to all the world. If I get out here in a demonstration against injustice, I'm preaching. I figure I can reach more of the world preaching a sermon that way than I could by just isolating myself before people in some hollow of a log somewhere. The Lord is in the business of saving souls, and I'd like to carry Lester Maddox up to heaven with me. I go to jail because I'm working for the Lord. They call it raising hell, but I call it working for the Lord. I don't think anybody, no agitator between here and hell or nowhere could be more of an agitator than Jesus. I just can't understand people when they think we are far from religion when we are demonstrating. I just don't see it.

The speaker's voice is rich and rhythmic. He is short, has immensely broad shoulders, dark, black skin, grey hair, and large, intense eyes. He has been a preacher, and his voice has all the range, depth, and command of a great preacher's voice. There are no weighted words or overly dramatic gestures.

He is fifty seven years old, and he has worked full-time in the Movement since 1963. As we spoke, we were seated at a table under a shade tree in the yard of a day care center. It was out in the country, very quiet except for the children who, at times, played around us and spoke to us.

He threw himself into talking and made his stories come alive. As he spoke, his voice and body were intensely focused on what he said. Much of the form, many of the metaphors, where those of a southern rural preacher, but the content was remarkably different. His faith and his conclusions were his own and led to action in the Movement and not "pie in the sky." His life was remarkably different from the life of a traditional southern preacher.

101

He has worked primarily in the area where he was born and spent his early years. There has been little progress and much violence in that area in the course of the Movement. We talked first about some people who had stayed with the Movement and about the many who had left it. Much of what he said about people leaving the Movement was based on his experience in this one area.

I believe that religion really helped people in the Movement. People had been taught through their religion to have patience. The invisible rewards of the Movement didn't discourage them too much because they had been taught their rewards would come later, after death. This served a great purpose: it gave struggling blacks the patience and the courage they needed, because the victories that have come out of the Movement are almost as empty, in a way, as the "pie in the sky." That isn't to say that "pie in the sky" doesn't exist, but just that it's not visible. It's about as visible as the rewards of sufferings and jailings. When we started in the Movement, many of us thought that we would accomplish first-class citizenship. We thought that the majority of the poor blacks would taste the fruits of the suffering, but there have been no rewards for them. Now the middle-class blacks are going into office, and blacks are able to register and vote, but this has not filtered down to the man on the bottom. That man has not tasted the fruit as yet. Until the majority of the poor can taste the fruits of a rich America, I don't think that we've come close to victory.

While I was in jail many times in the Movement, what kept me going was the hope of victory. After I would get out of jail, I had one little speech that I would make. I would say that before the year was out, we would have victory; we would become first-class citizens; we would have jobs; we would be able to go into places and be served; and we would be able to get in the front doors of businesses. I believed that at that time, and I kept fighting. I thought that when we put the pressure on the government, there would be a peak that we would reach, and then a breaking point—the opposition would break down and would give us what we wanted. That didn't happen.

There were quite a few people that got in and out of the Movement. It's a great sacrifice to be in the Movement. A lot of people see the light, and they understand what's going on, but they're like the rich man that came up to Jesus and said, "What can I

do to be saved?" Jesus said, "Sell out and divide among the poor." That man walked away from Jesus. A lot have walked away from the Movement.

Giving up money is a great sacrifice. Before the Movement, I made $9,000 a year, and I've never made near that much. I had three churches when the Movement started; I only have one now. I've worked all my days. I've worked as a skilled laborer, the type of labor that pays well. I have four children who are married now, but back then I had to make a living for them. If it hadn't been for my wife working, I don't know whether we could have eaten.

A lot of my blacks who were with us dropped out because of pressure. Many believed in what they were doing, but they were in business and borrowing money was difficult. They were identified with the Movement, and for that the whites penalized them. They couldn't get a loan. The whites allowed them to go so far and be kind of "Tomish," but when they get to pressing hard and hit some nerve points, they'd be penalized. They might have to pay a higher price for groceries. If someone were trying to run a little store, then the white suppliers might charge him higher prices. People couldn't compete, so they got squeezed out.

Another group walked away from the Movement because they thought that it would be over in a much shorter time. When it wasn't, they fell by the wayside. It's just like another parable. Jesus said, "A man went out to sow seed and some fell among the thorns and thistles and some fell on stony ground and some fell on good ground. Some of it sprang up and bore fruit a hundredfold." There were some in the Movement who didn't have patience. The white society went into a slump, a backlash.

Some white friends of mine started out with the Movement but dropped it. They thought we were going to beg a little; that some crumbs would be thrown to us, and that we would then settle back and be quiet. We just kept knocking on the door for public accommodations, and after they gave us that, they thought we would stop. But we wouldn't. So they turned on us and said, "You have gone too far." They stopped supporting us. A lot of them had been giving us money, but they never intended for us to reach first-class citizenship.

I know a whole church that had preachers coming in the front door and going out the back door almost in a line. They were firing them very fast during the days of the Movement because the ministers spoke out about what was right. One of the minis-

ters of the First Baptist Church went to California for a conference and came back to make a report. He started his report in the church, but he finished it somewhere else because they had him out of there so fast he didn't know what was happening.

People are being penalized all the way every day. There's a hundred and one reasons why people dropped out, but the biggest reason was because people weren't willing to pay the price. They just got tired of the pressure, and this society can put pressure on you.

For example, my car needs servicing, but I have to search for a mechanic like I'm in Russia. I'm just as scared to carry my car to certain white mechanics as I am to stick my head in a lion's mouth. Once I went for a wheel alignment. About three weeks later, those tires wore out. The mechanic knew me from the Movement, and he messed the car up. I'm scared to let him work on my car, work on my brakes.

There are times when I feel down and out because the road to freedom and justice seems as dark as seven nights. Most of us in the Movement had our hopes and our confidence in the courts, especially the Supreme Court. Then Nixon put those blind judges on the Supreme Court, judges who were dedicated to the society rather than justice. Although it's supposed to be justice, and it's written all over the courthouses all the way from here to Washington, D.C., 'JUSTICE,' what they give out is public opinion, not justice.

The road seemed to be blocked up when Nixon was elected. People have impeached him now, but I wanted to impeach him when he was campaigning. He said that he was going to make some black capitalists, but I knew that was just a whole lot of hogwash. They always hand one or two blacks a few dimes out of their hands backwards, to throw us off stride, to block the stride for freedom. I never campaigned against a man harder than I campaigned against Nixon. When he got in there, he was the first man, I'd say, who gave me the definition of talking out of both sides of his mouth. Some people go by the definition of the dictionary, but I pick up my definitions in action. He said one or two beautiful words that came out of one side, saying that he believed that all the citizens should have an education. Then, out of the other side of his mouth, he said he was against busing. Anybody who is against busing is against black people having a decent education. The election of Nixon said, "Stop the blacks."

I'll tell you why the school situation hurt me so much. Even

during the darkest days, I was saying that through the schools white children would understand black children and black children would understand white children. When that white child comes to be the chief of police and that black child gets in a fight with his wife, that white policeman wouldn't rush up to the scene, see the black man already mad at his wife, and say to him, "Boy, shut your mouth!" If the black talks back and says, "What the hell do you mean?" he won't be shot. Now, if you say that to a white man, he'll put a gun in your stomach and pull the trigger. Maybe that won't happen in the future.

During the Movement, several blacks were killed in this town over a period of about ten months. The white man feels that he is god of the earth. When blacks don't scrape and bow when speaking, he'll shoot them down. Blacks have been getting killed for the last 20 years for a loaf of bread all over the world and all over the United States. Right now they're falling! Whites don't want to cooperate with us. That wouldn't happen if we understood one another. That wouldn't happen if we went to school together. So school is the answer.

People are saying that blacks are lazy. Blacks get tired of reaching and coming down with a handful of air for 40 and 50 years. I get tired of telling high school children to stay in school, when they can't get a job when they come out. College graduates can't get a job, and you're telling them to stay in school. Blacks have been beaten and cheated out of their wages for years. Blacks have worked hard, and they don't have anything but a place to sleep! What kind of reward have they gotten for working hard?

I remember a book once that said, "Would the deacon have such perfect attendance in church if he weren't sitting in his frock and exercising authority over others? Would the school teacher be as dutiful if she weren't the one that headed the class and had the satisfaction of the enjoyment of teaching the class? Would the preacher be interested in the church if it weren't for the salaries and the power?" I thought about that. All of this is to consider that people do get rewards. Most of the whites who strive get ahead are rewarded. When people get ready to call somebody lazy, they should just look back over things and see how many rewards a black has gotten.

Also, an interpretation of religion has been used to fool us here, in Africa, and all over the world. It isn't a matter of the religion itself but the interpretation we got through the pressure of public

opinion in this society. Our preachers were writing their sermons after the wishes of the society.

I admire Castro for kicking preachers dead in the pants. He said to them, "You come here with your Bibles under your arm, shooting all this horse straw here. Get out. Cuba's going to be for Cubans!" I've got friends in the Movement who are afraid to say that. They say, "The guards of the United States think you're a communist if you talk like that. This is the United States! You're not supposed to admire a communist!" I've been working in the church since I was seventeen years old! I just admire Castro for what he did. But yet and still, I think the backbone of my keeping on is my religion.

I do have weak moments. I'd say maybe it's because I don't pray hard enough, or I become slack. I get down and out sometimes and feel that it's an impossible dead-end street we're on.

Sometimes I think understanding the Movement is like reading the Bible. Many people pick up the Bible, read it, and don't understand it. They don't know what they're reading. Only those who have the coloring, who have been given the insight of what's right and what's true, are given to know. When Jesus was asked, "Why do you speak in parables?" he answered, "That they may see and not see, that they may hear and not hear. It is given only to a few who will willingly accept it. Pearls are not cast before swine." It doesn't seem that it should be this way, but sometimes I think the Movement is almost as hard to interpret as the Bible. Through it all, though, the backbone of my keeping on is my religion."

We next talked of the course of his life's history, how he had grown up, and what he felt had led him to the positions he holds.

When I came to know myself, we were living in a town not far away from here. As for life as a youngster, I don't remember much. My mother was separated from my father. I don't remember him. After I had grown, I met him, but I didn't know him when I was young.

My mother worked in the kitchens doing domestic work. She left us home. I was the oldest of four children. I was kind of the nurse while she worked. I don't remember attending grammar school, but I do remember attending Sunday school. I went back to where I was born recently, looking for people who need housing. The same two churches I attended are still there. Even now, I find

myself singing the old songs I learned then. People get after me
for that in church, because hardly anybody sings them anymore.
Songs like, "You better mind how you walk, you better mind
what you talk, you've got to give an account at the Judgement.
You better mind." Songs like, "I know it was the blood, I know
it was the blood, I know it was the blood for me. One day when I
was lost, he died upon a tree. I know it was the blood. I know it
was the blood for me." Songs like, "What are you going to do
when the world's on fire? What are you going to do? You can't
hide." Long before I was converted, I was touched spiritually.

After a time, my mama met a fellow by the name of Rockwell.
We all were young, and she just called herself Rockwell. My father was really a Jones, and I'm really a Jones, but we called
ourselves Rockwell. Mr. Rockwell worked in a sawmill. When I
was about ten years old, we went to a place in Florida.

**He remembered clearly the first job he had had and how he
had gotten it. It was shortly after he moved to Florida, when
he was 11 years old.**

We played with the boss man's children. They were white. One
day the boss' wife sent me and her daughter down to the sawmill.
You could see us coming half a mile away. Black as I was, I came
strolling down the road with this white girl. As young as I was, I
was too dumb to know what I was doing. The boss saw the picture
and found me a job at the sawmill. I didn't have any objections
to going to work. I didn't understand that what happened to me
wasn't right. I don't reckon I was exposed to enough knowledge
of things to raise any protest in my mind about going to work. So,
I just worked. I was up on a belt that carried big blocks of wood
and slabs out to a pit. The train engines that pulled the timber
to town used the wood as fuel. My job was to throw that wood
off the belt. The blocks weighed 40 or 50 pounds.

We lived 20 miles from any town in low land. When the water
rose, we couldn't get out. We would be without food. A man told
us to eat gophers so we wouldn't go hungry. We ate gophers. I
worked there until the end of the sawmill. That was my first job.

In all the time I was growing up, Mr. Rockwell worked hard.
He didn't provide a fine car or a fine home, but he provided what
he could. I came up through '28 and '29, '30, '31, and '32. Those
were hard times. We moved back here in 1932, when I was sixteen. I remember because I joined the church when I was seventeen.

Before I was converted, I waited and I tried. The first experience I had was not a complete one. It was the first time I ever stayed out of my mama's house. I went down in a little creek where there used to be a railroad. I saw the sun go down, saw the moon rise, the moon go down, and then the sun come up the next morning. I prayed all that time and nothing happened. Another time, I went a little way from the house into some trees. It was still daylight, and I told the Lord, "Well, I have gone to all kinds of churches and listened to people. I have heard that some people are born for hell, that they're predestined. They are the hard-shelled type. Well, maybe that's the trouble, then, with me." I said, "Now, I don't know why you picked me to send to hell, but I want you to do me one favor. I want to get religion, and I want to serve you. But if I was picked to go to hell, I want you to let me die this year. I want you to let Reed the undertaker bury me this year. Let my mama put me in the ground this year." When I said that, a voice spoke clearly and said, "Every man has a right to the tree of life." I went home. That's all that happened that time.

The day I got religion, I was working on a white fellow's lawn, a man named Murphy. I had been praying very hard that morning. We had a revival going on in church at the time, and I had been to the mourner's bench. I shook people's hands and asked them to pray for me. I had become what you call a mourner. I was praying every day, all day and all night sometimes.

At ten o'clock this particular morning, I was working on this yard and something struck me. It just went all over me. I tried to be quiet and hold my peace, so I worked on until dinner. The first thing I said was, "Well, something finally happened." I went in to dinner and sat down. Mr. Murphy said, "Sam got religion." That knocked me off my feet. I didn't say a word. I didn't know he knew there was a God! I went on to the church and joined the church that Friday night. I went on to be very active in the church. I had had little schooling. After I joined the church, I studied the books of the Bible at Sunday school. Most of my being able to read came through daily studying of the Bible. Eventually they made me a teacher and then superintendent of the Sunday school.

I believe my religion unconsciously opened my mind toward the direction of the Movement. I believe the Movement was already under the surface of the hearts of many blacks who were suffering long before it flared up in the 1960s, or even earlier with Dr. King

in the 1950s. I was able to walk in the Movement in this town because of a fellow named Stewart. He was a black man who spoke out for and worked for voter registration in the 1930s. He's still living. I remember first meeting him, when he was speaking at a church, just a little old small church that hadn't been built long in the community back up there in a pecan grove. He talked about getting people registered to vote and taking part in elections. I was about twenty years old. I was very impressed with him, and I worked with him in voter registration. If I had to put my finger on any thing or person that most affected my mind in the way of leading me into civil rights, it would be this man and this experience.

It was hard doing the work then. It was dangerous. People were scared. It was frightening in those days. People would run and hide from you. You'd go to the front door, and they'd go out the back door. We had some rough times at that time. Fear keeps blacks under control, even today. Not only was it hard then, it's hard now! It's hard to get people to a meeting. There is so much pressure on blacks. You go to them and ask them to help with the Movement, and they don't. They try to explain it away, but the fear is still there.

As for my family, my mother never had any objections, but she never had been a person who led in the way of civil rights. My father would fight and get in jail if you messed with him, but as far as belonging to a group or organizing and talking about justice, he didn't lead me in this direction. Neither my sister nor my brother are active either. My brother has had trouble with drinking. He's off and on. He'll go to church and then he'll get caught up and stray off for awhile, then come back and beg the church's pardon. That's the kind of fellow he is. Now, my sisters, they are all church workers. My wife is a church worker and a member of the church.

From the time he started at age twelve, until the present, Reverend Rockwell has worked regularly. He said with great pride, I never received a penny from unemployment in my life. My sister always said that I worked so, she didn't know she had an older brother. I was gone when she got up in the morning, and she'd be asleep when I got back at night.

He has worked plowing land "from sunup to sundown," he has worked packing and transporting goods. He has had a variety of jobs.

He felt his religion, his work, and his voter registration activity were all important in the early part of his adulthood. In 1942 he was drafted and served for four years in the Army, much of it overseas. He said of his war experience:
When the war started out, they kept the blacks and whites separated. But when things got hot, they put us on a ship together. I was in the Pacific. On the ship we gambled together. We were hospitalized together in Okinawa. I don't know of any trouble. When we were hospitalized, if one black didn't feel like getting his dinner, he would tell his white buddy to, and *vice versa*. I know blacks and whites can live together because of this experience. Yet when it came time to come back, they separated us.

Shortly after returning from the service, he married. He now has four children. His wife lives and works in a city a few hours drive from where he lives. He sees her on weekends and whenever else he can. His children are now all grown and working. None is actively involved in the Movement at present.

In 1956 he became a preacher. Shortly before that, he had begun to work in a civil service job. Of being called to preach, he said, I remember, I felt I was called to preach before it actually happened . . . there was an old deacon, Deacon Convers, who I used to study with and read the Bible with. One time we were talking, and just out of the blue he asked me, "Aren't you called to preach?" I didn't have time to polish up my answer or anything, I just said "No." When I said that, something down in me said, "Don't you know you lied?" It was just as plain as I'm speaking now. After that I thought about "no" for a long time. I would sit up in the night school and think. It stayed on my mind so, that at times I felt like I was almost unable to catch my breath. For two or three years I walked around with that feeling, not submitting to the call to preach. Finally, I confessed to it. I told my church I was called to preach in 1955. They gave me a church, the Holly Grove Church, and after that I was called to several other churches.

Of the Movement's coming, he said, I think that the Movement's beginning in the late '50's and '60's was like an explosion when it came to this area. The Freedom Riders came to town and were jailed. Out of sympathy, the children from the college marched. I was on my job at the base. My boss let me off, and I joined the march. They locked me up.

I hadn't been arrested before and had never been in trouble. I just felt that blacks were suffering, and it shouldn't be that way. I knew that the situation for blacks should be changed.

When I went to jail even the first time, I was under the impression that America just had to know the truth about what was happening and how we felt. I felt that as soon as America's population knew what was going on, the masses of the people would rally for right and justice and fair play. I felt that I was going to jail and suffering for this reason. I didn't feel like I was doing it just to make trouble. After four years in the service, I came out with a good conduct medal. Nobody can say I've ever made trouble. My record shows that.

He quickly became involved, demonstrating, going to meetings, and going to jail. Some time after that first experience, he was fired from his job. That began his full-time involvement in the Movement.

When they fired me, I was out of the state. I was supposed to have been back to work that Monday morning but I was late coming in. They fired me on the grounds of my conviction in court. The case was this: we had been picketing a white groceryman's store to demonstrate the unfairness of jury selection. This man had been on a jury that had found the sheriff not guilty. I was picketing his store, and I was arrested and convicted. They said they fired me at the base because of my arrest. They said I was not fit on my civil service record. I fought them in court because I had a perfect record at work before the Movement. I hadn't missed a day. I had accumulated the maximum sick leave and vacation time that was allowed. I lost the battle. The firing was overturned much later, but my lawyer let me down; we didn't make them pay for the time I'd been out. I'm still not satisfied.

After losing his job, he became a full-time organizer with a large civil rights organization. He has worked in many different places across the South, directing voter registration drives, speaking at meetings and rallies, and has participated in numerous demonstrations, both those that attracted national attention and those on a local level. Now he works with a local day care center organized by the Movement, pastors a church, and continues to witness to his convictions about civil rights in his local area.

In the following, he describes only a few of his recollections of the Movement, those which seemed important to him.

Early in the Movement, I went to Washington, D.C. We went to talk to the attorney general about the situation here locally. We were being locked up every time we hit the streets with picket signs, even though we were peacefully demonstrating. So we went up there and said, "Now what is that?"

They didn't let us talk to the attorney general. They didn't respect us enough to answer our concerns. We talked with someone they let us see and were told what couldn't be done. I asked what was meant by "guaranteed rights" of the Constitution. The man couldn't answer. He told us in his office that, "The Civil Rights Bill is spelled out, but we don't have the spelling on the demonstrations, your unlawful assembly, and your picketing; and we can't help you."

We came back and suffered terribly. The Movement died. We filed for an injunction against the city so that they couldn't keep us from peacefully demonstrating. The blind judges sat on the decision for four years until the Movement died down. Then they said the city couldn't bother us for a peaceful demonstration.

It wasn't all bad. Sometimes the unexpected happened when I would feel most down. For example, when President Johnson signed that last stroke on that Accommodation Bill, I had a congregation watching him on television in the basement of the church. I had $300 in my pocket for nothing but steaks in places we had been shut out of before. When he made that last stroke, I turned them loose in all directions. I didn't allow anybody to carry weapons. I searched them and took all the knives. I was sending these boys everywhere, and when I decided to go, I forgot I had a switchblade in my pocket that I had got from one of them. I had a good steak with three ladies at a club. We got up, got in the car, and got about four blocks when the police came. We had to get out. They searched me and found the knife. One of them pulled out a big club and handcuffed me in the bottom of the car.

They had arrested me everyday, and they knew they didn't have to handcuff me. I was shocked out of my wits. I just didn't feel that they would go that low. They charged me with importing whiskey and carrying a concealed weapon, and set bond at $2500. They put it on the radio like I had had a machine gun, not a knife.

At twelve o'clock that night they came and unlocked the cell. They said, "Come on, you're getting out." Nobody had been to see me, nobody had told me anything. I didn't know if people knew where I was. They had taken so many blacks out and lynched them, that I didn't want to go. Then the manager of the

club where we had eaten, his lawyer, his bondsman, and the sheriff carried me over to the courthouse. The manager said, "When I found out what was going on, I didn't want any part of it. I got my bondsman to get you out." I said, "You just saved my faith! I was going in the opposite direction. I thought I was about to lose my faith!'" so sometimes the unexpected happened.

As part of marching and going to jail, people not only sang songs, but composed them as well. Reverend Rockwell showed me one of those songs from the Movement in his area. Some of its verses are the following:

The weather was fair and cold
The weather was fair and cold
Hundreds had promised to come
but only a few were there.

Standing in one place, standing in one place
We could see everyone face to face
With out-stretched hand and smiling face
We invited everyone to take their place.

The way out must lead in, the way out must lead in
No matter what's the price, we must pay
We must pay if we shall win.

The police just waited around
As we continued our march downtown
We moved in a single file
They moved around like ushers in an aisle.

We did not know our destination
It would be Highway 82
But the policemen standing there
Would not let us through.

Taking chances to get to the other side
Police just stood there with pistols on their side
They didn't care if we lived or died.

White like you, John, or black like me.
There was no hesitation in turning the key
If you show the least sign of wanting to be free
A wanting to be free, A wanting to be free.

Jail without bail is a sad story to tell
For day after day we peep through the cell
Day after day we peep through the cell
Peep through the cell, peep through the cell.

Watching other go by, watching others go by
Acting as if there was no bail
And we were the only ones, the only ones in jail.

The way out must lead in, the way out must lead in
Mo matter what's the price, we must pay
We must pay if we shall win.

Of the many large demonstrations he had taken part in, he talked especially about the Selma March. When the first March attempted to cross that bridge, I was in Montgomery organizing the people. On the second effort, when we started to walk, I went on the March from Selma to Montgomery.

When we went into Montgomery, there were all kinds of people and organizations in the group. After Governor Wallace refused to come out and talk, I saw each organization step to the front of the demonstrators to give leadership, then give it up and fall away. We stayed there until two o'clock in the morning. The organizations fell, except the SNCC group. I have always said that that SNCC group had the toughest minds, and that they knew when they reached their goals. They weren't sidetracked like a lot of organizations.

We stayed there, and the police got horses. We were sitting on the ground right before the Capitol. We formed a ring with the women and children on the inside. They charged with those horses; they'd raise up just like they was going to run us over. We took the test. Then they went and got a jeep filled with some kind of oil or something, a chemical, I don't know what it was, but it gave off perfume and smoke. They put it in the gas tank and parked that jeep right in front of use where the wind would blow the fumes on us. We didn't move. We just sat there. They raced that motor and burned that fuel and perfume and smoke until they got tired, and we just sat right there and didn't move. I thought the March was beautiful.

There were times in the Movement when I was frightened and scared. I remember I used to be scared in this town. The worst whipping I ever got was the time we demonstrated against the way we were railroaded through the courts, the way courts were set up, and how we had to pay bonds when it was not necessary. We called it cash register justice.

We started during the day. We wanted to sing and pray at the courthouse, but they wouldn't let us. When we started into town, they put up a barricade and stopped us about five blocks from

the courthouse. We marched up to the barricade.

The policemen were all lined up. One policeman walked up in front of me and drew back a fist. He caught me dead in the eye and knocked me flat. The reason I didn't duck was the nonviolent position I had taken. I got up and got on top of this little red Ford I had, and I ordered everybody back to the church. Then the policemen really started whipping us. The boys started throwing bricks, and that was the first time anyone had done that. The police started beating women with big sticks. That's the first time in my life I've seen a man hit a woman with all his might. I saw it all because I was standing up there trying to control the crowd.

After everyone had turned back toward the church, they attacked me again. This one policeman in particular, who I knew, knocked me down and hit me in the face with his stick.

That was in the daytime. We marched again that night. We started out singing *Nearer my God to Thee*. That's the song the people were singing when the Titanic sunk. The same policeman caught me the second time in the dark and hit me on the other side of the face. He stomped and kicked me so hard that I had pain in my side for years after that.

I didn't think anything about being beaten because I just figured that the policemen were agents for the system. They are not guilty to the degree we think they are. Because they are ministers for that system, I just felt like this was their duty. They were only following orders. The leaders of the community were the ones that were really responsible for what was going on. The policemen were just little henchmen. I didn't feel mad at them or feel like fighting them.

A lot of whites have the wrong impression of our work. They think we're just here to hate white folks and that we're trying to take over the country. We are not teaching hate. I was charged with insurrection here once. I was never for violence and never will be. I get mad like anybody else, but I have been able to stick to nonviolence as a tactic in the struggle. I think Jesus taught the same thing. I think that he taught that life in abundance will be on a much higher level than violence.

It was hard when the leaders were killed. When Kennedy was shot, I was on trial in the middle district court. I felt like there was no justice, even in the courts, as I stood before the judge. When King was shot, I just felt like we might not make it. That's a bad feeling for anybody to have. A person that has faith in God

certainly shouldn't come to that point. But I just felt like we'd lost the leader and that we weren't going to be able to finish our journey. It was raining that evening, and I drove in the rain alone all the way to Atlanta. It was a great loss. I was frightened because riots were creeping up. I had felt that the philosophy of Dr. King was holding down the violence but that after his death, if nobody were around to remind everybody, as Dr. King did, that nonviolence was the best way, I thought that we would have blood running in the streets. I think we were blessed that it didn't happen that way. There were some riots, but not many people were hurt. They stole a few T.V.'s and furniture.

In summing up, he said, I do not believe that you are rewarded for doing right through material gains. I believe it's right to fight for right even if you are losing or if there are no rewards. We kept moving because it was wrong for the whites to do what they were doing to us. Our cause was right, and it's just part of our religion to do right.

During the Movement, sometimes, we would be in jail for a long time and when we'd come out, people would just look at us and go on about their business like nothing was happening. There are times when I would go to a certain church about a mile from here. After all that struggle and jailing, I would look into the faces of the congregation, and it was like looking into the faces of people from a foreign country. To experience a situation like that, to be able to come back and keep going, you've got to have faith. You've got to be tough enough to know why you are fighting, to know what your goals are and to know when you reach your goals. If you don't know that, you can be sidetracked at any point. I try to look over and above the immediate obstacles. I just believe.

Chapter 10

Mrs. Washington

Mrs. Washington is a tall, well-proportioned, dark-skinned woman. She spoke carefully and brought the incidents of her story to life with a rich variety of gestures and accents. She spoke with an almost bemused self-assurance. She was, by far, the most charismatic speaker of all the men and women I interviewed. I almost felt in listening to her that she had lived through several different lives in one lifetime: one before entering the Movement, one in the early days of the Movement, and one in the present, so varied and complex were her experiences.

We talked about her early life and her struggle to survive the poverty and human frailty that surrounded her. We then talked about her initial involvement in the Movement, her later years in the Movement, and the present.

Mrs. Washington was born on a plantation. When she was five, her father was forced to leave the plantation because he refused to let the owner put his children to work in the fields. She has one sister. Her memories of her early years are punctuated by remembering many fights between her mother and father. The fights culminated in their separation about a year and a half after the move from the plantation, followed later by divorce.

My father didn't like my mother to go to church. She went so much that she was always having something at the church. He was jealous, so he would fuss and carry on and say she must be meeting another man. They would fuss and fight all the time. My mother was unhappy because she liked church, and my father didn't go. I think she went for strength. She had a hard time just physically trying to work and take care of my sister and me. She would work for white people.

My mother and father would argue and fight all the time. She left him because of the fighting. My father loved me, but he just pulled away. After we left, he came down one time and tried to get my mother to come back, but she wouldn't. She says now that

she hates the fact that she left him because she understands, 30 years later.

When we left my father, we went to the country. One time my mother ran off, and we had to go stay with an aunt. Then my mother came back, and we finally got a house. Then the house burned down. We lost everything. From the time I left my father (age seven), to the time I was twelve, I didn't have a brand new dress.

I remember one time I was doing something for my mother. I grabbed her shoes to clean them off, and I found that there wasn't any bottom on them. There was snow and ice outside on the ground. That just stood in my mind. I wished that I had money to buy her a pair of shoes. She wrapped her feet in croker sacks and went to work. We would get scraps from the white folks' table—that's what we'd eat. She'd bring that home, and we'd be glad to get it. But there was still something there. I'd say, one of these days we're going to be something. Those are the kinds of things that you remember.

My mother disciplined us, and I really knew she tried the best she could. She gave me strength about my being black. I was with children who were lighter than me. I had cousins, and there wasn't one of them that was as black as I was. At that time it was a stigma to be black with short hair. My mother just kept saying to me, "Black is honest." I came to know what she was talking about in the later years of the Movement. It was my mother's words and teachings and fussing and making us go to church and Sunday school, that gave me something to go back to eventually.

Mrs. Washington had some schooling interspersed with working in the fields. She left home at an early age, marrying at sixteen. The marriage lasted only a short time. After that she continued to search.

I got out on my own, worked from one thing to another, and started thinking about how to get somebody to take care of me. I had one boyfriend who was about seventy-two. It didn't work. We ended up fighting. I was trying to party and drink.

I moved through the cycle of saying that I wasn't going to be bothered by anybody, and I was going to be somebody. I was determined that I was going to be somebody, but I ended up with nothing because I didn't have a skill. I worked at this and that. I worked for some white folks. I worked a job at a lumber company. I had learned to read and write, mostly by teaching myself. I always loved to read books, and I just kept reading. I would listen

to somebody say a word I didn't know, and I would absorb that word. At the lumber yard, nobody could read or write, so I was special.

I went to stay with my sister. She was going through family troubles and separated from her husband. Then I worked for an old white man. He would drink all the time, and he wouldn't know what happened to his money half the time. He'd send me down to the store, and he wouldn't ask for change.

All this time, my mother was fussing for me to go to church, but I refused to deal with that. I was going to do my thing. I didn't know where to turn because I really didn't think anybody cared that much for me except for my family, and they were talking about the wrong stuff.

I got married at sixteen or seventeen, but I didn't stay with it any time. I was thinking I wasn't going to marry again, but I did. Along came this man, and I thought I was going to get some security. He worked on a boat and made $120 every two weeks. That was really some money. His friends would party and have liquor. So we got married.

We had to struggle for years and years. My husband was trying to work and have something. We tried migrant farming. My husband didn't work but four months out of the year on the boat, and the rest of the time he was drawing unemployment compensation. You scratch around, and you try to find something. Folks said that there was a lot of money in Florida. We had a car, and we figured that we weren't going to be able to make payments on it unless we got some money that winter. So we went to Florida.

We went down there, and there was nothing. We stayed in one room, and we had to cook in it. Three of us had to sleep in it because by then I had the baby, and we paid high prices, $10 a week for that room. We didn't know whether we were going to make it or not. If we had got a bigger room, it probably would have cost us $20 a week. We cooked over an oil stove. For two or three weeks, we didn't have anything but Irish potatoes, because they were so cheap. I know how to cook Irish potatoes every kind of way you can think of because of that.

The next year we went back there because we did survive. We thought we were going to do better because I learned how to peel tomatoes. I thought I was going to make $100 a week like some people, but they had been peeling tomatoes all their lives. I didn't make much because I couldn't work as fast. Migrant life was

going back and forth, trying to scratch up the money to get down to Florida and back, and sleeping anywhere along the way.

When her husband's mother died, she left them land. They stopped working as migrant farmers and settled down permanently. They got the land after a battle with the local justice of the peace who tried to take it from them. She was living in a small rural town when the civil rights workers came, and she got caught up in the Movement.

In this county there wasn't much else to do except work and join the Home Demonstration Club, where they show folks how to cook, to decorate, to keep clean, that kind of thing. Some people could do that, but it was boring to me to sit there and put a little macaroni on cigar boxes. I'm sitting there saying, "I'm going on home and cook this macaroni," because it just didn't make sense to have to buy the macaroni to put on a jewelry box and then have no jewelry to put in the box. Just nothing fit.

In 1964 I heard about the Freedom Riders on the radio. I said to my friend, "Corrine, I hope they come here." She said, "Honey, nothing happens in this county." I said, "Well, we'll see." Two or three weeks later, after all the commotion had gone on, I was sitting on the porch again with Corrine. We looked up and saw two young men coming down the street, and we knew who they were. They had a different walk. We walk one kind of way, and they had a fast walk and a kind of dip. They came by and said, "Hello there," and I said, "That's them, Corrine." Their voices were different. Being in a small community, you know everybody anyway, so we knew that they had to be the Freedom folks.

They moved around until that following Sunday. I was teaching Sunday school. I would use the Bible as a way of trying to get people to see that God don't want us to be down, and that all men are equals. At that time I didn't know I was talking Movement talk, but I wanted those folks to uplift themselves. One of the men came into the class. I kept watching him and he kept watching me. I didn't know whether he wanted to come over and speak or what his problem was. After I finished with our class, I asked if he wanted to speak. He got up and said, "Just like that lady was talking over there. Now God wants us to stand up." He talked pretty clearly. I liked it. He asked if he could come to the church, so we told him he'd have to ask at the 11:00 service if he could have a meeting in this church, just to talk to the people about

what their rights were. The preacher said, "Yes."

The Freedom folks came that next Thursday. That was my entering into the Movement. They asked who would go to the courthouse and try to register to vote. Up went my hand. My husband came over—he was going to draw unemployment compensation at the courthouse—and he said, "I'll go to the unemployment office first, then I'll come back and we'll go there together." There were eight of us that night who said we would go. That next day all the farmers were in town with guns. The sheriff and everybody showed up with guns. It was a frightening experience. We really never had had that kind of confrontation at all, even with white people. Four of us were going in the courthouse. That was the first time that any blacks had been in that courthouse to register except once. Two men had tried to register but were run out of town.

I was determined to see what this Movement was. It stirred an excitement as well as a hope. It looked like we were moving toward something. I didn't know what at that particular time. My days became filled with work and purpose instead of just going by.

Next, they set up a Freedom School. Mary, the teacher, was trying to figure out where she was going to stay, and I invited her to stay at our house. My husband supported me.

She'd sit and talk to us for hours. She told us about the history of black people. She told us exciting stories about ourselves. I didn't know anything about the history of black folks. I never related it to Africa on any terms because all we saw was the jungle movies—the folks going "booga, booga booga"—and we didn't want to be a part of that. We learned there was something more. She explained how we have our own culture. She told us how we should just relax and try to be ourselves, and that we don't have to be like white people. I didn't know at that time what she was doing like I do now. She was getting us ready.

Mary was a dark-skinned, nappy-headed child. I thought she hadn't washed her hair. I was going to get her to go down to get her hair pressed and get it fixed, but she kept putting me off and saying she'd do it tomorrow. She was very warm, and she was educated. I had never had contact with any educated person who talked and acted that way. She just shared our lives. She would eat whatever we had, beans or greens or whatever; we didn't have that much. She would sleep anywhere. If I had to wash, she'd help wash or whatever. She was just at home with us.

The Freedom folks told me to tell some people to register. I got some to go with me. The next two or three weeks, the Freedom folks said, "We're going to put you on staff. There's no money in it, but we think you should be staff. You go out and get your folks registered."

I became staff. I didn't quite know what I was doing, but I'd go back and ask, "What am I gonna say to the people?" They would say, "Just tell them anything that you feel, what you think should be done." A lot of people would tell me they were scared, and I'd tell them, "I am, too. What's the difference. We're going to die anyway, so it's best to be dying trying to do something." We got folks started, getting folks registered. Mary didn't know the people, and I knew them. She'd say, "You tell me how people act in this particular area." I had something to give her. It was a kind of relationship that I had never experienced before. We started off getting these folks out there, and I went over to the courthouse and was turned down.

At first we didn't have a car, but Mary and I would get to town in some way. I kept trying to get her hair fixed and then, when I finally got to town, I looked up, and there was a lot more people with hair that wasn't fixed, curls and everything. I thought it must be a style, so I let that alone. Finally I got up to her and said, "I want to ask you a question. Why is your hair like that?" She gave me a description. She did not try to cram not fixing it down my throat. Finally I learned. It took me quite some time, about a year and a half, before I could not have my hair fixed. I was comfortable with myself the way I was and she was comfortable. Finally I just got to the point where one day I just got up and washed it and walked out in the streets. Everybody looked. Now you walk around here and you're just liable to see hair fixed or not fixed. It was just that kind of breakthrough.

Also in the Movement, the relationship between black and white wasn't the hostility and hate of the whites that we had known. When the whites came into the community, they'd sit down with us and laugh and talk and we'd say, "Wow!" We just couldn't believe it because we never had had any contact with white folks except on another side of the fence. That whole thing had an effect psychologically on us. It got us to a point where we could confront the people that we had to deal with a little bit better.

We lived through some things. One night Mary went to some friends' house and came running back in the house to hide. We

had a garden, so we ran to the beanstalks. We had to stand in the beanstalks while the highway patrol was circling and just hunting us down for no reason whatsoever. We were up at night most of the time. When daylight came, until around nine or ten o'clock, we could get a little sleep, because the guns and the riders weren't coming. At other times we had to stay awake and get ready to move on the spur of the moment. Some nights there would be a cross burning in the yard, and the guns would be coming out. Folks would be getting ready to shoot. It was something.

I've really been thinking about what kept us going, and I think it was the songs and the spirit of the Movement. It was the people out there willing to die, and the people who had died for us. It was being raised in the Christian atmosphere, whether we practiced it or not. It was the feeling that God would take care of us. It was the feeling that we just had to keep going because it was wrong for people to live this way. Deep down in your heart you knew that you were not trying to hurt the white people.

There was also the spirit of the talks and the get-togethers that we used to have, the strength that we used to gain from one another. This kept us going. After something big would happen, I always had a center of people in the Movement and folks that were in the community. Immediately, folks would come to the rescue. I just couldn't stop. I'd have to go another day. Sometimes it was done that way, by saying, "I'm going to get through this day." That way I just kept doing, because something else was coming up.

There was a spirit of sureness. I knew that people were pulling for me. I knew that they would be there with whatever they had. I had never had that kind of closeness with any group of people, even in church. I think that's what kept me moving, too. I was scared to death sometimes. We had courage, but it was lined with justifiable fear. I have very often been scared to go out the door because I'd know that I just might meet a bullet outside the door.

The local people, as scared as they were, would come to those meetings shaking, reaching out for something. None of us knew exactly what it meant, but we were saying Freedom. It was just a feeling that things have got to be better. It was a long time before we actually got anybody registered to vote. We went through law suits and had to testify before the United States Civil Rights Commission. It was just a whole big commotion.

Mrs. Washington was rapidly recognized as a leader and led the organizing and voter registration efforts in her community. In 1966 a new problem confronted her, that of outside money coming in.

The Federal programs brought the money which was being given out. BOOM! The fights over who was going to get the money started at a whole different level. There wasn't but five jobs for the county, you see, but everybody was down there trying to get those five jobs. Well, I didn't want to, but I had to change to keep the folks. I became the organizer for this program. I had to change. It made my stomach turn when I got there and saw all the hoggy-haggy that was going on, after we had such clear goals and so forth and then everything got so fogged up.

In 1967 she had an opportunity to work with a middle-class, northern group that had some money but no idea how to use it.

Folks from that group were standing around talking about poor people needing some flower gardens. I said, "Hold it; people can't eat flowers." There's nothing wrong with flowers, but I saw those people getting carried away, and I spoke up. Before I knew it, I was tied up with that group. Here was a challenge of a group that had its hand on $300,000 and didn't know what to do with it. I decided to work on building community centers, using that money and getting other money to do the same.

I said to myself, "I'm going to do something concrete." That's the road I took. I got all excited to see the excitement in people's eyes as we got some things done in the community. I had some of my friends from the Movement out here screaming and hollering that the federal government was going to take over. I had a meeting with them, and I said, "Now look folks, if you all got something different to do, let me know and I'll be willing to work on it. But right now, this is all I know." They didn't have anything different. I went back to work on community development, and that helped me.

The work on that project helped her through the period after the deaths of Robert Kennedy and Martin Luther King, Jr. It was during this period that blacks and whites split apart in the Movement. Her understanding of this in her area was that, for the most part, the whites chose to return to work in the white communities. She was against forcing whites out. She did say that in her work in rural counties, she had first

sent in black workers, and only later white workers, because of the fear of whites in the communities. Thus the white organizers and black organizers had somewhat different roles in her area.

Some years later she took a job with a national, middle-class organization with civil rights ties. She has held that job since then. It involves much traveling, some public speaking, some fund-raising, and some organizing. She has continued to live in her rural community and has had to balance that experience with the experience of traveling and being active in a large organization.

Through the period of the Movement, she and her husband had been growing apart, and in 1971 they finally separated. In these years she found herself drinking more and more heavily.

I think I became very frustrated in the marriage. I was always conscious of being a woman and that a woman's place is over here and a woman's place is over there and a woman's place is this place and that place, and I stayed so busy trying to run from place to place until I never really expressed myself. My ex-husband was saying that I used to be a better person than I had become. I couldn't understand what he was talking about. One day he got angry and started cussing. He told me that I was too damned independent and overbearing. He said I was against everything. I think I was just supposed to do as I was told and keep moving on. I found out through the Movement that we had a lot of that, and I just didn't want to be told. I was making more money than he was, and he was struggling with his manhood. It just got to be too much of a hassle, so we separated.

People thought that I drank because I'd been through so much. But I knew I was getting on a merry-go-round inside of myself. I see that in so many things that have happened. I don't blame the Movement for this in any sense. For me it was a lot deeper than that. It was complexes and character defects that got to me. I know that the Movement compounded it, but I don't blame anybody. We were under so much stress, until drinking was somewhere to go just to relax. Drinking is the only thing we have in this country for some other kind of escape, and I had overdone it. It hindered me as well as kept me going. About two or three years before I came into the program for drinkers, I was at my wits end. I didn't want to drink, and yet there wasn't anything else

that would just give me some kind of satisfaction so I could keep functioning. I was working. I was doing all those big things.

All of us in the Movement paid for our sacrifices. The stress damaged us as individuals. You start out and live and work on the local level, but you have to deal with people that are on a national level. You have to find a little corner for yourself. I found a little corner with the bottle. I became spiritually detached. Suddenly I got blown to hell. The grace of God, or whatever it was, saw that He wasn't ready for my mind to go. I had to have something. I'm talking about my own life. Drinking is what I used as a prop. It got me through. It was a form of escapism.

Through the assistance of a friend and the help of a doctor she had met in the Movement, she entered a hospital and stayed for three weeks. Then she started in Alcoholics Anonymous. It was a different state of enlightenment, like the enlightenment in the Movement, but at a different stage," **she said. She said she had the same intense human experiences with the people she met through curing herself as she had with the people in the Movement.**

In 1971, when I got myself together, I felt that everything had happened for a reason, for the better. I had a hard time. I had to face myself. Some people don't ever get to the point where they have to face themselves. I say each of us has to go through our own form of insanity. I felt I went through it.

We talked about what had happened to others in the Movement. She illustrated what had become of some with a vivid description of a woman, like herself, who had taken a different route.

Mrs. Thompson's power started really picking up when she testified on television before one of the major federal committees. We had known her before in the state because of the Movement, but when people in the country saw this black woman and how she spoke, she went to gaining momentum. She came back to the state, and she went on a speaking tour. Things were set up by the civil rights organizations in different places, and money was raised from her story. She didn't gain anything else. She spoke in many different places. Her contact was with the media. She became famous without the understanding of what had happened to her. She didn't have time, I feel, to move from a lady in the cotton to a lady in Africa, or a lady in California. She would open her mouth, and then, BOOM! Everybody would turn. She just

got into that business of speaking and not learning until she came to find out, further down the road in 1968, that she was rejected.

Mrs. Thompson raised a lot of money, clothes, and food from her speaking tours, and she took the things and gave them out to people in the community. She built a new house with a big freezer. She made the mistake of giving these things out herself, in her own house. People would beat a path to her door to get things. All this time there was envy and jealousy building. Because of jealousy, people rejected her. She couldn't understand why they rejected her because she was so loving. She felt the rejection, and she felt the glory all at the same time, and she couldn't handle it. She got sick, and she didn't do nearly as much as she used to. She doesn't feel she has many friends.

See, she didn't have time to build, and the reason I know it so well is that I was headed in some of that same direction. Like Mrs. Thompson, I also started raising some stuff for my community, and the people started to turn on me. I stopped raising stuff, because I saw myself getting cut off. I came to see things much more clearly. This world was going to go on, and I just couldn't burn up all my energies in the way I had. I found I had limitations and abilities. I just can't solve all the problems; there are limits to what I can do as a human being. I don't have a staff of people that will write everybody and let them know I'm coming. I don't have everything prepared for me to go. I might get to more places if I had all these preparations, but I've got a boss swinging back on me. She wants me to work, and then she wants me to go here and there in less than 24 hours. I've learned to say, let somebody else go to Washington and speak to that group, or go to Texas and speak to that group. I try to hold down my job.

I have people I can really talk to now, and I know how to communicate. So often, people use that big word, communication, but there's no real communication. I can speak to five thousand people and it's entertainment. I can really entertain, because I can tell them about those people who got shot at, about the leaders that slept on the floor, about being in jail, and about how we didn't have anything to eat. I can tell how we got the grants, and that they're helping a little bit but we need more. People can sit there and clap their hands, but there's no deep thinking or even enjoyment left over for me.

We in the Movement are crisis-oriented people. Some of us have learned how to deal with that. Don't work the people you

organize to death before the crisis comes, and then when you get ready, they will move with you. It's more than that though. People have to learn to think, to know when the strategy changes, so that they won't crack up. Sometimes in the Movement our bodies would be so tired, that half of us would be in the hospitals with high blood pressure, hypertension, and everything; we would lose all the people who were sick. The same system kills off the folks that it has created. Many of the folks from the Movement are in the hospitals: one jumped off a building, some are out of the country, some are dead, some are in jail, and some are in Africa. Many that aren't drunk are on pot or something else—they're just out of it. Part of our weakness in the Movement was that people were strained to the breaking point. The system says that you have to work hard and make sacrifices. In the meanwhile, it doesn't say you need rest, relaxation, strength, and development in mental health. It drains you. The system waits. It waits for you to break.

I think about it. I say, "Now one thing I'm gonna do, now that I found a way, is just stay as sane as I can." I try to study the situation and know that there has to be a different way of work. So, I say I'm going to get some sleep, I'm going to eat, and I'm going to go to some meetings. I'm going to develop for the next ten years and see if I can't sit and talk and let people look at themselves and how they relate to what is going on. I'm going to try to see how many people we can develop in leadership roles in a county in a ten-year period. If we can have patience to work for ten years with one man, and he stands there for the next twenty, then that's better than coming up with five hundred people who will be dead in five years, or not working.

There's great things to come out of hard work and development. I think there is a period in this world now in which things have to happen, because the rest of the world is going to put the pressure on America to do better. The only thing that was relevant in this country over the past hundred years has been the Movement, people who are involved in the Movement will have much more to do, more to say, over the next period of years, than they have in the past, if they can get themselves developed. They will have more to say than anybody, because the rest of them folks is "Watergating." There's no trust that can be put into that kind of establishment.

The Movement that I see now is frustrating. People have made a lot of mistakes, but they've done a lot of good things. We've got

a lot of good folks who have their own personal hang-ups and problems, and it's going to keep us bogged down unless we change. We've got to understand that people can go only so far before they break. They have to take time out and develop themselves to approach another level. This has to happen.

Today, you hear that the Civil Rights Movement is dead, and that we're going down the drain. I don't believe that. I do think that the names are changing. The goals are the same, but we have to move to a different level of understanding. I've been through this whole thing, getting thousands of people registered in this state. We got some black officials elected, but I know that that is not the end. We need to have patience with ourselves and take time out to see and evaluate how we can move more effectively instead of jumping every time we react to a crisis.

We started out talking about equality and brotherhood, about people living as well as they possibly could with one another. That was my understanding. When we say equality, that means that people eat, live, and have jobs—and soon. Brotherhood means that people learn to live together with their differences and their weaknesses, and that people learn to respect each other as human beings. Well, some may say, that is a whole lot of pipe dreams or a whole lot of great imagination. I think that's what we have to have, in the first place, to survive. It might be a whole lot of whatever. But we'll see.

She talked about where she sees herself now and the key people in her life, her new husband and her son, and some reflections on her sources of strength.

The only reason that I married again is because I cared for the person. We have nothing. I mean security. I'm talking about the fact that I didn't ask for money or prestige or anything, just what we could give to one another. I didn't know how it was going to work out. I'm hoping, and that's where I am now.

I feel that women, for the last ten years I'd say, have had some trying times. Women have got to come out fighting. A lot of women who are the heads of households have needed that kind of strength to feel that they didn't have to go get any old Tom, Dick, or Harry just to have a man. Men are trying to improve in some ways, but they know now that women just don't have to be there with them. That's all I'm trying to say. It's good for women. In China, it's a beautiful kind of thing because the men support the women's liberation. That's what I'm trying to figure out—how

women can get these men to support us because that's the only way it's going to happen anyway, only if the whole family supports women with certain understandings. It has to open up so that people will understand that they're human beings.

Still, women don't want to be liberated from being women. If you can sit with your husband and talk out differences at periods of time, it helps a great deal. The liberated thing to me is that the person is honest with me and tells me what he likes and what he doesn't like. If my husband tells me he's not going to do such a thing, even if I don't agree, I know we can talk about it.

When my son John was eight, he got a good chance to go to camp in Vermont. He went every year until two years ago. He was around white people, all kinds of races of people, and that fear didn't set in. My son will talk to anybody, and he respects all people. I feel he learned a beautiful lesson, and he does, too, because he talks about it. He took the South and his experiences with him. The children there wanted to know all about the South and what it meant being black. He had something to give to this group of children, and they had something to give him because there were children from New Zealand, Spain, and other different countries. He was poor, and he told things that these kids hadn't been exposed to. Then they got other kids who were coming from Watts, and children from New York, Lexington, and all of the places that were called ghettos. He had a cross-section of all these minds and people. He never would have gotten that if it hadn't been for the Movement.

He wants to be a doctor. Being exposed to people has established hope. I think he sees his job as being productive and as something he can do himself. This is part of his self-learning.

I think the children have benefited even by being exposed to all of it—the desegregation of schools and the shake-ups. A lot of folks are saying, "There's nothing stable for the children." But children aren't stable anyway! Because of all this, my son doesn't hate white people. That's good that he doesn't have to carry this hate in him because hate would destroy him. He's not going to let anybody let him be less of a person either.

My roots are here where I got started in the Movement. Being in the Movement here was the start of another life-style for me. Here is where my eyes came open to another way of hope. I think most of the people here respect me just for me, because if I say something, I try to tell the truth. They enjoy that I'm somebody

who they have read about and who's been on television, but they talk to me like they would anybody else. This is the place where I found myself.

Right now, my stability point is here because all the rest is so unstable. I come back to this house which is not fabulous or anything. It's small and ordinary. Some of their houses are bigger and better than mine. I don't have a lot of fancy stuff. I may have to move toward fancy stuff, but I don't see myself moving too fast. I come out and cut the grass and people come by and sit and talk. We talk about nothing, but it's very interesting because that's where people are at. That's my roots. When I leave and go out and have to meet the monsters of Congress or whoever, I have strength that this is what the average, everyday person is like, without all the false faces and without all this other kind of stuff. It helps me stay much more myself.

Chapter 11

Sheriff Thomas Gilmore

I met the sheriff for the first time in the courthouse, a full-proportioned, old, white plaster building with long, narrow windows. It was set in the center of the town square, surrounded by green lawns and shade trees. The green was bounded on all sides by streets, and then rows of shops. There was a marker commemorating a Civil War march on one side.

The sheriff was young, slender, and black. His movements were lithe and graceful, yet he seemed to carry the responsibilities of his office carefully and heavily. He was dressed in a black suit, with no badge, no uniform, and no gun.

We talked in the office and then walked across the square to the jail. As we walked, he pointed out a large and aged hotel. During Reconstruction, the Union Army sent a judge down here. The local people hanged him there. He commented on a pattern across the rural South: the fewer whites there were in one area, the more intense the repression. There are many more blacks than whites living in his county.

We picked up a police car at the jail and drove through the town. The streets around the square were filled with memories for him. He showed me the one church where most of the mass meetings of the Movement had been held. He pointed out the route most of the demonstrations had taken, and the spot where he had once confronted the previous sheriff in a march. It was there that a woman had been badly beaten during a demonstration, and a group, including himself, had been beaten trying to file a complaint about the first beating. He showed me low-rent housing units and a community development center. He talked of one of the major difficulties now, namely, that of attracting industry, and said, Certain plants have a policy. They won't locate in the South in an area that is more than one-third black in population.

Out in the country, he talked about the land with great love. He had been born and raised in the rural part of the county. He emphasized that one of the greatest burdens of the Move-

132

ment had been when people were ousted from land they had farmed all of their lives, some even from land that their families had worked for three generations. It was a source of pride to him that few, if any, of those evicted had had to leave the county, but rather that they had been taken in and housed on others' land.

He said that the small, entirely black communities far outside the town were the strongest and most reliable communities in getting out the vote. These were the communities that had turned out to elect him.

He had to attend to one piece of sheriff's business, and I went with him. A youth had stolen $60 from the house of a neighbor, an older man. At the sheriff's request, the boy had returned almost all of what he had taken, as the sheriff was trying to avoid jailing the youth. The older man insisted that not all of the money had been returned. He also claimed that a ring was missing. The sheriff went to take care of it because, as he said, Folks don't want to see the deputy in many cases, they want to see the sheriff.

We talked with the older man, who was cantankerous and self-righteous, and then went to talk with the youth's father, as the youth was not at home. The father insisted that there was only one dollar yet to be paid back and no ring. As we talked to the youth's father, the older man drove up. It was a dark, rural, dirt road, and the youth's father and several friends, all drunk, crowded around the car. People came out of their houses to watch. Threats were exchanged. The sheriff quickly separated the two protagonists from the others and led then away. The two argued and finally agreed on a settlement. The sheriff commented that before he had been elected, the youth could have been jailed for months because of the crime. Afterwards, he commented that when he has to break up a crowd, he singles out the biggest man first and separates him. He said, though, that usually it is the smallest man in a crowd who starts a fight and makes trouble.

We then drove to his home where I met his wife and six children. We talked for a while, friends dropped by, and the children were constantly in evidence, clearly very fond of and very close to their father. At home the sheriff was quite different from what he was at work—relaxed, more joyful, gayer, freer.

He told me his life history clearly, and I did not ask many questions. He spoke slowly, with irony many times. There are no models for being the first black sheriff in a small community, and loneliness was the theme for much of our talk. He was eager to share what it has been like and to question me about medical and psychological problems he encountered in his work.

The counterpoint to our talk was his youngest daughter. She played around him continually. Her fast, high-pitched words contrasted with his slower, more carefully chosen words. She was constantly in motion, but the two were continually in touch with one another.

I was born about 5 miles south of here, close to the southern end of the county. I was raised by my grandmother. My mother was away in college, and my father was of very little assistance to me. There were five or six of my grandmother's children in the home with me.

I was no different from any other kids in this area. We farmed the fields. My grandmother had about 5 acres of cotton allotment at the time, which she grew on a farm that her grandparents had left for them. They had left some land for each of their children. She had kept her portion of it together and paid the taxes. In order to earn money from other farmers during the week, we farmed our land on weekends.

We also worked on the plantation nearby, almost as much as the people who lived there. This was the means for us to earn money. We had our 40 acres. We knew that we had somewhere to go, and that we were not going to get put off it. Even when I was a kid, whites would evict blacks for little or no reason. Some blacks probably got teed off with the system and exploded. If they didn't get killed, or almost killed, they'd get thrown off the farm.

He said with resignation, I think many whites were just mean, and they'd evict a black every so often to keep the others in line. Those evictions were very sad. Most of the time the family had six to ten children. They were friends of other children, friends of other women and men, and it was always sad to see them go. We really got attached to our land. As the family grew and as we needed more money, we would expand, you know, dig up some woods and farm a little bit more land.

My grandmother raised me. She's still living. She was in charge. I spent a lot of time with her. She was always exciting to me. She was tough when a situation called for it, but would laugh

just as hard as anyone else when she wanted to. She was a beacon of positive light to me until I was a teenager and really wanted to get out with the other fellows. She wouldn't let me go as much as I wanted to, and we fought about that.

I had this favorite cousin who was like an uncle to me, maybe more like a father, which probably affected my personality a lot, because I think of him often. This particular cousin had no legs at all, and sometimes I think he was responsible for my attitude toward the less fortunate people around me. He dominated the men in my life; he just came closer to me than any of my male relatives.

He was my grandmother's first cousin. He was the community's ombudsman. He did everything. He was a barber. He ran a store and a recreation center. His stage was broad. He was open-minded. He never thought for a day that he was handicapped; he needed no special attention from anyone. His store was a way-station for people when they got stranded. Sometimes when I would sleep there, I would see other people sleeping on the floor.

His store was right across from the school, so everyone got to know him. If they didn't have the money for something, he gave it to them anyway. It's no wonder he went broke. He died of some form of food poisoning or acute indigestion. It wasn't a hard death; he just kind of left us about 15 years ago.

I went to school. From the first to the sixth grade, the teachers were all women, and sometimes I wonder why I like so many women. **He smiled.** That was the beginning of my life. No man in the house, no men much in church. I walked to school for about six years with the rest of the kids, my buddies and my enemies, too. We had some real therapeutic sessions out there, morning and afternoon. We'd get our knuckles together.

I used to have a friend, a Methodist, who said that experiences formed a wheel; the negative ones are the broken places in the wheel. If you have too many negative experiences, you go through life bump, bump, bump, because there are too many broken places in the wheel. Only in the last few years have I learned to appreciate and cling to the good experiences.

My getting involved in the Movement was perhaps motivated by the many injustices I had seen. It was so commonplace for whites to treat you mean and dirty that, unless they killed you, there wasn't anything to be concerned with because it was a day-to-day thing.

We would go past this store, and the school bus would stop so that everybody could get out and go to the store. I didn't like it because I didn't have much money most of the time. The white lady's attitude was so snappy. As soon as you'd walk in the door, she'd snap, "What you want?" I'd think, Jesus Christ, my mom and grandmother teach me how to be nice, the folks up at the church teach me the church things, and here's this woman shouting at me. Another reason I didn't like going to this store was because I liked my uncle's store more.

Those experiences with the store kind of turned me against white people. There was little I could do about it, but I knew I didn't like them. You start growing, and you reflect. I remember other racial experiences. Once a black girl got shot in the leg. It was rumored that one of the big owners had had an affair with her, and he was upset that some black kid was walking with her. She was probably in the ninth grade at that time.

The plantation I used to work on imported people from the neighboring counties and brought them across the river in a rowboat. One time we were weighing cotton. The owner of the farm and his brother-in-law from Texas were standing around doing nothing. One of them grabbed this black kid to wrestle with him, and the black kid flipped him. He was embarrassed by that. People were laughing. That afternoon, the whites were taking the workers back across the river, and they turned the boat over and tried to drowned the kid. My mother stopped me from working on the farm for a long time because of that. After that I got a lot more deeply involved with the church. I got to be a favorite because I was attending Sunday school every Sunday. Many a time they needed me to help them read to the others. Some of them didn't understand the written words well.

As I got older, the plantation owner made things difficult for me generally. He was young, just out of college. If we were stacking hay, he'd put me up in the barn, in the hot spot. Or if I'd been riding the truck on the outside, stacking the hay on the truck, he would put me on the ground and have me throw it up. Or if the rain would start, I'd have to work outside longer than the others.

When I was in high school, I had an old truck. That really aggravated him. He was the plantation owner, and now that I am in law enforcement I understand how things were done. When I had the truck, the trooper would watch me all the time. I got all kinds of tickets for no muffler, no tail lights, things like that, not

tickets for speeding. I can remember one for not having a tag light when it was still during the day. They were harassing me.

For awhile I was an awkward teenager, and I didn't have much sense of anything. Everyone was in my way. I was restless. I lived a regular teenager's life, nothing sainted about it at all. I tried very hard to be the toughest guy in my classroom. If there was somebody in there who really challenged me, and the only way that I could deal with him was come up with a better grade, then I would study and get that better grade. I fluctuated from A to F to A—top to bottom—unless I was competing with someone, or unless I found a teacher who understood that I had the capacity to do the work and got me to do. Otherwise I wouldn't work.

I liked dancing and I took great pride in my dancing. Up until the twelfth grade, I wanted to be a professional dancer, with my own troupe and everything.

Late in high school, I had another terrible experience. My mother bought me the old truck I mentioned. It was for farm use down at my grandmother's, and I was in charge of it. When it wasn't used for farming, I'd use it for hauling and selling wood. I made enough money to get to my mother's in the city, or to get some money so that I could do other things that I was doing.

This lady started letting me credit my gasoline in my mother's name. She would never let me credit it in my name. My mother would come up and pay the bill once a month. One time it came out that I ran up a $50 gasoline bill. There's no way for me to know whether it was accurate or not. It could be that the bill was accurate, but I'll never believe it. I think that lady took advantage of my mother. My mother was really angered by the situation. We were getting closer to each other, and this made her very angry. So this created some friction between my mother and me, I think because of this lady cheating on the gasoline bill.

After high school, I wondered what I was going to do with my life. I knew I didn't want to be on the farm, and I really wasn't that excited about going to Detroit or some place like that. My mother didn't have that much, and I really didn't want to be a teacher. Other than my coaches, there was one teacher that stood out more than others, that I really learned to love. The rest I had just learned to play.

I had been going to church and trying to get some real religion, trying really to find out about Jesus and whether I could get some real relief—relief like the preacher had said I should have got when I joined the church. So I figured, well, I haven't gotten it

yet, and it's probably my fault. I'm going to go and get it now because I need it. I felt really messed up. Also, I had the job for the church of taking the poor offering to the poor. It might be $2. In one case I had to take some money to a person who had a serious operation for some type of tumor. This person was laying up in an open house in the winter. I wanted him to be warm, and I couldn't do it. Stuff like that got to me; I couldn't shut it out of my mind. I was looking for some relief for myself and others.

That summer at the high school, I decided to be a preacher. I enjoyed my preacher. I didn't get to see him too often, and he didn't ask me questions like the teachers did. Neither did he try to control my conduct in the same fashion, so I could tolerate him better. I thought that that's what I might want to be.

I decided to go to a small religion school in the South. Since I wanted to be a preacher, that's what I started working toward. I started preaching. People started talking to me, telling me their problems. Most of the stuff they'd tell me I really couldn't deal with. I found a way to talk out situations. I hadn't heard of some of their problems. I would sit up there and play and pretend that I had. I had doubts about the whole thing. Then I had an experience that almost convinced me that religion couldn't deal with the situation. This was after I had been in ministerial school for a while. A cousin of mine had gotten shot up. Another cousin of mine and I took him to the hospital. We found out later that he had been shot by a white fellow. I almost decided religion couldn't deal with the situation because of that. There wasn't any justice in it.

I got involved in a lawsuit challenging the jury selection system because of that accident with my cousin. There was a lot of pressure on my family because of my involvement. Also, later on, the Freedom Riders had come through the place where I was in school. I got involved in protesting in school, and I was threatened with suspension.

After a couple of years, I dropped out of the ministerial school. I just got disillusioned. I wanted to get away from school. Even though I felt that with my preaching I could make people feel good, and that was all right with me, I asked myself, am I really changing anything or just making people feel good. I decided I would get away, get lost, as I had seen many people do.

I got married to my high school sweetheart as soon as we reached legal age. My wife has been my best support. She has

demonstrated more than one person's share of patience and understanding.

I just wanted to hide, and I thought the Air Force was the best place. I volunteered. My physical condition required me to have to take an additional test after the regular physical. I had to wait another day, and that gave me enough time to change my mind about going into the Air Force. It was right at the time of the Freedom Rides. I think the violence inflicted upon my brothers and sisters changed my attitude toward military service.

We went to a nearby city, and I worked for awhile. Then I met a friend of mine who'd been to California and came back with nothing but wild, exciting stories to tell. I thought, "Jesus, Jesus, Jesus! I don't know where I'm going to live, but I'm going! " So we went out to California.

California was an education. If going to Detroit was like getting a master's degree, then California was like a Ph.D., or even an M.D. The first time I was ever called "nigger" by a police officer was in L. A.

Our second and third sons were born there. I never fell in love with L. A.; in fact, I worked two jobs in order to live and save so that we could get home.

When I got back here, the Movement in my home county was starting up again. I recognized that I had been running away from facing up to all the injustice in my home county, and finally I faced it.

The incident that drove me core deep in the Movement happened just after I got back home from L.A. I drove 3 miles to Demopolis to get milk for my youngest son, Ronald. While turning around at a service station, I put mud on a state trooper's auto. The state trooper got out of his auto and demanded that I wash it. I told him that I had money and I would pay for his car being washed. He cursed me, called me "nigger," and told me he knew I was headed to Selma to demonstrate. He said if he saw me again he would blow my brains out. I knew then that I would never be forced to run from my home county again.

One of my better experiences was to have walked, marched, and led people on to the sheriff of this county. He had a reputation of being able to literally tear men apart with his hands. He had been a football player for the state university and then became a pro. I walked up to him and said, "We're going to school over at the white school." It was several blocks away. I said to

him, "We're going to ask you all to just move aside and let us go."
And the people would go, "Yeah, yeah, yeah." He said "No," and
then he went through his ranting and raving and I said, "Well, if
you're going to stand in the way, maybe the next time we're going
to have to think about getting another sheriff." You know, I had
never dreamed of getting myself in this position at all, being
sheriff.

One thing that was good in the Movement, even though the
brothers got loud and nasty sometimes, was that during the whole
Movement, no Movement person killed another within the Movement. We had some fantastic times. I remember one lady, eighty-
three years old, picketed every day from ten o'clock to two
o'clock, the hottest time of the day. Sometimes her daughter and
granddaughter would join her, three generations at once. I used
to kid her, "If you and she can do it from ten to two, God knows,
I don't have to ever sleep." Sometimes I would go through the
night and then through the day without sleeping. I did most of
the mobilizing. My friends handled the legal maneuvers. We were
saying and doing things that made people feel they were somebody. People were able to see the different levels of this thing.
That was enough. That was where it ought to have been.

We decided in the Movement that politics was the way. We
needed to put someone into the sheriff's race. I was out of town
when they did the nominating. Jim called and said, "You got it,
and you aren't going to have any problem, 'cause nobody else
wanted it." I accepted because I wanted my chance on a different
level than those we had confronted on the streets in my county
and other counties.

I ran in 1966, and the whites took the election. I don't concede
yet that I lost that election. They cheated and stole. Losing the
election was a difficult thing for me because of all the work people
had done in the campaign. One reverend even fainted in the
voting line, it was so long and hot, and they rushed him to the
hospital. They wanted to keep him, but he convinced them to let
him come back and vote. He did vote and then went back to the
hospital. I figured the majority of people in the county were being
pushed around, and I never enjoyed being pushed around. There's
something about being pushed around in that election that made
me come back again. They had taken the election.

I got involved with the Meredith March, and it was frustrating.
I saw the serious conflict between SCLC, SNCC, and CORE, and

the creation of Black Power. I leaned toward SNCC. They were saying, "Well, let's really look at this thing. We talked about nonviolence as a tactic. Maybe integration wouldn't work."

It was a frustrating time. Several times when I was near giving up, people from outside organizations came and got me to work for them. One man, Randolph Blackwell, sought me out, offered me a job, and for a year I worked with the Southern Rural Action Project, trying to get a black economic base. In Greene County we worked hard, but the attempt failed. It was hard.

Dr. King asked me to help on the Poor People's Campaign. Then he was killed. I had known him well. After he was killed, I had that "I can't believe it! " attitude for a week or so. I went to a staff meeting of SCLC, a retreat, really, where I saw most of the staff members breaking down in tears. I'm talking about several days after Dr. King had been buried. I don't think I cried at all, but I don't know if anybody was more upset or lonely than I was at that time. I think I decided when I saw all these people crying—men, women, boys, girls—that that wasn't the kind of thing I wanted to do. I wanted to get back to my community and do something in memory of him.

I learned to fast; I heard what Dick Gregory was saying. He represented a lot of strength to me. He was in jail with some type of fast at the time, and I kind of stayed with what he was doing for awhile. I think I got my strength from fasting and keeping my mind on a particular project that I could work toward, and it was good for my mind. So I didn't fall apart in the process. I know some friends who may never be any good anymore after that time.

I had worked on the Poor People's Campaign and had been in jail in Resurrection City. After that, the American Friends Service Committee came along with open arms and helped me over another hurdle by showing me many opportunities to serve, not only in the U.S., but also abroad.

I feel that being able to win some battles every so often kept me hanging on. I felt that I had won some minor battles in the streets of Eutaw. I felt a sense of victory from the battle streets of Birmingham and Selma, but there was no sense of victory in local or area politics for blacks. An opportunity was provided by whites who were bent on violating the law. The judge of probate left all of the black candidates' names off the ballot of the 1968 election—four commissioners and two board members.

The American Civil Liberties Union and Charles Morgan took us through several courts and finally to the Supreme Court. They

got a new election for us on July 29, 1969. We won the election. This victory put me back into the political ballgame again and helped me to appreciate and understand Chuck Morgan's saying, "When you work hard and do right, you'll win." I felt that just simply living another year would almost ensure me a political victory.

I sometimes treat my job as if I am the county's pastor—like those old country preachers just running around the circuit, seeing about their members and their problems. I suspect that that has kept me from having an unnatural dependence on a weapon. I want to be able, in my work, to come off my head faster than I come off my hip, and I've been trying to do that. In religion we say, "Out of the heart." I have learned, as sheriff, a real lesson in humility.

Being sheriff has permitted me to be a real student; it's afforded me a real learning opportunity. I've seen people at their best and at their worst. I've seen people when they're real. I used to take the attitude that the Lord was punishing me, but now that attitude has changed, and I feel I'm kind of privileged to have an opportunity to really learn the truth. I've learned how families get along, how different it is from what's on the television set. Men do beat their children half to death, and women do the same.

I get called a lot when there are family fights. A lot of times just talking to the people is enough. I've seen some situations that are fantastic. I get a kick out of knowing I've helped. One way you know is that you see husband and wife back talking to each other, and after a while you see those smiles coming back. You see love, whatever it is, connecting. Then you see a little hostility towards you and you know it's time to leave.

I don't consider myself to be one to use violent force to correct any kind of behavior. I just let my actions speak and the way I work speak, and let people know I'm not going to give them a bad deal.

At the high end of the spectrum, I've seen people work together when a problem threatens more than one person. I've seen justice. Justice for me if I stole an automobile, and justice for you if you stole an automobile might be very different things. I think in the courts we have to give some consideration to everything that's involved. We have to look at the person involved. We have to give people second chances. I've had several second chances in my life. If you're rich, you'll get a million chances. But people sometimes

get punished because they're poor. Blacks and minorities are punished because they are who they are.

I've seen some good situations recently. There was a manslaughter charge where a young black guy killed a black minister by accident with his car. I don't know whether he had been drinking or not, but I know he wouldn't have wanted to go out and kill the man. The kid got probation in this case, and that's highly unusual. I've seen similar cases where a man got five years in prison.

I guess the things that are hardest . . . well, are the suicides, for instance. One particular suicide that shook me most was a young black kid who was supposed to be going to work for me on Friday and shot himself on Tuesday.

When you've got something to fight for, you haven't got time to go crazy. I talked with a white public offical about it, who said there weren't nearly as many suicides among the whites during the Black Movement as there are now. We've had half a dozen since I've been sheriff.

The first time that I've been attacked since I've been sheriff happened recently. It happened down at the A&P lot. One of the shoppers called us down because a guy was throwing bottles at people. I knew it was coming. I could just sense it.

I drove my car up to within 20 feet of him, and he said, "Don't come any closer." I said to my deputy, "Better get ready to hit the floor." I figured it was time for me to get out of my necktie. I started easing it down, threw it on the seat, and eased out of the car. Sure enough, the bottles came; swish, bang, they hit the car twice. By that time I had two officers with me, one on my right and one on my left, and we started pushing towards him. He went back to where there were 150 bottles stacked, where he had plenty of ammunition. He let the first bottle go at me about waist high, and missed. I never moved or jumped, and I made a couple of steps toward him. The second bottle came toward my feet and didn't bother me. He never threatened me again. I guess he threw 15 or 20 bottles at the policemen beside me. I was thinking when I drove up there that when he was attacking the car he was attacking the authority figures. When I came out of the car, I was just a man to him, no uniform, no gun, nothing but me. I got close enough to be the first to grab him. God! I had to fight the other officers to get them off him. One of them was spraying Mace, and it got in my eyes. This is another lesson when you get three or four officers involved. You obviously think about your own life and

your own well-being as a police officer. You think people will kill you. They have killed other police officers. You can do some things that you'll regret, as a police officer, because of this thinking pattern.

The other thing that bugged me the most and made me angry, really, was the crowd. When I first stepped out there were a half-dozen people. When I got my eyes clear from the Mace, there must have been 50 people. I just didn't think they'd be there at that time and not only were they there, they were expressing their views rather loudly.

We took him to jail, and the guy never said another word. It turned out that he was disturbed; he thought he was going to die; he was confused; he thought people had killed his little white dog. He needed to be in a hospital more than a jail, but no mental hospital had a bed for him. We arranged for the family to get bail and counseling for him from the mental health organization in our community until the next day when there would be a hospital bed available.

After I had got halfway to him, he looked just like an uncle of mine who had been sick all of his life after a fall when he was five years old. The uncle never really functioned past a second grade level. Seeing this man brought all that home to me.

In summing up he said, I consider myself a little mystical. I think most of us who came through the Movement would say, "I'm going to do what the spirits say do, because I can't really predict what's going to happen tomorrow. I'm going to be guided by some feelings of life." To me that is the spirit I'd been introduced to when I was younger. That was the spirit my grandmother was talking about, the Holy Spirit that would make her shout.

In the Movement I got a kind of inner strength that I wanted during my high school days when I was in the process of becoming awake, or had been awakened and was frustrated by what I had seen. I got strength from facing the sheriff because he was the biggest man in the county. He had the money; he had the guns. We whipped this man in open battle in the election. You really get the feeling that somebody bigger than you is walking beside you, and you feel that, well, man, nobody can hurt you if he wanted to.

God is real, like grandma said. Not only did the spirit help me to deal with the sheriff situation, it helped me find homes for the

people who were evicted, abandoned. He makes those other people feel good through you. He takes care of you.

I think faith in myself was increased by being with these people who responded to me in the Movement. I think I must have increased my faith in God as I increased my faith in myself and others.

It seems to me that if a religion does not help you deal with the facts of life, it's no good. I guess the hardest and most difficult fact of life is dealing with the question of death. If a religion can't help you deal with the question of death, to me, the religion isn't much good. Supposedly we had dealt with the question of death as we entered the church. But I didn't. I found that I had to deal with the question of death more so in the Movement than anywhere else, and I dealt with it. To me, that was the real religious experience. I learned that death is as sure as life; I can't escape it. I learned not to fear it.

Nonviolence is related to this. I think when Dr. King was killed I must have dealt with this question. I am still dealing with it, for sometimes I feel the real need for my gun. I would strap on my shoulder holster and then would end up talking my way out. I would straighten out the situation without ever pulling out the gun. I think I've only pulled the gun once in three years and that time the person I was looking for wasn't where I was looking for him. He'd shot somebody. It's fair to say I'm still tossing nonviolence around.

I'm trying to imitate some of Mahatma Gandhi's practices. I fast. I fasted about the war in Vietnam. I fasted and prayed for a young guy admitted to a mental hospital near here and for strength for myself and others.

I enjoy my family. We go out together quite a lot to games, movies, and church. Can you imagine all of us in one place together? You ought to see the people visiting someone looking at all of us. We do what we want to do. We demand to be free, as free as we possibly can in a given situation. My wife and I love each other; we fight each other, not physically, but we sit and argue and enjoy it. We act like human beings. We love each other. She's my goddess and I'm the god. The children keep us living and searching for more life.

I don't necessarily pray very much any more, but I do ask my God to grant me the serenity to accept the things I cannot change. I also pray for courage, wisdom, and patience. I believe Dr. King's

whole teaching about love and Jesus Christ and nonviolence.

From the trail that I have trod, and the groups and individuals I have known, worked with, read about or observed, I have decided that man is called upon to have the capacity to love his fellow man and his God, and through his faith and work to develop that capacity to its fullest.

Chapter 12

The Way Out Must Lead In

The way out must lead in. These words of Reverend Rockwell's song meant literally that the way out of discrimination and segregation was to go to jail. The way out had to lead to a deep and lasting commitment. What I hear in the words, and in reading the histories, is that the way out led people in, not just into jail, but into self-examination, into fundamental changes in the ways they viewed themselves and others, and into major, new relationships. For those people with whom I spoke, the way out led into lasting personal growth.

Each historian is an individual, and each story is unique. There is no single conclusion or condensation in psychiatric terms that suffices to sum up what happened to the historians. What I feel in reading the histories is primarily a deep respect for their efforts and for the ways they have found to maintain their commitments. The main answers to the question of how to keep working and maintain a commitment are the people's own individual ones.

Nonetheless, as the workers were primarily organizers and leaders, their roles were similar, and they faced certain major problems in common. Just as they faced certain problems in common, there are certain common themes that run through most, if not all, of the histories. It is useful to examine these themes.

One theme is the stress that the historians felt because of being organizers in the Movement. Another is the importance of certain childhood figures, while another is the impact of joining the Movement. An important theme in their accounts both initially and throughout their involvements is the human closeness they shared within the Movement, as is the development of a new consciousness of self-worth. Major themes in the reflections in looking back over ten years of work are the evolution of faith in the work and the reconciliation of the Movement experience with the rest of their experience.

Reverend Caldwell, Joe, George, and Mrs. Washington each described what happened to those not able to withstand the stress of the Movement. Many workers left the Movement because of

it. Many others became ill or incapacitated for periods of time. Obviously, the relationship between being in the Movement and having difficulties is complex. Many who had difficulties and left did so for reasons other than the stress of the Movement. For example, some left because of problems they had before joining the Movement. But it is undeniable that being active in the Movement, because of the physical violence, the uncertainty, and the rapid pace of change, was stressful. George and Mrs. Washington describe periods in their own lives when they felt overwhelmed. One stopped functioning, and the other had a bout of alcoholism. As several of the historians said, the stress continued; there was no way to get away from the Movement for a time, to rest and take stock of the situation before continuing.

Experiencing losses was a part of the stress, and dealing with loss a significant part of their lives. Throughout the years of the Movement, many workers were killed, and many were beaten and maimed. Mrs. Williams' words as she described learning that a friend had been killed was one clear statement of this common experience of pain and loss. "After I heard the news, I couldn't even relax. It seemed to me I could scarcely think. I was just one great sore inside. When you've known someone that well, and you've lived around them, and they've just poured out all their life stories to you, and then something like that happens, sometimes you wonder if it's worth it. That life is gone and that person can't do anything anymore. Then you wonder if all he really did amounted to anything. You wonder if any of it is really worth it. It gives you just an all-gone feeling."

Each of the workers has described the impact of having a friend or a leader die. As several said, being unable to get over the death of a friend or a leader led to many other workers' falling apart. Being able to grieve and keep working was a necessity.

Beyond grieving for those who had died or were hurt, the workers had repeatedly to deal with the sense of loss about what they had hoped for through the Movement, but had not been accomplished, what they had envisioned, but had not been realized. This became increasingly important as time passed, and it became clear that the early dreams of the Movement, of rapid change, would not be fulfilled.

Concerning the theme of childhood figures, Reverend Caldwell attributed his becoming a minister in large part to his grandmother's call. Mrs. Johnson said that the relationship she had with her father, and her father's protection of her, gave her

strength to keep fighting in the Movement. George said that the greatest influence on his development was his grandfather. Sheriff Gilmore saw his concern for the people in his district as coming in part from the relationship with his cousin, who he says was like a father to him. Some of the historians are more complete than others in describing their childhood and its influences. Nonetheless, in looking over the whole group, it is clear that most feel that they got loving and caring from parental figures, and that the memory of such love and caring is real for them today, and is consciously acknowledged by them as an important factor in their own development.

Most of the historians described their initial involvements in similar terms. This is striking considering the diversity of backgrounds, of ages, and of reasons for getting involved that the people represented. Mrs. Johnson became active after writing a letter challenging the discrimination in the giving of loans to farmers. Sheriff Gilmore became totally involved only after several partial involvements and only after leaving the South for a time. Joe got involved while in high school. Several others joined after college, and some were even older.

In spite of this diversity, the work that they did, organizing, was similar. Organizing consisted of living in a community, getting to know the people in that community, going from door to door presenting issues, and trying to change the community. The organizers often worked 15, 16, 17 hours a day. Moreover, the local communities carefully scrutinized the organizers, and so all they did in the community had to be acceptable. Thus, for them, there could be no commitment that was more important than the commitment to the Movement. Being involved was a powerful experience, like a religious conversion. Involvement consumed the workers' time and energy. They were gripped with a vision of change, both in themselves and in the society around them. They lived this vision, trying to realize it in the way they ordered their personal lives as well as in the way they communicated it to others.

For the communities they worked in, they actually embodied, lived out, and represented a new consciousness of self-worth and growth, just as they also represented the possibility of concrete changes in registering, voting, and the like. Thus their relationships to others changed. Every gesture, every action was seen against the background of their being organizers and was mea-

sured by the standard of how much it would contribute to the Movement. They broke away from traditional roles, away from following traditional models. They gave up jobs, educational opportunities, material possessions, money, and often personal safety. They gave up family ties and other close relationships in many cases.

They were aware of being gripped by and part of something new and strange and good. Mrs. Washington put it well, "I was determined to see what this Movement was. It stirred an excitement as well as a hope. It looked like we were moving to something. I didn't know what at that particular time. My days were filled with work and purpose instead of just going by."

Even though the traditional roles, the models, in southern society were limited and confining, nonetheless to break away from them required a great effort. In breaking with them, the people vaulted into the unknown psychologically, just as they did physically, in going to desegregate lunch counters or to register to vote. Change for them had an external dimension in that they gave up the regular pattern of their lives for the uncertainty of being organizers; correspondingly, change had an internal dimension in that they gave themselves over totally to believing in the ideology of the Movement. As they rejected traditional roles, they gradually formed new roles and new patterns for themselves. The availability of certain people as models, experienced Movement leaders like Dr. King, helped, but much of it they did by themselves.

How were the people able to sustain themselves after giving up so many of the traditional supports of society? The way out led into deep and lasting change in the personal relationships of those who got involved. The way out led into intense human closeness. Pat Watters describes the Movement as "extra-cultural, beyond the normal limits of American culture."[1] This word applies well to the intensity of closeness within the Movement. It was extraordinary. The closeness had two dimensions. One was that the organizers became very dependent on and shared with the few other organizers with whom they worked. The other was that organizing led to new relationships with people in the community that was being organized. It led to knowing a great deal about and sharing much with those people. Both of these aspects were important, not only in the early stages of the Movement, but also throughout the whole Movement.

As one example of the first dimension, Mrs. Washington said, ". . . I always had a center of people in the Movement, and folks that were in the community . . . . Folks would come to my rescue, I just couldn't stop . . . . There was a spirit of sureness, I knew that people were pulling for me; I knew that they would be there with whatever they had. I never had this kind of closeness relationship with any group of people, even in church. I think that's what kept me moving, too."

For some, such as Joe, this kind of closeness took place within one particular civil rights organization and with the people of that organization. For others it took place not within a particular organization, but within a geographical area. John Lewis said that the community of Movement people was his family for a period of time. He describes the group as a band of brothers and emphasizes the importance of the closeness. "The community was tremendously important. There was a kind of togetherness. . . . If something happened to one person, it happened to all of us. If one person would go to jail, we would all go; and if one person suffered we all shared in the suffering." Joe also compared the Movement community to a family. Part of getting involved meant breaking with their own families for some, but more importantly, there was a positive attraction to the closeness and sharing within the Movement circle.

Throughout the Movement, music was tremendously important. Reverend Caldwell offered a cogent explanation of one reason music was so important. "The songs that we sang had more influence than anything else in enabling us to endure what the white people put on us. . . . Music does tend to bring the spirit together. Music is what kept the slaves together, enabling them to endure the lash. While I am sitting down here with you our spirit is separate, you might say. When music moves, we move to the same spirit. So, in that sense we feel that our spirit is moving together. We look at one another and communicate . . . ." He said that music enabled people to share with one another. Music was so important precisely because it was the expression of the intensity of the closeness.

Another kind of new closeness developed between the organizers and the people they were trying to organize. The organizers gave much, but also felt they got a great deal in return. Joe states this when he says, "People acted out love. . . . I wonder how I could take it, and how the people could stand it; then I remember these experiences, and I have some idea. The community would

just open up, it would just embrace the Movement workers."

George described something of the learning through getting inside of the world of others and seeing it from their eyes, when he talked of the joys of organizing. "There was much joy in participating with the people. . . . I think I became part of the people. I never did try to assume leadership . . . . The joy was talking with the old people. I always listened very, very closely to the old people. . . . I've done a strange kind of organizing. I've picked cotton and talked with people. I have cut weeds and talked. I've fished. I've camped. . . . I found out what made them endure, and I became a part of that."

It was one thing to get involved in the Movement initially, and quite another to keep going for more than ten years. The closeness was a sustaining force all through the Movement. Reverend Caldwell put this perhaps most succinctly: "I didn't lose hope, although it was and is a very troubled hope, and I kept a group. I think the group is the biggest thing we've got going for us, and I always told everybody else to do that. You can't make it in this kind of thing by yourself. You have to have something to reassure you. Not only that, you have to have something to keep you straight so you don't give in to the rewards of society . . . . The group is working amid all the failures as the source of comfort and support for us."

The group of other organizers was the major source of human relationships for those completely committed to the Movement. Even such relationships as marriage were deeply affected. Several of the organizers married other Movement workers; several postponed marriage because of the Movement. Others that did neither of these were at least married to people sympathetic to the Movement.

A second major theme in the people's descriptions of what sustained them is a new consciousness of their own worth and of their own power to bring about change. The whole of the segregationist culture had as its goal the passivity and acquiescence of blacks: any action might threaten the status quo. Involvement in the Movement was involvement in action, action which broke the pattern of ingrained acquiescence and acceptance. There was a great joy and sense of accomplishment in this. Taking action, not being passive, was the visible expression of this new consciousness. Moreover, all of the workers had become angry, many enraged, by their own humiliation and oppression, as they have stated. They were well aware of the oppression and humiliation

of their parents and grandparents, of the legacy of slavery and lynchings. Taking part in the Movement was a positive way of dealing with this anger and rage. For Sheriff Gilmore, the expression of action came in a confrontation in a demonstration: "One of my better experiences was to have walked, marched, and led people on to the sheriff of this county. He had a reputation of being able to literally tear men apart with his hands. . . . I said to him, 'We're going to ask you all to move aside and let us go!' . . . And he said 'No' . . . and I said 'Well if you're going to stand in the way, maybe the next time we're going to have to think about getting another sheriff." For many others, it also came in demonstrations, as well as in other ways.

This new consciousness developed through the course of the Movement. It was supported in part by the fact that the people were able to see results from their action: there was legislation, voters were registered, and some black candidates were elected, for example. It was supported in part by the Movement community of which the workers were a part. Beyond this, however, what I hear in the histories is that the stance of being active and of having a positive sense of self-worth made inner psychological sense to the workers, far more sense than the passive stance of repressed, denied anger and inaction that segregation demanded. Therefore, the new consciousness grew and developed.

One of the pressures George spoke of was having to contain his anger in the face of a situation that was extremely provocative and seemed to demand to be changed. There was a tension for all the workers between the realization of what was wrong in segregation, or in the country as a whole, and the inability to change the situation quickly. What is remarkable about the workers is that they were not overwhelmed by their rage and that they did not lash out blindly. Just as the capacity to grieve and keep working was a necessity for the workers, so was the capacity to be angry and feel outrage, and at the same time put those feelings into action toward the goals of the Movement. The workers possessed both of these capacities in an unusual degree. I do not have any simple explanation of why they had these qualities, but I feel that it is important to note them. Both are related to another theme in the worker's accounts. This theme, also relevant later, is the workers' ability to accept their own limitations. In order to stay in the Movement, the workers had to accept that they could not bring about change quickly, or totally, no matter how compelling the need for change.

Over time and out of the new consciousness of self-worth, the workers developed a faith, both in themselves and in the worth of what they were doing. By faith I mean that the people came to believe fully and totally in what they were doing, regardless of their gains and losses, regardless of the consequences of having the faith. If, as Lillian Smith has suggested, there were many forces and people at work to kill the dream in southern society, these people were the antithesis, they were the keepers of the dream.

Some of the historians came to see their faith within a religious context, others did not. Mrs. Williams' and George's are the best examples of faith not expressed within a religious framework. Mrs. Williams had had first-hand political experience with black politics and black movements before the 1960s. She had lived through a move toward separatism, through conflicts between blacks and whites, through violence, and through the effects of failure and repression. She was quite articulate about having been involved many times before, and she drew on her experiences to advise others. In spite of feeling that she had seen so much that she could not tell all of her experiences, for fear of disillusioning those she was with, she did become fully involved. Her reason she put directly and simply, "What keeps me going? I guess it just is a feeling that there are certain basic human rights and you're going to exercise them, regardless. You hope you can do something to cause somebody to see the error of his ways . . . I still believe change is possible. . . ."

George also had past political experiences as one of the bases for his involvement: his talks with his grandfather about the black past and the future. He believed strongly in what he was doing. He rejected two of the major ideological positions that many people used in the Movement, nonviolence and Christianity, and worked from a political ideological stance instead. As with Mrs. Williams, he did not become absorbed in or dominated by a political ideology. "A lot of people were very scholarly, and I'm not a very scholarly person. . . . I always looked at the things we were immediately working toward . . . . But I limited myself . . . . I'm basically geared toward the land."

Many linked involvement in the Movement with early or continuing religious experience. Some repeatedly used religious metaphors in describing the well-springs of their actions in the Movement. There are two intertwined strains to that religious experience: that of traditional Christianity and that of nonviolence.

This is not to deny the varieties and importance of other religious experiences to political activists outside the South, such as the awareness of African religion, the development of the Muslim faith, or the growth of interest in eastern mystical experience. But these kinds of religious experience were not identified by the organizers with whom I spoke.

Visionary religious experience is an integral part of much southern rural life, for both blacks and whites. Many people grew up in the South within a religious framework but did not get involved in the Movement. Many who did, did not break with the metaphors of traditional religion in becoming involved, but rather they gave a new meaning or interpretation to the religion. This interpretation was consistent with the demands of the Movement.

A good example is Reverend Rockwell, a minister and an organizer. He had profound, early, religious experiences, as he has described. He was a preacher and the pastor of several churches before becoming involved in the Movement in the 1960s, and he has continued to be the pastor of at least one church. He said that he felt his religion was crucial for his commitment and said religion was the "backbone" of his keeping on in the Movement.

As much as he is a part of southern religious tradition, his actions and his faith are his own creation, and have led him into political action, jailings, and the like. In his words, his religion and the need for action are one: ". . . I feel like I'm working for the Lord. The Lord told me to preach to all the world. If I get out here in a demonstration against injustice, I'm preaching. . . . I don't think nobody, no agitator between here or hell or nowhere could be more of an agitator than Jesus."

Reverend Rockwell's stance, deeply religious as it is, allows for a cogent political analysis of what has happened to the Movement. His religious faith does not blind him to the importance of other kinds of experiences. Thus he says that his experiences in voter registration in the 1930s and his involvement in World War II are important factors in his own current involvements. Likewise, in assessing why people left the Movement, he points to economic factors in what amounts to a Marxist analysis. In explaining why blacks appear at times to lack initiative, he again cites economic factors. He does not say the people who left the Movement are irreligious or evil. He is religious, but his religion does not bind him to a narrow world view. Likewise, Reverend Caldwell describes his involvement in the Movement as religious,

especially his first experience in jail. Yet he has been totally involved for the last several years in securing land on which to build a stable political and economic base. Sheriff Gilmore reports that he had profound religious experiences in the Movement. Yet he has also run and won a political campaign, and now works full-time as a sheriff.

For some, the commitment to the Movement and to religious belief became expressed through nonviolent action. This is certainly true for both Reverend Caldwell and the sheriff. For a few, such as John Lewis, the belief in nonviolence was a belief that became a way of life, a total commitment.

Whether the faith was based on religion or on political analysis, what is important is that all the people developed a faith which was not theoretical or absorbing in and of itself. Had they become too involved in articulating the theoretical aspects of that faith, they would have lost touch with the concrete political realities they were trying to change, and with the lives of the people they were trying to change. This characteristic of the faith people developed sets the Civil Rights Movement in sharp contrast to movements based on dogmatic ideological systems, and to intense visionary religions which emphasize total obedience to a rigid code of behavior.

How decisions were made in the Movement reflects the characteristic of not adhering rigidly to a fixed ideology and being open to experience in the present. Decision making was a matter of consensus. The workers came together, talked, sang, argued, and then decided together what action to take. It was not done in an autocratic manner with a clearly defined leader. John Lewis emphasizes this in relation to decisions within the organization of which he was a part. Joe emphasizes this in field organizing: "I would be faced with a decision that might affect four or five hundred lives directly . . . I would take it to the people . . . . They would decide."

Finally, all those who stayed in the Movement over the long haul made sense of, or combined experience in the Movement with the rest of their experiences, and accepted themselves, with their limitations. Many of the people of religious backgrounds stated their understandings in religious terms. Others did not. What did happen is that all came to understand the Movement experience as a continuation of earlier experiences, while also recognizing its importance. Several said clearly that what they expressed through the Movement was what they had been feeling

before the Movement came along. For example, Mrs. Washington saw her mother as laying the groundwork for her later pride in being black with the insistence that black was honest. Reverend Caldwell said that the call that his grandmother gave him became real and was answered only through the Movement. Sheriff Gilmore said, "In the Movement I got a kind of inner strength that I had wanted. . . .I think my faith in myself was increased by being with these people who responded to me in the Movement. I think I must have increased my faith in God as I increased my faith in myself and others . . . . I guess the hardest and most difficult fact of life is dealing with the question of death . . . . Supposedly we had dealt with the question of death as we entered the church. . . . I found that I had to deal with the question of death more so in the Movement than anywhere else, and I dealt with it. To me, that was the real religious experience." The experience in the Movement was essential in his understanding of his own life, his religion, and his history.

Mrs. Washington perhaps most clearly states the sense of having to come to grips with her own limitations in order to keep working. She also emphasizes the importance of having roots: "My roots are here where I got started in the Movement. Being in the Movement here was the start of another life-style for me. Here is where my eyes came open to another way of hope . . . . This is the place where I found myself."

Being an organizer over ten years meant being able to meet the basic human needs for love and support within the framework of the Movement. It meant putting economic and physical security aside in favor of the human relationships and the possibilities of change that the Movement afforded.

Two factors are noticeably absent from the workers' accounts of what kept them going: economic reward and realization of political ambition. It is conceivable that at certain stages being in the Movement was economically attractive. For some, at least, it provided the way of getting a subsistence wage in a rural agricultural region that was severely depressed economically. But for the people I have described, it is fair to say that the motive of economic profit does not explain their actions. Certainly for most of them, being in the Movement was not economically profitable, especially not in comparison to what they could get, or were offered, in other jobs outside the Movement. Moreover, there was a strong, conscious rejection of individual economic gains by most of the people throughout the Mvoement. Giving up financial re-

ward was part of the discipline of being an organizer, as Jim, John Lewis, and Reverend Caldwell attest in different ways.

Some of the workers realized political ambitions through the Movement. New opportunities opened up for many, although they had no way of knowing that when they first became involved. But as with not making money, one of the major commitments of being in the Movement for these historians was not to place personal gain, such as the realization of ambition, above the needs of the Movement, and they did not. Thus, as with economic profit, the motive of the realization of ambition does not account for the people's continued commitment.

Of course, these histories are representative of only a small group of workers, those who stayed in the South and the Movement over a long period of time. Their experiences are not typical of the majority of people in the Movement who were involved for a period of time and then left. Nor do these histories explain how or why some people who were in the Movement became permanently incapacitated, although the historians do at times describe such people.

In reading over the histories, it is clear that the historians underwent inner psychological change. The concept of identity is relevant to this change. John Lewis gave a description of identity in relating his and others' experiences in being in the Movement. "Being involved tended to free you. You saw segregation, you saw discrimination, and you had to solve the problem, but you saw yourself also the free man, as the free agent, able to act. . . .After what Martin Luther King, Jr. had to say, what he did. . .as an individual you couldn't feel alone again. . . .It (being in the Movement) gave a sense of pride and it was a new sense of identity, really. You felt a sense of control over what was happening and what was going to happen."

In more traditional psychological terms, but not in conflict with Mr. Lewis' observation, much has been written about the process of identity formation and the normative identity crisis of adolescence, most incisively by Erik Erikson. He describes ego identity in the following way: "The sense of ego identity, then, is the accrued confidence that one's ability to maintain inner sameness and continuity (one's ego in the psychological sense) is matched by the sameness and continuity of one's meaning for others."[2] He sees the formation of a stable ego identity as the major developmental task of the stage of adolescence. Identity formation and a stable identity involve many different factors. In

forming an identity, young people must make sense of their own physical endowments, past experience from birth on, and present opportunities in a way that allows them to function in the world and to have a sense of certainty about themselves. Young people must come to grips with three major developmental areas: (1) relationship to others, both sexual and nonsexual; (2) independence of and relation to family; (3) choice of work and career.

The process of identity formation, as Erikson describes it, is a general developmental phenomenon: all young people go through it. Experience in the Movement was only a part, but an essential part, of the process for some young people. The Movement experience, especially the role of organizer, was part of the set of the present opportunities of some of the younger workers. Put another way, Erikson stresses that the external reality in which adolescents find themselves, the historical actuality, is important in either allowing or preventing adolescents from developing normally and finding a healthy sense of identity, and in influencing the nature of that identity. The context of the Movement was the historical actuality for some of the younger civil rights workers. He also says that the process of identity formation continues throughout life, although with nowhere near the intensity that it does in adolescence.

Regarding the three areas Erikson mentioned, some young people in the Movement found their major source of relationships with others in the Movement. Through being in the Movement, they achieved independence from family and made, by being organizers, the choice of a definite kind of work. These young people, then, consolidated their identities while in the Movement. Their role as organizers shaped their identities; it became an essential part of their identities. Joe is an example.

What of those who were beyond adolescence when the Movement began? Not all, but some, forged not a new identity, but a changed identity. As discussed before, externally, their lives changed as they gave up jobs and family ties and took up organizing and new intense relationships. In terms of their inner sense of themselves, they changed as they made permanent the new consciousness of self they had experienced in joining the Movement. In Erikson's terms, they acquired fundamental inner confidence in themselves as organizers and in the fact that this inner sense was matched by their meaning as organizers for others.

One might argue that the histories really represent only the psychological concomitants of being in the Movement, that what

the people said about themselves is too psychologically based, and that a sufficient explanation of the Movement would be to define the set of conditions, or opportunities, that occurred in the South and the country at large.

Both internal change and external opportunity were necessary for the Movement to happen, and neither one is solely sufficient to explain what happened. The histories are not a total explanation of the whole process but provide one perspective that is an essential part of the explanation. This perspective is perhaps too often left out or ignored in analyses of the larger forces.

Obviously, the external situation, the set of opportunities and obstacles presented to the individuals, was very important and had a great impact. Parts of the external situation were the broader historical forces: the mood of optimism in the country is an example, as is the simple and terrible reality of the centuries of oppression, humiliation, and subjugation of blacks. In a more narrow sense, for example, had there been no CORE Freedom Ride in 1961, John Lewis would not have gone on it or have been so deeply moved by it. But what happened in the Movement was more than just the presentation of opportunities. The workers had a major role in shaping the important accomplishments of the Movement, whether in relationships with others, in demonstrations, or in legislative action. John Lewis, through his own actions, provided leadership so that the Freedom Ride continued after it faltered. It is the perspective of the ten-year involvement that is useful here. For if conditions were favorable in many ways for the emergence of the Movement in the early 1960s, they were certainly unfavorable to its continuance in the late 1960s and early 1970s. The external reality, the set of opportunities, became very limited. Yet the people maintained their efforts. This is because they had an inner awareness, commitment, and faith, which was not dependent just on the external opportunities. It is in this sense that the inner changes are so important. Because of those inner changes, the people kept working in spite of the changed external reality. There is a deep irony here, for being intensely commited and changed by the Movement created difficulties for many workers, as they have stated. One of the major problems for the workers was what to do when the Movement seemed to fall apart in the late 1960s. This was particularly difficult for those who were young, who had formed their own identities in the Movement, and who, as Joe said, grew up in the Movement. There was no continuous Movement as people had known

it. This is what Joe meant when he said there was no place for these people to go. Those who were able to adjust for the most part did so with much pain, and did so by finding a niche where they could continue in some form to be Movement organizers. They could not give up the identities they had so recently formed.

Repeatedly the historians emphasized the dimension of close relationships to others in describing what they felt had kept them going. There is a direct connection between the inner psychological change that the historians describe, and this closeness. Relationships with others drew people into the Movement. Once people were involved, the relationships, the closeness provided the glue, the matrix, the support for the people so that they were able to change the way they felt about themselves and their actions. Moreover, relationships with others (along with self-understanding, which will be discussed later) provided a stabilizing influence, something secure and reliable, in the midst of all the uncertainties with which they had to deal.

The importance of relationships is also a reflection of what the Movement was: both in its goals and in its structure, it tried to foster dignity, equality, and closeness amongst its adherents. This emphasis on relationships, rather than ideology, is one of the ways in which the Civil Rights Movement is distinctly different from many other political movements.

Many theorists of development emphasize that a young child develops in major ways through relationships to others, and that the patterns of relationship in childhood, for example, between mother and child, have life-long effects. What is emphasized by the experience of the civil rights workers is the importance of relationships with others, at stages other than childhood, in enabling people to change. The intense relationships with others, which for a time superseded those even within the family and were among the most intense that the person had experienced, were a necessary part of the process of change.

These workers' lives demonstrate the possibility of remaking or changing identity beyond adolescence. Some histories show an unusual kind, or way, of growing and developing through adulthood. I suspect that this process of change beyond childhood through intense human closeness that is evident in the histories can well be found in other situations, although I have not explored this at this time.

What about the quality of the people's understanding of themselves and of their needs for such understanding? They certainly

felt that understanding themselves was a necessary and important process. In interviewing them, I often sensed I was tapping into the on-going process of their trying to understand themselves. They were aware of their own feelings and had wrestled with the questions I raised before I met with them.

The uncertainty in their lives is a contributing factor to the importance of their self-understanding. They were constantly tossed about by forces and changes beyond their control. What they did have, in addition to their relationships with others, was themselves, their own histories, their own memories, and their own reactions about what was happening to them, and, eventually, their own understandings of themselves. Self-understanding, along with relationships to others, provided a kind of stability.

Finally, the historians were under considerable stress through being in the Movement. Understanding themselves, making sense of the disparate parts of their experience, helped them to deal with the stress and function effectively.

The way out led in, then, not just to jail, but into new relationships, into a new consciousness of self-worth, and into self-understanding.

Chapter 13

Continued Growth

Over the years since the men and women were first interviewed, I have stayed in touch with most of them, and have followed up on all of them for the second edition. All but one were recontacted and reinterviewed during 1980. The basic principles of what they said about what sustained them, the common themes in their accounts, remain similar to those expressed before. Many were working in exactly the same communities, in the same ways as before. Others were not. Some have had or were having a much more difficult time than before, as is reflected in their accounts.

For this chapter I have not presented the entirety of the interviews. I have not presented material that was presented before, but rather have focused on what has happened to them in the years since I originally talked to them.

They are different in some ways from before. They are older. Many of them now have children, and concerns about the world that these children will grow up in and how to raise them now figure prominently in their work. Several have advanced to positions of considerable prominence and are well known publicly. As before, I have not concentrated at all on their public work, but rather on their individual experiences and on what has sustained them.

I have not added another set of conclusions. The fundamental concerns they voiced before—the overwhelming importance of closeness to others, both initially and throughout the Movement, the handling of anger, the new sense of self, the taking of action rather than being passive, the development of faith in the work over time, the reconciliation of Movement experience with the rest of their own life experiences, and the acceptance of self with limitations—all remain true. What is different, and in some ways even more unusual than in the original observations, is the length of the commitment of these men and women, now extending over twenty years in most cases. The length of their commitment, and the fact that most of their observations

about what sustained them over that time have remained stable over the past six years, give added weight to the importance of these observations in understanding how they were able to keep going. The length of the commitment also reinforces the notion that these men and women have forged a new or changed identity, in which they now feel secure, and which is stable. Their experiences have molded them, changed them; they could not, in any sense, go back and become what they once were. That they have kept working over the past six years, years that have been even more unfavorable politically and economically to the ideas of social change and justice which they support, also reinforces the importance of their commitment. Their identities are now fully bound up with their roles as activists and leaders within the Movement.

Three areas of their lives deserve special mention in this follow-up. The first is the handling of anger. These men and women are continually exposed to social and political conditions and to a lack of change that make them angry, and to conditions that cry out to be changed. Their ability to *not* shut out that anger—to see the conditions and to work in limited ways to try to change them, while not being so overwhelmed by their rage that they quit and/or lose control—is remarkable. They have an unusual capacity in this regard. The sources are unclear, but the nature of it is clear and deserves mention.

Secondly, this second set of follow-up interviews confirms the overwhelming importance in these men's and women's lives of their relationships to others. They talk about their relationship to others as their main sustaining force. Many of the relationships first established when they joined the Movement are still ongoing and important to them. These relationships are intimately linked to the process of psychological changes undergone by these men and women. The relationships initially drew people into the Movement; and they provided a context, a matrix, a haven, a stability, that was essential, even necessary, for these men and women to undergo psychological changes while they were in the Movement. Certainly, the relationships with others within the Movement superseded all other relationships in their lives, assumed more importance than relationships to mother, father, siblings, and friends; and this fact is directly related to the ability of these men and women to change.

Finally, in reinterviewing these men and women, I came to understand that I was tapping into the ongoing process of their own self-understanding and was dealing with questions they had wrestled with many times themselves before. They valued highly their own understanding of themselves. Both the process of self-understanding and the understanding itself were important to these men and women. The connection between self-understanding and deep involvement in political or social movements in other contexts remains to be examined; but the study of these men and women's lives undeniably emphasizes the fundamental importance of self-understanding and self-awareness to enabling men and women to make major changes in their lives and to enabling them to sustain themselves in difficult circumstances over a long period of time.

The study of these men and women's lives is unfinished; that is, their lives are evolving and developing. Their lives are in process, and some of the historians are in transition, both now and at the time that they were interviewed. But there is a certainty and a stability to their commitment, as there are also hardship, loss, anguish, rage, and faith. They are continuing to develop and change, and this capacity to develop and change, to adapt to the rapidly changing political and economic conditions while maintaining an inner stability and certainty about the long-range goals of the Movement, is both characteristic of them and also remarkable.

Mr. John Lewis left the Voter Education Project in Atlanta to work in the Carter Administration for three years as the Associate Director for Domestic and Anti-Poverty Operations of the ACTION agency. He left this agency in the summer of 1980, before the presidential election, to return to the South and a job in a co-operative bank in Atlanta. When I talked with him, he said he stood by what he had said in earlier interviews. He retained a sense of the possible in the South and felt that a movement like that of the early Sixties might emerge in the South and he felt that he wanted to be there, with it, in the South.

In response to questions about how he had sustained himself, he said, "I don't really think I've deviated from those feelings and ideas I had before. The philosophy of nonviolence is still very much with me, and was, even while I was in the

government. In my confirmation hearing I spoke about the beloved community and what gives me faith and hope to go on. I think it's the people I've worked with. Many times in the work in the government, I went to the deep South and saw old friends from the Movement. Yes, they do keep me going.

"The best part of the work in the government was the time I've spend with the people. For example, talking with an elderly native American couple in Navaho, through a translator. To see them, the people, their faces, to learn what they want for their children and grandchildren, this has been the best. I've done the same thing with people in the deep South, with Chicanos, with people from Appalachia. It made me realize what Dr. King was trying to do with the Poor People's campaign. The worst part was having to deal with the insensitivity of Congress. The whole time I was there, we never received a single appropriation for our department. We made it though on the standing budget, just a continuing resolution. During those three years, the concerns of poor people were not on the Congressional agenda. The people in Congress do not consider poor people 'in.' They don't have much money or much voting power. It was hard to get people to listen. We were always going out begging. What you can do is so limited."

In the time since he was last interviewed, Mr. Lewis and his wife had a son, who is now four. When I asked him what he wanted for his son, he said, "I would like for my son, and for all children, to grow up in a country that is a little more peaceful, that is free of violence—personal violence and social violence—and where children will have the opportunity to live the fullness of their lives, not in fear of something happening in the streets. I don't want him to live his life in the threat of war. I've taken him with me on a number of trips. I've told him about the Civil rights Movement and about the beloved community. I've shown him pictures. I've taken him to Mississippi with me. I think he understands as much as a four-year-old can.

"If anything, I believe in the philosophy of nonviolence more strongly than before. Somehow we've got to find a way to continue to move the nation to think about some kind of peaceful solution. We've got to start working for peace, for a nonviolent world. One of my greatest fears is that if we don't respond, we will have outbreaks of violence from time to time.

When people become desperate, they do desperate things.

"I've continued to be faithful. I continue to go to church. I don't think my faith has changed that much. In terms of my personal life, I think through being in Washington I've become more of a private person. I never got caught up in going to the parties, the receptions. I just went to work. If not, I'd either go home or get involved in community action. I had a few friends, and I tried to do my best."

Mary Ann Logan Davidson, called Ann Williams in the first edition, has continued to be active in supporting local political candidates, working for political change, and supporting the poor in the town in which she lives. She said much of what she'd done over the last six years had been in helping and defending poor people who didn't understand the legal system. She commented, "I think there will be a resurgence of the Movement. It's just a case of 'here we go again.' They open one gate and they close another for us through all the avenues of life. There are big demonstrations all over the state now. There'll be a lot of political activity and a lot of fights. There's been some killing. Four colored women were shot in Chattanooga; a nine-year-old girl was shot somewhere else. There's been resistance to change locally, and there's resistance in the state as a whole. For example, in this state, they will not pass a compulsory attendance law. They'd rather have poor whites grow up ignorant, not going to school, than to have poor black children educated. There's so much delinquency here among young people as to make a strong man weep. Things are just the same, only different." Ms. Davidson's main efforts when I spoke with her were to work for a redistricting plan which would allow the first black commissioner to be elected in her area. As she said, "for the first time since Surrender."

As with Ms. Davidson, Reverend Charles Sherrod, called Reverend Caldwell in the book, was in the thick of things in action when I spoke to him. He directs the New Community's farming operation in southwest Georgia. There has been and continues to be a major struggle to make the farm, now over four thousand acres of prime land, a viable commercial operation. Sherrod explained that his major ongoing concern was meeting

the monthly payment on the debt. Sadly, the group had to sell off over a thousand acres of farm land last year to refinance the debt. He has had major troubles with the bureaucracy in Washington in terms of getting FHA and other support due him as a farmer, as well as trouble locally. Much of our talk was about the economics of farming, how to make the operation go.

"If we ever get adequately financed, we'll be in good shape. We're planning soybeans, corn and vegetables. We've got pecans, as well as fruit trees, apples, figs and so forth. We've got eight acres of grapes; we've got sugar cane; we raise hogs, and we cure them ourselves. We try to get rid of the middleman by selling directly to the consumer. We sell through the farmer's market.

"We still have cooperative ownership down here. We do now have some people who are on money jobs, people who work for a check, but we also have some who work and share in owning the land. They have an opportunity to direct how their land is utilized. We have a committee of workers, and everyone has one vote. If a policy decision is being made, they can vote against it. If the supervisor makes a mistake, the workers bring it to the committee. We've obliterated the position of manager and employee. Essentially, there are only workers.

"The most important thing about what I'm doing is the people who surround me. They give me the strength to keep on. I've been able to keep on and have hope that things will be better. If this were simply a personal struggle, it would have been too difficult. The group provides leisure amid turmoil. I know I can go away and the whole of the operation will not break down. If I'm away a week, the whole thing won't fail. I don't have to look over everyone, to look at the farmer's market, or at the paint shop, or at the tractor driver, because now we have people who are as intimately involved as I am, and we continue to have a community.

"As I look over things, I feel some short range goals are out of our reach. It's a disappointment which causes me to be frustrated. It's a frustrating ordeal, year after year, to know that there are twenty-five years of mortgage. If no one sees us and sees how this model can be reduplicated all over the country for distributing power, it will be very bad.

"At the same time, we are rearing our children, having fun, speaking to people, having political success in various counties,

and helping people. These small opportunities keep us going, and we keep our eyes on the prize. I was elected city commissioner. The only thing that's changed because of that is the way I dress. I cut my hair and I shine my shoes, but the things I've always done I always do. In this position I'm just able to do more things for more people. I've been able to use a phone call where I might have had to have a demonstration in the past to get something accomplished. The political power, the structure and the balance of power are still in the same hands."

When I asked him about nonviolence he said, "My feelings haven't changed about nonviolence. We still have some demonstrations. Last time we were in Plains demonstrating against the Food Stamp cut-off. We don't have as many demonstrations as we used to, but they're still a legitimate means for us. People are still taught to demonstrate nonviolently.

"I don't think there's a mass rising of the Klan here, except in the minds of some people. There've been a few manifestations of it close together in time—the killing of some blacks in North Carolina and South Carolina. We still have the same tough white opposition down here, and there's still strong opposition in economics and politics.

"The overriding priority in my life has always been the search for truth. In the last few years the priority has been the acquisition and holding of the land. Some of the philosophical goals of my being have changed. I yearn for the nourishment of the university, but have not been able to reach out and touch it, because so much holds me to the priority of the Movement. My faith remains. I go through the Bible once every two years. I have children now. We're not willing to turn them over to the culture or even to the church. I don't mean to put down all churches. I'm trying to teach them myself, the good I learned from those churches. I just try to treat each child as an individual on his own. What I want for them is more than we have now. Much less of the unnecessary hindrance that we have, the stupid laws, and all the bad to us, the prohibiting institutions. Hopefully, they will be strong enough to deal with them internally before the system gets to them. Hopefully, they'll have protective mechanisms inside and not be changed by the institutions."

In summing up, he said, "I want to make a plea to people. I want to see this country remain whole and sensitive enough to

make room for all the kinds of actions, not experiments but the actual life that this farm presents. I want to make a plea for ways of sharing power in this country. There has to be a redistribution of wealth in this country; there has to be or else there will be little drippings of blood or a great explosion. If it's not pouring out of the heart, it may be by guerrilla warfare. My group is committed to nonviolence, but just think what would happen if some group like ours were committed to violence. That almost happened, in a sense, with the Panthers. If they had done some other things, had not carried them out with such an air of braggadoccio, if they hadn't used the ego need to claim what they did, they could have devastated this country because of the resources of disgruntled people. We're trying to obtain fundamental change without upsetting the apple cart. We can share part of the power, the land, and that sharing doesn't have to be too painful. But I want to make a plea to people. I want to see our country remain whole and be sensitive enough to make room for the kind of action we're engaged in."

George had been interviewed after leaving Southern rural town where he had worked for ten years. He had been in a period of crisis, and he simply had not found it possible to keep working. When I talked with him again, he was back working actively as an organizer and leader in the same state, in a rural area. The crisis in his life had passed, and he felt deeply committed to what he was doing. He'd come to a position of training leaders, working in leadership development and coordinating the activities of various programs such as legal assistance for the poor. He had a particular interest in the disenfranchisement of small farmers and had worked to provide assistance in management and legal help. He felt poor organization had been the downfall of many civil rights groups, and he was working to help local groups to develop sound organizations, as well as to coordinate countrywide and statewide organizations. He had also been very active politically. He had run workshops, trained leaders, and provided management expertise and support to groups. He emphasized the importance of the election of black committeemen to the Agricultural Conservation and Stabilization Service. That service determines how much people can plant on their land, and the allotments of various crops they may have.

Of his work he said, "I feel we've been able to save some land for the time being. Land ownership or retention is not enough. It must be productive or it becomes a liability, not an asset. We've been trying to address federal programs which now have services for small farmes. In the past, all the technology was geared toward the biggest farmers. FHA approval hinges on the Conservation Service criteria. Small farmers can't qualify for FHA, and this is of great concern."

In terms of politics, he said, "The riot in Miami came as no surprise. A lot of it had to do with the economy. When they say we have unemployment of 20 percent as a national figure, I believe in rural areas that there's 45 or 50 percent, perhaps even more. There simply is no employment in many places. The climate here is like the sixties. A big eruption is possible. It might be a recession now for white folks, but it's a depression for black folks. What happened in Miami was a manifestation of a greater problem. It happens not just to blacks, but to poor whites. The climate dictates that kind of thing. Here in the deep South we have the poor attacking the poor. The problems are the same as in the urban areas. As the small farm disappears, the only choice for people here is to go to New York, Chicago, and Cleveland and try to compete in an already overburdened job market. It's one and the same problem for me. The rural areas have been neglected in terms of the federal budget.

"What I see in the air is that we have a return to the sixties but much worse. People are more aware now. People are watching. When you bring Cubans and misfits, people are watching. People look at how the people from Haiti are being treated. They are being treated differently, and blacks are aware of that.

"A lot of people have the rhetoric, but unless you've been through the frustrations and through the Movement, you can't understand it. A few of the basic things that need to be understood. We have a generation now that missed the glory of the Civil Rights Movement. They missed that experience. They don't know who Martin Luther King was. Things are very different now. What will happen when these people get very frustrated? Cities are at risk—Philadelphia, New York, Detroit. I don't know how much difference black leadership in a place like Detroit will make."

In talking of what sustained him, George said, "Well, it's not been easy. Because of my Movement experience and my

commitments, our family's been bound to do without things that other people deem a necessity . . . that's been one of those things . . . and I have two children. Groups of people have been helpful. I'm not a practicing Christian, but I have learned to follow my instincts. I'm one who believes in a supreme being, and that's where my strength comes from.

"I have friends that I consult on various matters. I just have a determination to survive. My greatest inspiration was my mother's father. He was a strong person. I come from a very strong family, extremely strong. I was taught to survive from an early age. I had to carry my own load. When a crisis comes up, I just don't get bogged down. I go off and fish and think about it. Most of the time it works out, sometimes not, and then I try something else. I've been on my own since an early age, that's the way my father was. We had to pay rent at age twelve in our house. It was a strength, both negative and positive. I grew old before I grew up. I missed a childhood. I don't see it as a negative thing. I am able to build. I am very good with my hands at things like carpentry. I know a lot about food preservation, and I am basically able to be self-sufficient.

"With my children I try to teach them very basic things. My daughter is fifteen. I'm trying to teach her by example. I try to lead an open life. There is very little we don't expose them to in our relationship. If one of us has a problem, we all have a problem. I don't ever tell her things. Her interests go way beyond that of material things. She's a very good reader. She knows several languages. Her political development is different than mine. I don't try to alter that.

"My wife is involved in the Movement too. Her interests are in the children. She has a degree in child development. She used to do a lot of organizing. Recently she's been striken with rheumatoid arthritis. She's been in a wheelchair for over a year. That's presented a lot of problems, because she's been extremely active. She's better now sometimes, but there's not a cure. She's tried everything. That's created problems. We've no money. All that we had I've spent on medical bills. We've been through it, and she just can't contribute the way she used to.

"In terms of a hard time in the Movement, much of it is the way you handle it. I handled things differently when I was younger. Experience is the best teacher. You learn how to handle a confrontation. Sometimes it's a must; sometimes it's not. This state is different than in 1963, when registering to vote was

an act of bravery. I don't experience that now about registering to vote. That's changed, but overall I don't think things have changed. I have no wish to go back to the town I was in. If you go back to a place, you should go back with a different image, represent something different. You become a myth. People have expectations of you because you were brave, you challenged the system and you had things on your side. Sometimes there was rapid achievement. It's not possible now because the problems are so complex. The powers have been to school, too.

"I'm hoping that we can move beyond the question of color, hoping that there will come a movement that will unite the poor, the dispossessed, that will take a serious look at how lives are damaged. I can see it coming. There's gonna have to be some more struggle, that's sure. I can see it brewing whenever I go to New York or go to Harlem. I have friends in Detroit. I don't know that the result will be. Some basic things will have to be nationalized. There has to be some change.

"In terms of why I stay here, I just stay. That's all I know. This is all I know. It's the only thing I'm basically interested in. I've made the decision to spend the rest of my life doing this. I don't think there'll be a basic change in this country in my lifetime. This is just where I am and where I will be."

Mr. Leon Hall, called Joe in the book, worked for several years as the civil rights coordinator for a large union's boycott of J. P. Stevens Co., trying to bridge the gap between organized labor and the Civil Rights Movement after he stopped working with the School Desegregation Project. He then became chief of staff and secretary of the board of directors of the Martin Luther King Center and then a member of Mayor Maynard Jackson's cabinet. He was working there when he was interviewed. Mr. Hall's life has continued to be bound up with the King Center and the influence of Dr. Martin Luther King's nonviolent philosophy. He was particularly involved in the fiftieth-anniversary tribute to Martin Luther King, and indeed had traveled to Eastern Europe to speak to the World Peace Council during the year of its celebration, as well as serving as an aide to Mrs. King at the United Nations during that year. He had developed much broader political awareness and international perspective than when I first talked to him.

Of his visit to the World Peace Council in Eastern Europe he said, "I was invited to give a tribute to Dr. King at the meeting

of the World Peace Council. It was one of the most fascinating things I've been to. I didn't end up a believer in their system at all, but I certainly learned a great deal. There are some strengths there, for example, guarantees of health care, jobs, education, and housing that we don't have, although there are also many things wrong there. They look at Dr. King almost in awe.

"The Peace Council itself involves a hundred different countries, three quarters of which are nonwhite, 60 percent of which are nonaffluent. Many are locked in struggle with their governments. The tribute to Dr. King was the highlight of the conference. There were people there from the PLO; there were Israeli freedom fighters; there were people there from Zimbabwe. All the people were universally supportive of Dr. Martin Luther King. His life and work had touched people all over the world, even in different political systems. Even those who chose not to be nonviolent took inspiration from him.

"I said to them nonviolence was the key, that it was the psychology Dr. King had instilled, the psychology of hope, the ultimate right, and it would prevail. An undying faith, an undying hope for happiness is not a fad, it's a commitment to struggle. We always know there will be light at the end of the tunnel.

"I talked with people from Zimbabwe. I knew there would be victory there. You knew they would win, but they didn't know it then. They made the decision simply to fight till the end of their days. We knew Rhodesia was on its last legs, but those inside found it hard to see; those in the belly of the whale wouldn't see it.

"I talked with people from Haiti and other Caribbean nations. It's important for the superpowers to realize that there is a fundamental inequality. Those people desire a higher quality of life. The world is interdependent; what happens in one place influences others. How we are viewed abroad is not something to be proud of. We're a source of pain. People at that conference each had the greatest pride and love for their country, whether from Africa, India, or Israel. I can't share that pride in my country, because of the pain and history of my people in relationship to this country. With the exception of Andy Young's effort to get on the side of the Rhodesian struggle, we are supporting the oppressor. For example, we supported the Shah. We Americans sit in a very precarious position because of our relationship with dictators, and a rigid indifference to the plight of the common person."

In thinking about the future, he said he had done more and more thinking about the next twenty to twenty-five years. "I think to myself, what will it be like when my sons are thirty years old? What will it be like to go to the Caribbean, the Middle East, or Africa? There is an increasing arrogance and almost contempt for poor people in this country. I came home feeling, and I still feel, we need to prepare ourselves better; I've got to prepare myself better. We have to live in much closer relationships with others, with other countries. On a local level, in this town, I do what I can. We've got to maintain our commitments, we've got to progress. In 1962, Martin Luther King had a long vision. We couldn't even vote. Now, in 1980, living in Atlanta, we need the same long vision. In 1962, they began to hire black policemen here. The officers had to dress at the YMCA. Now we have a black chief of police.

"I am increasingly concerned with the increased economic difficulties. All of our gains may be jeopardized. Now services may have to be cut, and poor people will suffer. There is a more important role for activists than ever before."

When asked what kept him going, he said, "It all goes back to Dr. King, Dr. King and the philosophy of nonviolence. It is a psychology of hope. I find myself falling back on this hope. It's a force behind us, within us. I know about Gandhi. The chords are struck. I try to be concerned with truth. In terms of what he wanted, he certainly would want people to know that the Movement continued.

"And it does. There are networks of people that are in touch. People come out of the woodwork to support the Movement. The Movement cannot die as long as there are those of us who keep working, as long as one person can take the initiative. We know who each other are. We continue to struggle. People would like to see the Movement fail, but it hangs on."

Jim has remained active in the same town, doing the same kind of work in economic development that he did when he was initially interviewed.

Mrs. Johnson reported, "Things are worse here than they were in the sixties. The unemployment rate is very high, and it affects blacks more than whites. School integration is still token. Black teachers are not being promoted very much. In terms of voting, we can't elect a black candidate; the only thing

we can do is swing the vote. We set up a block vote in the last election. Eighty-five to ninety-five percent of the blacks voted in the block, and we were able to decide most of the election. For example, there was a supervisor who had been here for twenty-eight years; we voted together and were able to get him out."

In terms of violence, she said, "It's not like it used to be. There's no night-riding, but they deal with you in other ways. It's harder in some ways because it's hard to find exactly the person who's opposing you. You at least could do that in the sixties."

She talked a little bit about Head Start and the Child Development Group which Mrs. Johnson had been deeply involved in. The Child Development Group was being cut off for lack of funds. "They were out to get us. Head Start will continue, I hope. It's been good and successful here, but we didn't take advantage of it as we should. Everyone wanted to have a job, and those that didn't get them, didn't have much to do with the program."

Mrs. Johnson has been active all over the state. She named over twenty boards on which she served, including the local county Democratic Committee, in which she was co-chairman with a white person, the Community Action Program Board, the Council on Aging Board, a Health Systems Group, and many others. She had set up a three-county family health center in her area through federal grants. She said people bring their kids into the Health Center, but the problem is "that they simply cannot get aid. We can't hold enough doctors."

When asked why she kept going, she said, "Somebody has to be in there. I just like it." Then she recalled her starting out in the Movement, when she'd written a letter to the Farmers' Home Administration, complaining about discrimination in the giving of funds to blacks and whites, and then spoke about the founding of the local NAACP chapter in her area. In terms of what keeps her going, she said, "The good Lord, and I just try not to let something get to me. I visit churches regularly; I don't have any one special church. I get good support from the black community; I get good support. You have to stand by people until they will stand with you. You have to not be greedy for money. A lot of people have done that—have gotten money and moved on. I don't have much push for money. When you want to be a leader, you have to let people make you one; you can't make yourself. You have to stand with them until they choose

you." She said that on all these boards and so on, she drives her own car and pays her own way so that she can maintain her independence.

"I'm so busy, sometimes I feel good when I can stay home two or three times a week. I have one daughter who is with me now, and I still have my farm; I love it. I had to give up my cattle because I couldn't grow hay because I was out so much. I like the land the best. I love land. I'm trying to get people together about land and farming. That's what keeps me going. That's what kept me going through the Movement. We didn't have a dime, but we could grow on our own land, and get food. I guess another thing that keeps me going, I just got a lot of teaching from my father. He said, 'Don't let nothing get you down; a quitter never wins, and a winner never quits.' And then, too, the support from my friends. People know me as one who has changed the South. I feel real proud about it, and I couldn't say no. I say, everywhere black people need to get together, more than ever before. We've got such a little bit, Head Start and so on, we really need to get together; then I say, 'if you don't know where you came from, you don't know where you should go. People who don't have a past don't have a future.' If children today knew the struggle we had, they would unite; but they don't have it in public schools. We try to tell them about it, but I'm not sure we are able to. We can't even have a Black History week." Mrs. Johnson then went on to say that she thought documenting and describing the struggle and how people survived were important. She is writing a book about her own life history. She recalled several of the instances about her own history—her grandmother being a slave, how the grandmother had talked, the circumstances of her father's birth, and illustrated, as she had before, their importance. She hopes to have more time now to write and to try to pass on the knowledge of the struggle to others. Her house burned recently, and much of her writing had been destroyed, but she keeps working nonetheless.

When interviewed, Reverend Dean was pastor of a church in Memphis. Since being interviewed last, he had run for Congress in Mississippi, in a campaign that brought blacks and whites together, although he was not successful in gaining election. Working with a group, Reverend Dean had obtained a license for a television station in Jackson, Mississippi, and

helped to create the first fully integrated, partially black-owned television network in Mississippi. He was engaged in a similar endeavor in Memphis. He commented, "I do not let the externals of the Movement or the external place become controlling for me. It is imperative for me to have an internal place. It is easy for liberals to have a romanticism about racism in the South, and to let that blind them. I'm a thousand percent for the Movement.

"The last four years have been the hardest in my life. I've had a lot of grief over civil rights activities. A particular person in Mississippi who, for his own reasons, I think became overcome with guilt after being on many bombing missions in Vietnam, decided he would become the purger of the Movement. He decided he would find out who had cooperated with the FBI and the CIA during the Movement and he decided it was me. When I was running in my campaign, someone who was working with me was shot and killed. I cooperated with the FBI, of course—very publicly, because I wanted to catch the murderer, that's all. Yet now he's turned that into something much more, and has publicly accused me of cooperating with them. He's also turned Jewish people in Jackson against me because of my work of trying to minister to the Klan. There's such an irony or pain in being accused.

"There's a basic issue concerning faith that's important. The Movement was set up on an ideal. I'm not sure the Movement took into consideration the reality of evil that exists in society. Liberalism tended to emphasize the good to the denial of evil. In fact, the Civil Rights Movement really didn't deal with the problem of evil. I realized that when I created a biracial television station. That primarily Black station had immediately to deal with the same structure of selfishness that any other TV station had to deal with. There was some good achieved, but there was immediately also a return to the more basic problem of selfishness.

"I am deeply aware that life is a process; you don't get finished with it. I'm very much at the point of trying to understand what the whole matter of faith is, in terms of what's good and what's evil. Khoumeini and Begin and the right-wing here in America preach that evil lies out there in someone else, and they will have to wipe it out.

"The last four years have been the toughest years of my life. It's been a real struggle. It's been a real learning experience.

I don't really have here in Memphis a critical mass or community of friends, less so than I did in Jackson."

Reflecting on the civil rights Movement, he said, "People tend to become the roles they play. The civil rights Movement was such a primary experience. It did affect who people became, and who they are. You can't shut off that intensity; it makes you a certain way. It made me, too. The community doesn't let you forget it. There's a stigma to it—not negative, but you're not able to cut it off. It is not easy. It is not possible to move back into a faceless role in the typical community. There are experiences . . . not necessarily scars . . . that affect the way one relates to the community. Your involvement always seems to be there. I guess it's like going through psychoanalysis: once you've been through it, you're just aware of certain things you would not have been aware of. If you went through the Movement in an intense way, you are always sensitive to the things that are happening in the community. That awareness sets you off from others. You have to be guarded in what you say. Communication can go awry. On the other hand, if you're aware, you can also be a teacher and use it. It is a primary experience."

Reverend Samuel Welles, called Reverend Rockwell in the book, had worked with several different groups since I had spoken last with him, and had gone through hard times. "The last regular Movement job I had was with Southern Rural Action. I worked in housing with them, trying to get some houses together, some new houses built after a big tornado. I worked with Southern Rural Action until September 1979, then their grant ran out of funds. For the first time in my life I'm working in private business. I'm a maintenance man for an apartment complex. I'm not in full-time activity the way I was, but of course I'm active.

"I'm still pastoring in Southwest Georgia. I go down there several times a month. I'm speaking out down there whenever I get an opportunity. I'm still actively involved in political campaigns down there.

"I hope there's a way of picking up demonstrations again. The time is ripe. We would like to believe we have made some gains through the Movement, but the system will just not allow it. A lot of people criticize us, but nothing has got us home yet. Who can say what we should do? Nothing has made this country give black people an equal share. They give us something,

and then they take it back. Like in Miami—in some ways, they are only doing what the rest of us should be doing. They're the battleground for the nation, for the way I'm treated, for the way black people are treated. I don't make an apology for what they did.

"I will not preach violence, I do not preach violence, and I will not participate in violence. But I also will not criticize my brothers for anything. I will not condemn my brothers for anything. Before I think blacks should let white racists turn the clock back, I think blacks should die and go to our graves. All blacks should be killed before they are comfortable being slaves. I don't have any grief for the loss of a brother who died fighting for freedom. Before I'll be a slave, I'm not going to rule out anything. I feel like white America has had the chance—it had its chance in the 1960's when Dr. King spoke the truth, preached, told them the truth, how we feel as we are black.

"The white power structure has made blacks a little more comfortable in some areas, and they try to embarrass us, using Uncle Toms to discourage us. We've done no wrong. I'm saying, in a way, we can't do anything wrong. Three hundred and fifty years we've tried everything we know how to try. There should be some kind of Movement going on. The President said that violence would not do anything, yet just as he was saying it, he was sending the Attorney General down there to Miami. They would not have moved a finger if people had not looted, had not burned. They would not have given a damn about a nigger beaten to death by four white policemen. I get mad as a six-shooter whenever somebody starts saying something about being on the wrong side of the fence, about violence. It makes me mad.

"We are 10 percent of the population till wartime, when we become 22 or 23 percent of the population. The system doesn't speak my language. The language should be freedom for all.

"The leadership speaks for the racist majority, and they will continue to, until they are educated. The first step toward educating the whites is the integration of the schools. That's the ugliest thing the racists keep going. In 1954, there was a Supreme court decision that said segregation was wrong, yet people have been fighting and breaking the law since then. It's just no different than it was.

"My children sense that. People wonder why this younger generation is going wild. We have sown rebellion and ugliness.

That's all we've let our children see. How am I going to train my child one way, when the reality is different? It's the opposite of the home of the free and the land of the brave. As far as the reality, how can I teach them anything different? They'd have to be blind fools. People across America break every law in the book. They change the law every day. Richard Nixon put all those blind fools on the Supreme Court.

"We've almost lost hope. I see thousands of blacks walking around every day. They don't have the initiative, we're told. We're always told blacks are asking for a hand-out, yet it's impossible for me to make a living. I'm working now, sweeping floors. I've swept floors all my life. My son may not want to. He might not want to sweep the floor. He might want to be a senator or a bank president. Children don't want to sweep floors because their daddy sweeps floors. Just because I have, doesn't mean my son is going to tolerate this bull. I don't know what's going to help but people better straighten up. There's going to be a slaughter in this country if people don't straighten up somewhat. But black folks will be slaughtered. We can't win, and we will die. The clock is turning back at breakneck speed. In some ways we're further away than we were in the sixties. There are a few parts where a few black people have gotten good jobs. We've made some gains overall, but they will be erased. Down in the rural area, every chance they get, they're putting in white principals in the schools rather than blacks.

"I don't blame the blacks in Miami because nothing we have done has worked. I don't blame those people because anything we've done, anything we know how to do, hasn't worked. I don't blame anyone for trying anything, at this point.

"Down in the rural area, where I preach, is where I'm from. It's my hometown. I don't think people have moved up very much at all. In some other cities, they have made some gains. I think we have more Ku Klux Klansmen down there than any-place in the world. There are some black people who have made a few gains, but the white power structure is getting a grip on the black leaders now. I went to an Emancipation Proclama-tion Day in Albany, down there. They lined up all the black preachers, and gave each one of them a $100 check. That's what I mean about getting a grip. Most of the people listen to the preacher in the rural areas. There isn't any other means by which people communicate. People don't read the papers or whatever, so much. The white power structure got to the

ministers. They had them posing for a picture in the paper. I couldn't do that; I wouldn't be in that line for anything. They were so blind and dumb, I feel like they sold their souls to the devil.

"There's one area down there still with a strong group which was able to elect an alderman. I still work with that group and with him, a black alderman. There will be a black majority of registered voters down there, if we work. The blacks will become a majority and we can elect some people. I still work in his campaigns.

"I don't know what keeps me going. I've counted the Movement as part of my religion. I was pastoring three churches when the Movement began. I've been pastoring one now. I've had that church since 1959. I've been there twenty years. Not all the total membership of the church is in agreement. I'm not sure these people are with me. I wouldn't say there are many of them with me. Nonetheless, I do feel like I'm doing the Lord's work to make the world better. I just believe keeping on is a part of my religion, and being in the Movement is a part of my religion. I don't believe I can work out salvation for my soul unless I continue in the Movement. I've got to keep going. If I was right then, I'm right now.

"Also, I'm a black man that just doesn't believe in letting people walk over him. I don't think I should let anyone fight my own battles. Certain parts of the Bible, one story in particular, the story of Moses, has particular meaning for me. Before God called him, he had to know his attitude about his brother. He had killed a man, and had to flee the country, and God called him. God did not endorse that part of him, but God was for the total effect. The word came. I've heard them cry, 'Let my people go.' Let them go. I cling to that. What I ask for, is hands off and open the door. Don't give me anything, just open the door. Don't block the door. Give me an opportunity, don't deny me that opportunity."

When asked about Dr. King, he said, "It's hard for me to have any ground to criticize the leadership of SCLC, because no part of leadership has any ways of speeding things to anywhere. When Dr. King's movement was broken up into splinter groups, I didn't want to criticize. Mrs. King took part of it. I wish that things had stayed together. Maybe things would have been better, but I'm still not sure we would have been any closer to

freedom; it's hard to criticize. I have Dr. King's tapes; I still listen to them. Sometimes I hear new things on the radio that people report he'd said. He's still very much there in my thoughts. Messages are still being unfolded. I keep getting the message every day. We really can't let his death be in vain. We've got to keep the wheel turning at all costs. Sometimes, when I go back to the rural area, I'm bitter. I may have changed, having a little more knowledge when I go back, I still see nothing much has changed. They're still killing black folks down there, and if a black man goes with a white woman, they come up dead. I'm bitter; in some ways, not so bitter. I do know where I am and and what's supposed to be."

Mrs. Washington has remained in the small town where she worked in the Movement, and where she was living when I first interviewed her. She is now a public official of that town. Mrs. Washington's first involvement in the Movement came in trying to register in that small county and town. Of being a public official, she said, "In a small town, they say it's a part-time job, but you really work full-time. This town needs everything; that's why I'm there. I'm involved with everything—water, sewage, and so forth. I only get paid a hundred dollars a month. My whole involvement is to try to get people participating and voting, and trying to register.

"In addition to that, I've been traveling. I've been to China four times, and I've become the national president of the U.S.-China Friendship Association. I've been negotiating in terms of exchanges of visits. I'll be going to Tibet in July. China has a quarter of the world's population. There's a kind of people-to-people relationship. People are still in need. They have a lot on the ball in terms of learning how to survive, ancient ways. Being an old country, there's lots of human skills. We have a lot of things other people can learn from. We have technology, we're faster than most people. In China, 90 percent of the land is agricultural. The whole system is public. That's what I come from—the land—and I can identify with the people. I'm close to the land. I've made new friends through that. There's just a certain affinity."

In terms of her own county and her own work, she said, "I'm still at work, trying to get people down to register to vote, and to vote.

"It's still hard work. The main key is political participation. Programs and projects are all tied into the vote. The only thing that keeps being really important is the vote. The only thing that keeps the Klan down is the vote. They can shoot up a lot of people, but the vote stops the shooting. Our country is run by a certain kind of system. There is a vote in Congress now on food stamps and Head Start, also on what's going to happen with farm allotments. It all goes back to the vote; it keeps coming back. What equalizes the whole thing about who has money and who doesn't, the vote decides it.

"In this country, I've hired workers for different jobs, all kinds of things because I'm a public servant elected by the vote. I've gotten homes from plantation owners to fix up for people in the country; that's because of the vote. The Movement has got to go back to the core, to ground zero, and come from that; and that's the vote. What we need to do is to vote and know why. I'm now co-chairman of the Democratic party for the county. I'm a Democrat now, but it doesn't necessarily mean we have to be that forever. I'm on the Democratic Executive Committee. People who participate in the political process pay attention to us. The governor has spoken a number of times. He told us what he had on his heart; we even had what we call a dialogue—even that is because we have the vote."

She repeated the importance of her roots, which she had emphasized when I had first spoken to her. "I'm in a town where I don't have a lot of relatives, but it's a place to come back to, where I came up out of a political stronghold, and peace, and so on. People still ask me, and talk to me. I incorporated this town, and now I'm elected. My spiritual roots are here in terms of something that actually happened here for me. I was in poverty. The sense of the Movement manifested itself here to me. Right now, I don't have any plans to leave."

When I asked what was sustaining her, in addition, she said, "I feel like some people just give up and go out. There's not a lot of outward satisfaction in this world. You do sometimes find yourself sort of isolated, pushing through various things. That makes it really important to have a circle of people that are very close. We call on one another for strength. That's what sustains people. They do hang on with that commitment. We were about something; we are about something. It is worth it. It was either you get out and fight for freedom, or you become part of the lagging grass. It gets to be part of your blood. You continue to

work with the things in your roots; that is your sustaining thing. What keeps me going? Either you do what you believe in, or you will feel terribly bad. A lot of people didn't make it; a lot have not done well. Different things happen. Some got depressed. For some, things weren't going fast enough. Everybody wanted to be important. Some go on, some pick up and leave. I see somebody now, every once in a while, who's dropped out. I tell him, 'You did your part. If you don't have it now, you have to go on your way.'

"Commitment to yourself, not just to the other people, sustains a person. You have to start to act for yourself; it soaks into you. You have to go back into yourself all the time, if it gets discouraging. After all, a movement is change. You have to see it from a broader perspective. Everything changes. If you are to remain a part of it, you have to change yourself, too. I'm a person who believes in a spiritual way of living. You have to get yourself together spiritually, whatever your hook-up is, whatever it is you have to be a part."

Sheriff Gilmore remains sheriff in Eutaw, Alabama. He was re-elected in 1978 to another four-year term. He was satisfied with what he had said in the previous interviews about what enabled him to keep going, and added some observations from his current experience.

"You realize how vast the ocean is sometimes, and how small your boat is; much more so than you thought. I've had a few problems with the job, and I want to stay here. I want to work more with juveniles, and I want to work more with police officers, provide help to those that get hung up. Sometime, perhaps I'd like to get into making laws. Things are more political now than ever, but there is a sort of living spirit here. However much trouble it is, it still keeps on, still abides in me and others.

"It takes a total commitment to keep the Movement going. We in this country just don't want to deal with the problem of crimes, we just don't want to make any changes. All kinds of things have an effect—schools, churches, industry. I got a work-release program started. Many people in jail have physical abnormalities. Many need counseling for family problems. More than half of those have drinking problems. We have to address those. I've got the feeling we can work on it if we're serious about it. Since I've seen you last, I've been to Europe, South America, and Africa. I'd like to travel to the Orient and

Eastern Europe. What impressed me most was Africa—parts of West Africa—Gambia, particularly. In terms of my profession, the police officers there didn't wear guns. They had this set-up where they could put guns on if they needed them, but they didn't carry them. I was impressed with how they handle mental illness and law enforcement there. There was a very small amount of crime. Then, too, I'd read *Roots,* about Gambia, and I visited the place where Alex Haley claims his folks are from; that really impressed me. I was impressed with the ability of blacks in Nigeria, how they handle things."

Of the Movement, he said, "It will never be like it used to be. I wouldn't want it to be. I know some of what will be, will be sticky stuff. A small, committed group like we were in the beginning in SNCC can make a world of difference. It can make a change in the right direction. We made it possible for a lot of people. I think we can do more.

"It gets lonely out here sometimes. That can be worse than the KKK. That kind of loneliness stays with me sometimes on the journey. As the song says, 'Nobody said it would be easy.' I don't believe He brought me to this place to leave me. A lot of us were close in the earlier days, and we would speak out together. We don't meet as we used to. We expected some would have to go their separate ways physically, but not spiritually. For a while, here in this town, some of us were on opposite sides of the fence politically, who had been in the Movement. We were embarrassed by that. We now try to stay close together. We often talk about tomorrow, about how we want to make tomorrow know that we are living now.

"That's the way it's been. When I'm lonely, I can think of others who are going on in another level. I feel a sort of closeness there. You have to allow your spirit freedom."

Summing up, he said, "That early period of the Movement, coupled with my religious spirit and the faith I have in people, are the things that keep me hanging on."

Notes

CHAPTER 3

1. This material appeared in a slightly different form in T. Manschreck and A. Kleinman, editors, *Renewal in Psychiatry: A Critical Rational Perspective*, Hemisphere Publishing Corporation, Washington, D.C., 1977, and is used here by permission of the publisher.

CHAPTER 12

1. Watters, Pat, *Down to Now*, Pantheon Books, New York, 1971, p.10.
2. Erickson, E., "Identity and the Life Cycle," *Psychological Issues*, International Universities Press, N.Y., 1959, p. 89.

Selected Readings

Agee, James. *A Death in the Family*. New York: Avon Books, 1966.

Agee, James. *The Morning Watch*. New York: Avon Books, 1976.

Agee, James and Evans, Walker. *Let Us Now Praise Famous Men*. New York: Ballantine Books, 1966.

Allport, Gordon W. *The Nature of Prejudice*. New York: Anchor Books, Doubleday and Co., 1958.

Angelou, Maya. *I Know Why the Caged Bird Sings*. New York: Bantam Books, 1970.

Baldwin, James. *Go Tell It On the Mountain*. New York: Dell Books, 1970.

Bellack, Leopold A. and Sheehy, Michael A. "The Broad Role of Ego Functions Assessment." *American Journal of Psychiatry*, Vol. 133, 1976, No. 11, p. 1259.

Berrigan, Daniel and Coles, Robert. *The Geography of Faith*. Boston: Beacon Press, 1971.

Campbell, Will D. "The Faith of a Fatalist." *New South*, Vol. 23, 1968, No. 2, p. 51.

Campbell, Will D. "The World of the Redneck." *Katallagete*, Vol. 5, 1974, No. 1, p. 34.

Campbell, Will D. "Vocation As Grace." *Katallagete*, Vol. 4, 1972, No. 2-3, p. 80.

Cash, W.J. *The Mind of the South*. New York: Vintage Books, 1941.

Caudill, Harry M. *Night Comes to the Cumberlands, A Biography of a Depressed Area*. Boston: Atlantic—Little, Brown and Co., 1963.

Coelho, George V., Hamburg, David A., and Adams, John E., (eds.). *Coping and Adaptation*. New York: Basic Books, 1974.

Coles, Robert. "A House of Truth." *The American Scholar*, Vol. 34, 1965, No. 4, p. 620.

Coles, Robert. *Children of Crisis, A Study of Courage and Fear*. Boston: Atlantic—Little, Brown and Co., 1967.

Coles, Robert. *Farewell to the South*. Boston: Atlantic—Little, Brown and Co., 1972.

Coles, Robert. *Migrants, Sharecroppers, Mountaineers, Volume II of Children of Crisis*. Boston: Atlantic—Little Brown and Co., 1971.

Coles, Robert. "On Courage." *Contemporary Psychoanalysis*, Vol. 1, 1965, No. 2, p. 85.

Coles, Robert. "The End of the Affair." *Katallagete*, Vol. 4, 1972, No. 2-3, p. 46.

Coles, Robert and Brenner, Joseph. "American Youth in a Social Struggle: The Mississippi Summer Project." *American Journal of Orthopsychiatry*, Vol. 35, 1965, No. 5, p. 909.

Coles, Robert and Clayton, Al. *Still Hungry in America*. Cleveland, Ohio: World Publishing Co., 1969.

Dabbs, James McBride. "Haunted by God." *New South*, Vol. 27, 1972, No. 4, p. 2.

Dollard, J. *Caste and Class in a Southern Town*. New York: Doubleday, 1957.

Dunbar, Leslie W. *A Republic of Equals*. Ann Arbor, Michigan: The University of Michigan Press, 1966.

Dunbar, Leslie W. "The Annealing of the South." *The Virginia Quarterly Review*, Vol. 37, 1961, No. 4.

Dunbar, Leslie W. "The Changing Mind of the South: The Exposed Nerve." *The Journal of Politics*, Vol. 26, 1964, p. 3.

Dunbar, Tony. *Our Land Too*. New York: Vintage Books, 1971.

Eisenberg, Leon. "Racism, the Family, and Society: A Crisis in Values." *Mental Hygiene*, Vol. 2, 1968, No. 4, p. 512.

Eisenberg, Leon. "Student Unrest: Sources and Consequences." *Science*, Vol. 167, 1970, p. 1688.

Eisenberg, Leon. "The *Human* Nature of Human Nature." *Science*, Vol. 176, 1972, p. 123.

Elkins, Stanley M. *Slavery*. New York: Grosset and Dunlop, 1963.

Ellison, Ralph. *Invisible Man*. New York: Random House, 1947.

Erikson, Erik H. *Childhood and Society*. Second Edition. New York: W.W. Norton and Co., Inc., 1963.

Erikson, Erik H. "Identity and the Life Cycle." *Psychological Issues*, Vol. 1, 1959, No. 1.

Erickson, Erik H. *Identity, Youth and Crisis*. New York: W.W. Norton and Co., Inc., 1968.

Erickson, Erik H. *Insight and Responsibility*. New York: W.W. Norton and Co., Inc., 1964.

Fanon, Franz. *A Dying Colonialism*. New York: Grove Press, 1967.

Faulkner, William. *The Hamlet*. New York: Vintage Books,

Random House, n.d.*

Faulkner, William. *The Mansion.* New York: Vintage Books, Random House, n.d.

Faulkner, William. *The Sound and the Fury,* New York: Vintage Books, Random House, n.d.

Faulkner, William. *The Town.* New York: Vintage Books, Random House, 1961.

Frazier, E. Franklin. *Black Bourgeois.* Glencoe, Ill.: Free Press, 1957.

Freud, Anna. *The Ego and the Mechanism of Defense.* New York: International Universities Press, Inc., 1946.

Freud, Anna. *Normalcy and Pathology in Childhood: Assessments of Developments.* New York: International Universities Press, Inc., 1965.

Georgia Writers Project. *Drums and Shadows, Survival Studies Among the Georgia Coastal Negroes.* New York: Anchor Books, Doubleday and Co., Inc., 1972.

Good, Paul. "Poverty in the Rural South." *New South.* Vol. 23, 1968. No. 1, p. 2.

Good, Paul. "The American Dream of Cleveland Sellers." *New South,* Vol. 28, 1973, No. 2, p. 21.

Hughes, Langston. *The Movement, Documentary of a Struggle for Equality.* New York: Simon and Schuster, 1964.

Huttie, Joseph, Jr. "'New Federalism' and the Death of a Dream in Mound Bayou, Mississippi." *New South,* Vol. 28, 1973, No. 4, p. 20.

Kardiner, Abraham and Ovesey, Lionel. *The Mark of Oppression.* New York: W.W. Norton and Co., Inc., 1951.

King, Martin Luther, Jr. *Strength to Love.* New York: Harper and Row, 1963.

King, Martin Luther, Jr. *The Trumpet of Conscience.* New York: Harper and Row, 1967.

King, Martin Luther, Jr. *Where Do We Go From Here: Chaos or Community?* Boston: Beacon Press, 1968.

King, Martin Luther, Jr. *Why We Can't Wait.* New York: Signet, New American Library, 1964.

Lester, Julius. *To Be A Slave.* New York: Dial Press, 1968.

Lewis, John. "Religion and Human Rights: A Final Appeal to the Church." *New South,* Vol. 23, 1968, No. 2, p. 57.

Lewis, John and Allen, Archie, E. "Black Voter Registration

---

* n.d.No date.

Efforts in the South." *Notre Dame Lawyer*, Vol. 48, 1972, No. 1, p. 109.

Lewis, Oscar. *The Children of Sanchez*. New York: Random House, 1964.

Lynd, Staughton, (ed.). *Nonviolence in America: A Documentary History*. New York: Bobbs-Merrill Company, Inc., 1966.

Malcolm X. *The Autobiography of Malcolm X*. New York: Grove Press, 1966.

McGill, Ralph. *The South and the Southerner*. Boston: Little, Brown and Co., 1963.

O'Conner, Flannery. *Everything That Rises Must Converge*. New York: Farrar, Straus, and Giroux, 1965.

O'Conner, Flannery. *Mystery and Manners*. New York: Noonday Press, Farrar, Straus, and Giroux, 1970.

O'Conner, Flannery. *Wise Blood. A Good Man is Hard to Find. The Violent Bear It Away*. New York: Signet Books, n.d. (3 books in one edition.)

Percy, Walker. *Love in the Ruins*. New York: Farrar, Straus, and Giroux, 1971.

Percy, Walker. *The Last Gentleman*. New York: Farrar, Straus, and Giroux, 1966.

Percy, Walker. *The Moviegoer*. New York: Noonday Press, Farrar, Straus, and Giroux, 1967.

Pierce, C.M. "Psychiatric Problems of the Black Minority." In *American Handbook of Psychiatry*, G. Caplan (ed.). Vol. 3, p. 512. New York: Basic Books, 1975.

Pierce, Chester M., and West, Louis Jolyon. "Six Years of Sit-ins: Psychodynamic Causes and Effects." *The International Journal of Social Psychiatry*, Vol. 7, 1966, No. 1, p. 29-34.

Pierce, C.M. "Violence and Counterviolence: the Need for a Children's Domestic Exchange." *American Journal of Orthopsychiatry*, Vol. 39, July, 1969, p. 553-568.

Pettigrew, Thomas. *Profile of the American Negro*. Princeton: D. Van Nostrand Co., Inc., 1964.

Poussaint, A.F. "Problems of White Civil Rights Workers in the South." *Psychiatric Opinion*, Vol. 3, 1966, No. 6, p. 18.

Poussaint, A.F. *Why Blacks Kill Blacks*. New York: Emerson Hall Publishers, 1972.

Poussaint, A.F. and Ladner, Joyce. "Black Power: A Failure For Integration Within the Civil Rights Movement." *Archives of General Psychiatry*, Vol. 18, 1968, No. 4, p. 385.

Rainwater, Lee. "Crucible of Identity: The Negro Lower Class Family. *Daedalus,* Vol. 95, Winter, 1966, p. 172.

Rose, Thomas, (ed.). *Violence in America.* New York: Vintage Books, Random House, 1970.

Silver, James W. "Mississippi: The Closed Society." *The Journal of Southern History,* Vol. 30, 1964, No. 1, p. 3.

Smith, Lillian. *Killers of the Dream.* Garden City, New York: Anchor Books, Doubleday and Co., 1963.

Size, William C., (ed.). *Human Life Cycle.* New York: Jason Aronson, Inc., 1975.

U.S. Senate, "Hearing Before the Subcommittee on Employment, Manpower and Poverty, on S. Resolution 281. to Establish a Select Committee on Nutrition and Human Needs." U.S. Government Printing Office, 1968.

Vaillant, G.E., (ed.). "The Human Life Cycle, A Review of Major Prospective Studies of Human Development." *Seminars in Psychiatry,* Vol. 4, 1972, No. 4.

Walker, Alice. *In Love and Trouble.* New York: Harcourt Brace Jovanovich, Inc., 1973.

Walker, Alice. *Once.* New York: Harcourt, Brace Jovanovich, Inc., 1968.

Walker, Alice. *Revolutionary Petunias and Other Poems.* New York: Harcourt Brace Jovanovich, Inc., 1973.

Walls, Dwayne. "The Chickenbone Special." Southern Regional Council, *Leadership Series No. 2.* Atlanta, Georgia: 1970.

Watters, Pat. *Down to Now, Reflections on the Southern Civil Rights Movement.* New York: Pantheon Books, Random House, 1971.

Watters, Pat. "Encounter With the Future." *New South,* Vol. 20, 1965, No. 5, p. 1.

Watters, Pat. *The South and the Nation.* New York, Pantheon Books, Random House, 1969.

Watters, P. and Cleghorn, R. *Climbing Jacob's Ladder, The Arrival of Negroes in Southern Politics.* New York: Harcourt, Brace and World, 1967.

Welty, Eudora. *A Curtain of Green and Other Stories.* New York: Harcourt, Brace and World, 1941.

Woodward, C. Vann. "What Happened to the Civil Rights Movement in *The Civil Rights Movement Re-examined.* A. Philip Randolph Educational Fund, 1967.

Wolfgang, Marvin E. *Crime and Race, Conceptions and*

Misconceptions. New York: Institute of Human Relations Press, Pamphlet No. 6, 1964.

Zinn, Howard. *Albany, A Study in National Responsibility.* Southern Regional Council, Atlanta, Georgia: 1962.

Zinn, Howard. *The Southern Mystique.* New York: Alfred A. Knopf, 1964.